The English,
The French and
THE
OYSTER

To the OG
and to the memory of Christopher Dilke,
for so long its illustrious doyen.

The English,
The French and
THE
OYSTER

Robert Neild

Quiller Press
London

First published 1995 by
Quiller Press Limited.
46 Lillie Road, London SW6 1TN

Designed by Jim Reader
Jacket designed by Tim McPhee

Produced by Book Production Consultants PLC,
25–27 High Street, Chesterton, Cambridge
Printed and bound by St Edmundsbury Press, Bury St Edmunds, Suffolk.

Contents

Acknowledgements

I am grateful to the publishers and authors who gave me permission to quote from the following books:

Apes, Angels and Victorians: a Joint Biography of Darwin and Huxley by William Irvine, published by Messrs Weidenfeld and Nicholson; *Shells* by Mary Saul, published by the Hamlyn Publishing Group; *The Letters of Charles Dickens*, edited by Madeline House, Graham Storey and Kathleen Tillotson published by Oxford University Press.

I am also grateful to the following for permission to reproduce pictures:

M. Daniel Roux of the Section Régionale Ostréicole de Marennes-Oléron
M. Pichot-Louvet of Cancale
Illustrated London News
Christies, Picture Library (Claesz)
Nat Gallery Washington DC (Manet)
Musee Condée (de Troy)
Kishorn Shellfish
Loch Fyne Oysters
Mr Jim Bamber
Dr Eric Edwards
Mr Steven Jones
Virginia Matheson
Silvia Thompson

Preface

A S AN OYSTER lover, I used to wonder why it was that oysters were so scarce in Britain. One was told that they had been cheap and plentiful in the 19th century, and visibly they were still cheap and plentiful in France. Unable to find any book or article that answered the question, I decided in retirement to look into the history of the oyster. I found that oyster production in Britain is now a fraction of what it was in the mid-19th century, whereas in France it is much higher; and that this difference is not the inevitable consequence of climate or of other physical differences between the two countries. In fact both countries have faced similar oyster problems. These have been caused as much by man as by nature – for example, they have been caused by over-fishing, by pollution that poisons oysters and by pollution that poisons those who eat oysters. But our two countries have reacted very differently to these common problems, each repeatedly behaving in a way that epitomises its national approach to life and to economic government. I have therefore found, to my surprise, that in writing a history of the oyster in the two countries I have written a history of how the two countries manage their affairs – seen with respect to their treatment of the oyster. It has been an amusing and instructive task.

As I went along, I learnt about oysters and how to enjoy them, and I learnt about the myths surrounding oysters and the way they are depicted in the arts. It seemed a pity to leave out these gleanings, even though they are peripheral to a book on the history of the oyster. I have therefore included them at the start in two chapters which will, I hope, serve to whet the appetite of the reader for the oyster and for subsequent chapters about its history.

Perhaps because nobody had explored the history of the oyster for a century or more, I found that almost everyone I approached in England and France was extraordinarily friendly, was interested to know more about the subject and was most helpful. Those who have helped me include civil servants, biologists in fishery laboratories, oyster growers, historians, lawyers, a bibliographer, not to mention archivists and librarians. It is impossible to name them all, but I must name some.

First and foremost I am indebted to Dr Eric Edwards, director of the Shellfish Association of Great Britain and Brian Spencer of the Conwy fisheries laboratory. At the start of this enquiry, they gave me written material, explanations and introductions to people in and around the oyster industry, all of which were invaluable; when later I turned to them, they patiently answered my questions; and when my typescript was ready in draft, they read it and commented on it. I should also thank three friends, John Bury, Jeremy Maule and Tony Weir, who most kindly read part or all of what I have written.

Many oyster growers I visited round the British coast were most generous with their time. Some invited me to meals or to stay; many kept sending me information when they came across things that might help me. Already I have been back to visit some of them when I have been in their neighbourhood. In particular, I want to thank Mark Pattinson, John Noble and Douglas McLeod in Scotland; and, in the rest of Britain, John Bayes, Philip Gibbon, Len Hodges, David Hugh-Jones and Christopher Kerrison.

For information about the ownership of the foreshore and the problem of obtaining oyster concessions, I am indebted to Frank Parrish, Martin Gravestock and Peter McGovern of the Crown Estate offices in London and Edinburgh; to Sherriff D.B. Smith for his advice on the Scottish law of the foreshore; and to Lord Courtney and David Jarrad.

Others I must mention are Noel Wilkins for giving me permission to draw freely on his book on aquaculture in Victorian Ireland and for vetting what I wrote about Ireland; Mark Whitley for explaining to me the work of the Southern Sea Fisheries Committee; Jim Bamber for telling me his memories of oyster stalls in Blackpool; Christopher Leftwich, the Fishmongers' Company's Chief Fisheries Inspector at Billingsgate; Lord Butterfield for advice on the aphrodisiac properties of oysters; Peter and Trish Wright for finding material for me in the United States; the staff of the Cambridge University Library, in particular those in the Official Publications Department: their efficiency and courtesy in finding and fetching old official reports and papers is quite remarkable; and last but not least the Fishmongers' Company for their support and encouragement.

In France I am indebted to: M. Bernard Lecomte of the *Ministère de l'Agriculture at de la Pêche*; M. Yves Fauvel, Dr Henri Grizel, M. Ravoux and Mlle Radinac of IFREMER; M. Max Thibault of INRA; M. Trouvez of the *Département des Affaires Maritimes* at Cherbourg; M. Quetier, mayor of Agon-Coutainville; M. Claude Gatignol, deputy for la Manche; Dr Raymond Guilhem of the *Services Vétérinaires* at Arcachon; M. François Cadoret, M. Eric Dalaran, M. François Hélie, M. Jean-Marie Merenna and M. Pichot-Louvet, all oyster growers; M. Roland Roucher, organiser of the competition for *l'Huître d'Or de Bretagne*, 1994; and Mogador Empson, the most generous of hosts, on whom I descended in Normandy. He opened for me the doors of the Norman oyster world, the starting point for my exploration of oysters in France.

9.1.95
R.R.N.

CHAPTER ONE

Oysters, love and the arts

THERE IS NOW the possibility of a revival of oyster eating in Britain after a long period in which oysters have not been seen at our tables or on the marble slabs of our fishmongers. Technical developments and improved standards of hygiene have made a revival possible, but if it is to occur the taste for oysters must be revived. Oysters are no ordinary food: they are eaten raw and live; they are associated with festivity and with love; they have been gathered and eaten in Britain and other parts of the world since prehistoric time: there is a special aura about them.

Oysters and love

Oysters have the reputation of being an aphrodisiac, and they have often been associated with seduction. Indeed there used to be a slight tinge of the naughty-nineties about oyster eating in England. As moral standards have eased, that has gone, but the oyster's aphrodisiac reputation lives on, not just in Britain but also in France and other parts of the world.

The most convincing explanation for the oyster's aphrodisiac reputation is psychological. All over the world people from primitive times have believed that shells have magical properties connected with fertility. Mary Saul, in an excellent book on shells, has suggested that these beliefs 'most likely originated with the first man to pick up a cowry on the shores of the Red Sea and to discern, in the shape, colour and form of its aperture, a fancied resemblance to the sexual parts of woman, the door through which a precious child enters the world.' She goes on to explain that:

> Two basic needs dominated the life of early man; the need to find food and the need for children to perpetuate his race. His reasoning led him to believe that an object which appeared to resemble a part of the human

body could magically influence that part, and that the object itself possessed vital and magical powers.

The cowry, therefore, was believed to have the power of conferring fertility, to be a protection against sterility and to increase sexual potency. It was the repository of the vital principle or 'soul substance', the ensurer of life and of resurrection, which is life's continuance. It became the symbol of womanhood, the source of life, dwelling place of the deity who made fertile both the women and the crops.... Such shells have been found among the most prized possessions of primitive peoples all over the world.

So the shell of the cowry, with its power of ensuring fertility and easy delivery, was hung as near as possible to the reproductive parts, on aprons or girdles, and became regarded as the most suitable gift to be presented to girls when they reached puberty or when they married.[1]

The idea of magical powers was transferred to other shells and spread through the world, giving rise to beliefs in a god in a shell and to legends of the birth of a woman or a female child from a shell, a goddess from the sea. The most famous of these is the myth of the birth of Aphrodite (whom the Romans identified with Venus) to whom we owe the word aphrodisiac. The scallop shell figures in the mythologies of ancient Greece and Rome, and it was in a scallop shell that Aphrodite, the Greek goddess of love, marriage and family life, was carried to shore, having risen naked from the foam in the sea, the scene depicted by Botticelli in his 'Birth of Venus' which hangs in the Uffizi Gallery in Florence.

Those who attribute aphrodisiac powers to the oyster may merely be repeating a notion derived from these ancient myths, but a more common explanation is that when they look at open oysters they see a resemblance to the intimate parts of the female body, as their ancestors did when they looked at cowry shells.

There are two possible scientific explanations for the aphrodisiac reputation of the oyster. One is that they contain many desirable nutrients and may have served to boost the vitality of ill-nourished men and women in days when diets were often deficient. The other is modern. In the course of research into ways of relieving the constriction of the blood vessels suffered by diabetics, trials were conducted with a chemical which, besides serving that purpose, was reported by a male patient to have restored his potency, a phenomenon which is not surprising since the commonest cause of non-psychological impotence is congestion of the blood vessels leading to the male sexual organ. It was later noted by Lord Butterfield, a distinguished expert on diabetes and an oyster lover, that the chemical used in the trials was one that occurs naturally in the native oyster.[2] So it is conceivable that the aphrodisiac reputation of the oyster has depended on its effect on the nerves or constricted blood vessels of diabetics and old men. But both these scientific explanations have limited application. Together they are scarcely sufficient to explain the persistent reputation of the oyster as an aphrodisiac for people of all ages, of both sexes and all stations in life. It is easier to believe the psychological explanation based on mythology and on the feminine characteristics of the oyster. But it may equally well be that the aphrodisiac reputation of the oyster is just a matter of thinking it is so, a matter of self-fulfilling suggestion.

The oyster and the arts

The oyster has been portrayed more satisfactorily in painting than in prose or verse, probably for the simple reason that the artist can please us by showing us the appearance of a food – a plate of oysters, a fish on a dish, a loaf of bread, a pile of fruit or some game in the feather – whereas the writer who attempts to describe the appearance and taste of the same oysters, fish, bread, fruit or game will be hard put to it not to bore or irritate us. Since taste is personal and is almost impossible to describe, few readers are likely to feel that an author's attempt to describe a taste is satisfactory. And if he dwells long on the appearance of a food, he risks sounding false and greedy.

Dickens is the British writer who really warms the heart of an oyster lover. His liking for oysters, evident in his fiction, became exuberant when he visited America in 1842. In Boston he made friends with Cornelius Felton, Professor of Greek at Harvard, another oyster enthusiast. Together they went 'roistering and oystering' in New York. The people of New York, who gave Dickens a tumultuous reception, paid tribute to him at a 'Boz Ball' attended by three thousand people; the fare included 50,000 oysters. After Dickens returned to England he wrote letters to Felton punctuated with banter about oysters. He played with the question, what happens to the New York oyster openers out of season:

> Do they commit suicide in despair, or wrench open tight drawers and cupboards and hermetically-sealed bottles – for practice? Perhaps they are dentists out of the oyster season. Who knows![3]

And he told Felton the story of Dando, a notorious London oyster thief:

> He used to go into oyster shops, without a farthing of money, and stand at the counter, eating Natives, until the man who opened them grew pale, cast down his knife, staggered backward, struck his white forehead with his open hand, and cried 'You are Dando!!!'. He has been known to eat twenty dozen at one sitting; and would have eaten forty, if the truth had not flashed upon the shop-keeper. For these offences he was constantly committed to the House of Correction. During his last imprisonment, he was taken ill – got worse and worse – and at last began knocking violent double knocks at Death's Door. The Doctor stood beside his bed, with his fingers on his pulse. 'He is going,' says the doctor. 'I see it in his eye. There is only one thing that would keep him alive for another hour, and that is – oysters.' They were immediately brought. Dando swallowed eight, and feebly took a ninth. He held it in his mouth, and looked round the bed, strangely. 'Not a bad one, is it?' says the doctor. The patient shook his head, rubbed his trembling hand upon his stomach, bolted the oyster and fell back – Dead. They buried him in the Prison Yard, and paved his Grave with oyster shells.[4]

Dando was so notorious for his oyster guzzling that his name apparently became a household word. He was the subject of many cartoons; a play was written about him in 1838; and in 1850 Macaulay, after taking out his niece, Alice, wrote 'I was Dando at a pastry-cook's, and then at an oyster shop' – meaning presumably that he over-ate, not that he refused to pay his bill. George Otto Trevelyan, the editor of Macaulay's letters, published in 1876, added a footnote:

> A generation has arisen of whom not one in fifty knows Dando; the 'bouncing, seedy, swell'; hero of a hundred ballads; who was at least twice in every month brought before the magistrates for having refused to settle his bill after over-eating himself in an oyster-shop.[5]

Apart from Dickens, British writers tend to use the oyster as an image for an enclosed world, or to make macabre jokes about it, dwelling on the fact that oysters are eaten alive. The worst is Lewis Carroll in *The Walrus and the Carpenter*, a tale of naive young oysters being taken for a walk along the beach and chatted up by the walrus and the carpenter whose only purpose is to eat them. We laugh at the last verse, but it is really very ghoulish:

The Walrus and the Carpenter, Tenniel.

'O Oysters,' said the Carpenter,
'You've had a pleasant run!
Shall we be trotting home again?'
But answer came there none
And this was scarcely odd, because
They'd eaten every one.[6]

The macabre impression created by the words is reinforced by the bleak and angular way in which Tenniel depicted the walrus and the carpenter in his illustrations.

Saki is no better, though his ironical style is totally different from that of Lewis Carroll:

I think oysters are more beautiful than any religion…. They not only forgive our unkindness to them; they justify it, they incite us to go on being perfectly horrid to them. Once they arrive at the supper-table they seem to enter thoroughly into the spirit of the thing. There's nothing in Christianity or Buddhism that quite matches the sympathetic unselfishness of an oyster.[7]

But across the Atlantic one finds oyster verses of a jollier spirit. The best is by Ogden Nash:

What, No Oysters?

There is no R in the month of May,
There's none in the month of June,
And the days of the dog, July and Aug.,
Glide past on R-less shoon.
Then where are you going, my pretty maid,
And what will you find to eat
While the oyster broods in inedible moods
In his lonely bridal suite?

'I'm going a-feasting, sir,' she said,
'I am on my way to dine.
Let the succulent bivalve cling to its bed,
Methinks I am doing fine.
For the chowder laves the fragrant clam
In the old New England style,
And if corn on the cob with my teeth plays hob,
I'll remember not to smile.

The baby lobster scarlet gleams
Next a mound of fresh asparagus;
While the blue point dreams connubial dreams,
I'll munch till my veins are varacus.
Lo, luscious now as an infant's lisp,
The strawberry, tart and juicy,
And soft-shell crabs as sweet and crisp
As a nocturne by Debussy.

"Though there is no R in the month of May
And none in the month of June,
Nor the days of the dog, July and Aug.,
You can stuff till you're fit to swoon –
Who's that a-ringing the doorbell so,
Louder than doorbell ought to ring?
Why, its half a dozen oysters, bowing low,
and their mouths are simply watering."[8]

Perhaps I am too hard on British oyster versifiers; they are not all dismal. Consider these lines by John Gay, written early in the 18th century:

> Be sure observe where brown *Ostrea* stands,
> Who boasts her shelly Ware from *Wallfleet* Sands;
> There may'st thou pass, with safe unmiry Feet,
> Where the rais'd Pavement leads athwart the Street.
> If where *Fleet-Ditch* with muddy Current flows,
> You chance to roam; where Oyster-Tubs in Rows
> Are rang'd beside the Posts; there stay thy Haste,
> And with sav'ry Fish indulge thy Taste:
> The Damsel's Knife the gaping Shell commands,
> While the salt Liquor streams between her Hands.
>
> The Man had sure a Palate cover'd o'er
> With Brass or Steel, that on the rocky Shore
> First broke the oozy Oyster's pearly Coat,
> And risqu'd the living Morsel down his Throat.
> What will not Lux'ry taste? Earth, Sea, and Air
> Are daily ransack'd for the Bill of Fare.
> Blood stuff'd in Skins is *British* Christians Food,
> And *France* robs Marshes of the croaking Brood;
> Spungy Morells in strong *Ragousts* are found,
> And in the Soupe the slimy Snail is drown'd.[9]

And then there is a canto in *Don Juan* where Byron plays with the notion of an oyster crossed in love (which first occurs in Sheridan's play, *The Critic*, in the mad rigmarole of the mock heroine, Tilburina) and manages, in keeping with the mood of Protestants at that time, to take a swipe at Catholic monks:

> "An oyster may be crossed in love" – and why?
> Because he mopeth idly in his shell,
> And heaves a lonely subterraqueous sigh,
> Much as a monk may do within his cell:
> And *à-propos* of monks, their Piety
> With Sloth hath found it difficult to dwell:
> Those vegetables of the Catholic creed
> Are apt to run exceedingly to seed.[10]

The best known pieces in French about the oyster are two fables by La Fontaine. One, *Le Rat et l'Huître,* is a warning against being nosey: a country rat of little brain, seeing an open oyster with something edible inside, put his head into it, only to have the oyster close its shell and trap him. (This may have a foundation in fact: one comes across accounts of a dead rat or mouse with its head caught in an oyster shell.) The second, *L'Huître et les Plaideurs,* is a warning against going to court: two pilgrims, unable to agree which of them should eat a single oyster they had found on a beach, submitted to the judgement of a passer-by who, having opened the oyster, ate it and handed them each one half shell.

Oysters in painting

By far the best pictures of oysters are the still lifes painted in the Netherlands in the 17th century. Oysters are rarely to be found in the art of earlier periods. When Renaissance painters wanted to represent the shell as a symbol, and when architects at that time and later adorned a niche over a door or any curved recess with a shell, they followed the Romans and depicted the scallop shell, not the oyster. The choice is understandable. The scallop shell, with the appearance of a fan with wings at its base, is so perfectly shaped as to be aesthetically pleasing and structurally convenient to the artist and the architect. By comparison, the shell of the oyster, even the native oyster, is a clumsy irregular thing. When painters turned their attention to the oyster they were attracted not to its shell but to its delicate edible interior. Moreover the scallop shell became the badge of pilgrims, allegedly because of its part in a miracle that occurred off the coast of Portugal as the body of St James the Apostle was on its way from the Holy Land to Spain, where, at Compostela, it became a most important object of devotion and pilgrimage. According to the legend, a rider whose bolting horse carried him into the sea was believed lost till he and the horse miraculously emerged from the sea covered in scallop shells near the boat carrying the relics of the apostle.

Before the Reformation, the artists of the Netherlands had developed great skill in painting animals, flowers and other natural objects which they introduced into religious pictures. When in the Reformation the country split and the representation of religious subjects became taboo in Protestant Holland, the artists were well equipped to concentrate their skills on the representation of the world around them; and, fortunately for them, there was a market amongst the rising class of merchants and amongst other parts of the Dutch population for paintings of such things as flowers and food, as well as for landscapes, seascapes, portraits and interiors of houses. The Dutch term *still-leven*, meaning a still or dead object, was coined to describe pictures of this kind. In their still lifes the artists displayed their extraordinary ability to depict the textures and surfaces of objects – of textiles, of light on a glass, of the petals of flowers and of foods, including oysters. Oyster lovers who look at Dutch and Flemish pictures of oysters of this period cannot but be tempted by the appearance before their eyes of such perfect native oysters and marvel at the skill of the painters. Still lifes of oysters are to be found in most major art galleries; the galleries of

St James the Great,
Albrecht Durer.

the Low Countries are of course rich in them; and so, as a result of Spain's links with the Low Countries, is the Prado in Madrid.

In Holland two of the best known painters of oysters were Pieter Claesz (1590-1661) and Willem Claesz Heda (1594-1680), both of Haarlem, a town which specialised in so-called 'breakfast pieces', meaning still lifes of food; another was Jan Steen (1626-1679). But the most perfect oyster painting I have seen (see colour section) was produced by a Flemish artist, Osias Beert (1580-1624), of whom it has been said that he 'loved the grey tones of Oysters'.[11]

Since the 17th century, oyster paintings have been few. There is a still life by Manet and another by Braque; and earlier there is the most exuberant and famous of all oyster paintings, *Le Déjeuner d'Huîtres* (the oyster lunch) by the 18th century French painter Jean-François de Troy (see colour section). It shows young bloods consuming oysters and champagne, and is believed to be the first painting of champagne, which had only just been invented by Dom Pérignon: a cork is shown sailing up in the air, watched in amazement by the servants.

9

This painting and another, *le Déjeuner de Jambon* (the lunch of ham) by Lancret, were commissioned by Louis XV to decorate a dining room at Versailles which was used after hunting expeditions. Both paintings can now be seen at the Château de Chantilly.

CHAPTER TWO

Advice to the oyster eater

WHILE WORKING ON this book, I have tasted a lot of oysters and discussed their merits with oyster growers and experts in Britain and France. I shall try to pass on to the reader what I have learnt. The most valuable experience I had was when I read in *l'Ostréiculteur Français*, the journal of the French oyster growers, that a competition for the best Pacific oysters grown in Brittany was to be held as part of a food and wine fair; Breton oyster growers were invited to send in baskets of 50 oysters to be judged by a panel of 8 judges according to 5 criteria listed in the announcement. I rang up the organiser and asked if I might come along and see how to judge oysters. Not only was I invited along and treated in the friendliest possible way, but when the day came I was invited to join the panel in place of a Frenchman who did not turn up. I thus became one of the judges of *l'Huître d'Or de Bretagne*. What an honour! And what fun it was. It all took place in a modern agricultural college and research establishment in Rennes. In a laboratory each batch of oysters was given a code number and every oyster was weighed to see if it was within the stipulated weight limits. Next twenty were opened and, as a measure of quality, the weight of the flesh within the twenty was compared with their weight before they were opened. From each batch a tray of ten was laid out for inspection unopened, then ten from each batch open, and then ten open but empty so that the shells could be examined. Finally came the tasting of the oysters one after another in separate booths in a special darkened tasting room; and then lunch and wine and eloquent speeches. It was after four o'clock before we rose from the table.

But back to useful advice about oysters.

The two types of oyster and their prices
Nowadays there are two types of oyster on offer in Britain. They are shown on

page 15. The classic type, now very scarce and expensive, for reasons we explore in this book, is round in shape, rather like a scallop, and rather flat. Oysters of this type are called 'natives' (or rarely 'edulis' from their Latin name *Ostrea edulis*); and are also known colloquially as 'flats'. Sometimes the name of the place from which they have come is added. In the past Colchester and Whitstable were the dominant names, but nowadays sources in Ireland and the west of England are more common. The French use the word *Belons* for native oysters, after an estuary in Brittany that was once a famous source of supply, or less usually *plates* (meaning flat).

Oysters of the less expensive type have a deeply cupped lower shell and flat top shell; they are more long than round; and their shell is crenellated and of a coarse texture. They are usually called 'rock oysters', or just plain 'oysters'. Occasionally you will find them called 'Pacific oysters' or 'gigas' (from their Latin name *Crassostrea gigas*). As with natives, the place where they were grown is sometimes added in the belief that it will sound attractive. For example, you may find the word 'Scottish' or 'Irish' or the name of a county or the name of a Scottish loch used as a descriptor. In French they are often just called *huîtres* but they are also referred to as *huîtres creuses* (cupped oysters) or just *creuses*.

'Natives' (and the French *Belons)* is a prestigious word reserved for that type of oyster, and restaurants and other suppliers do not fail so to use it. Anything that is not called a native will be a rock oyster, whatever fancy name it may be given.

Whether to go for natives or for rock oysters is a matter of taste and the depth of your pocket. The difference in taste between the two types of oyster has been likened to the difference between the sole and the plaice. Both those flat fish are excellent, but the first is more highly esteemed and much more expensive than the second. The native oyster, like the sole, has firm flesh and a taste that is subtle. The rock oyster has a more watery flesh and a taste that is sharper and ever so slightly metallic. Connoisseurs will say that the native is unquestionably superior. But it is a matter of taste. Rock oysters can be delicious.

The sort of retail price you have to pay for oysters to consume at home is now 40p to 50p each for rock oysters, 60p to 90p each for natives of moderate size; in restaurants you will have to pay more. For large oysters you will pay more than for small, but it is hard to say how much more. There is a scale on which native oysters have traditionally been graded in Britain according to their size (i.e. area) which, since they are of fairly regular shape, was measured by putting them through a ring or by looking at them. For each size there was a typical average weight per oyster to which reference could be made. The scale and average weights ran from No 1's for the largest oysters (120 grams each or more) down to No 5's for the smallest (55 grams average weight). Rock oysters are of such irregular shape that they can be measured only by weight, but when you find rock oysters in a shop, supermarket or restaurant in Britain, they are not offered to you in different categories according to weight and the average weight of what you are offered is generally not specified. What is offered to you can vary a lot but will usually be in the range 70 to 120 grams.

In France, as in Britain, a smaller number means a larger oyster but, apart from that, matters are very different. The French system of classifiying oysters is formal, rational and rather elaborate. Thus in the classification of rock oysters three characterisitics are taken into account and tested by sampling: the unopened weight, which is indicated on a menu or in a fish shop by the number appropriate to that size; the ratio of the weight of flesh to the unopened weight, which is the basis of the descriptors *Fines* and *Spéciales*; and, thirdly, whether the oysters have been fattened in *claires* (where, besides putting on weight, they may get a special flavour and colour; see page 49). It is these descriptors which, combined, produce terms such as *Fines de claires*. There is a different and older system for classifying *Belons* (natives), in which the size scale starts with 000 (equivalent to our No. 1's) and proceeds 00, then 0 and then 1, 2 and so on to No. 5's, the average weight of which is only 33 grams, much less than the average weight of British No. 5's (55 grams). For the benefit of readers who go to France, the French system of grading rock oysters is explained more fully in Appendix A (page 183). Once you understand its logic, everything makes sense. If the EU were to standardise the grading of rock oysters in member countries on French lines, the British oyster eater would be better off at home and less confused when he went to France. In the meantime, the point to remember is that in both countries a higher number means a smaller oyster, but the scales and everything else are different.

Where to buy

It is not easy to buy oysters in England. Not many fishmongers sell oysters and, if they do, they usually know very little about them. Moreover they assume, rightly, that their customers know no more than they do. The risk is not that you will be sold oysters that are infected; the new EU regulations have taken care of that. It is that you will be sold oysters that are too big or too milky or are stunted; or that the oysters will be wrongly described if you ask what sort they are. For example, when I asked a fishmonger if he had any natives, he paused for a minute, obviously baffled by the meaning of the word, and then pointing to some oysters said, 'Yes, these are natives; they come from Norfolk.' They were rock oysters.

There are four possible ways of buying oysters:

1. Buy from a reputable supermarket that stocks oysters. For example, Waitrose, Tesco and ASDA have begun to sell rock oysters.

2. Buy direct from growers, a number of whom deliver oysters in excellent condition using 24 hour delivery services. Do not be put off by distance. Some of the best oysters to be had come in perfect condition from Ireland and Northern Ireland, from the west of England and from Scotland. And be warned that there are substantial differences in the prices charged by different suppliers for the same type of oyster (i.e. for natives and for rock oysters), differences that bear no relationship to the quality of the oysters you are sent. Do not be influenced either by sales literature that is lyrical about the place where the oysters are grown or by the place name. A list of suppliers can be obtained from the Shellfish Association of Great Britain at the Fishmongers' Hall, London EC4R 9EL. Try different suppliers in turn until you find the combination of oysters you like and price that is, for you, the 'best buy'. If you go to an oyster bar or restaurant and find oysters you like, ask where those oysters come from, track down the grower and try ordering direct from him.

3. Choose a fishmonger you know and feel you can trust.

4. Go in the early morning to Billingsgate.

In fishmongers and supermarkets you will usually be offered only rock oysters. Natives, being scarce and about twice as expensive as Pacific oysters, are stocked only by top fishmongers, for example Harrods and Selfridges; they are best ordered direct from growers.

If consumption and production of rock oysters are expanded substantially, as they now could be, oysters may come to be stocked and understood by every fishmonger, as they are in France. But until that happens, direct ordering from growers and buying from supermarkets will generally be the most reliable way to obtain good oysters.

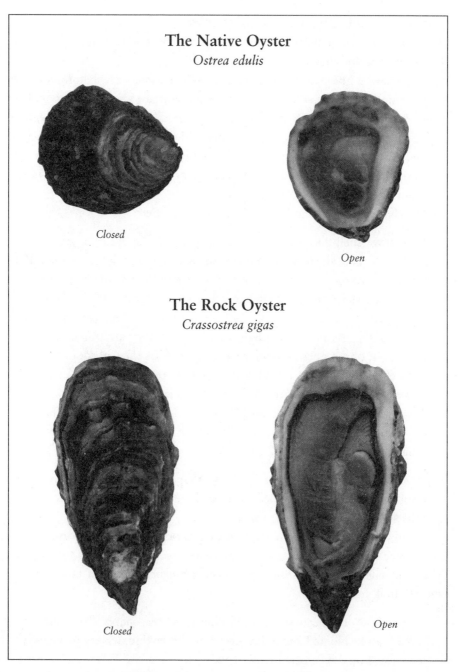

The Native Oyster
Ostrea edulis

Closed

Open

The Rock Oyster
Crassostrea gigas

Closed

Open

The native and the rock oyster compared.

Assessing the condition of oysters

With both types of oyster it is important that they should be in good condition. This is what to look for.

First there is the external appearance. When oysters are before you in a shop, or have been delivered to you, or when you are about to open and eat them, the first thing to establish is that they are alive. See if any of them are gaping open with a gap between its upper and lower shells. If any of them is gaping, tap it with your finger or with a coin or pencil and see if it closes. If it does not close, it is dead or dying and should not be eaten. If many are in this condition, reject the lot.

The characteristics to look for in a rock oyster are:

1. A lower shell that is deep, affording space for the oyster to grow.
2. A shell that widens out from the hinge and is slightly fan-shaped. If the shell is narrow and no wider at the far end than at the hinge, there will not be space for the oyster to grow satisfactorily. Oysters become misshapen like this, and sometimes bent, if they have been crammed too close together in the plastic mesh bags in which they are usually grown nowadays, or have been crowded close together on the seabed. In France these elongated oysters (which are despised) are called *oreilles de lapin* (rabbits' ears); in English they are sometimes called bananas.
3. The shell should be undamaged; it should be solid, not flaky; it should not be dead in appearance. Barnacles on the shell do not matter but are usually removed for appearances' sake.

For natives, the same criteria apply, but the shape you look for is different. You look for depth in the lower shell or, in colloquial terms, for oysters that are 'well-heeled'; and for a circular shape.

Secondly there is the internal appearance, though you will probably be able to examine the internal appearance only when you have brought your oysters home, or when you have some open oysters put before you at table. Here is what to look for:

1. The body of the oyster should consist of reasonably firm flesh; it should not be bloated and milky, nor should it be thin, watery or stringy; the flesh should be creamy white.
2. The inside of the shell should, ideally, be shiny white and smooth. If it is discoloured, usually grey or green, that does not matter. Occasionally

you may see a blister where mud has entered and the oyster has grown a layer of shell over it. Such blisters are harmless, provided you do not puncture them with your knife when opening the oyster or with your fork when eating it, so releasing the stale mud and a nasty smell.

Judging the taste of oysters

There are three elements to the taste of an oyster – salinity, texture and pure taste. All will be influenced by the quality of the waters from which the oyster has come. Oysters like estuaries and other coastal areas where there is a mixture of sweet and salt water in which plankton grow well. The water at each place will have its own characteristics. These can be permanently damaged by industrialisation, the building of harbours and coastal works, and other acts of man. And they can be temporarily affected in a manner that will cause temporary variations in the quality and taste of oysters from a growing area by natural variations in rainfall (which changes the supply of freshwater) and in the temperature.

The salinity of an oyster should be neither so high as to make the oyster sharply salty, nor so low as to make it insipid. The texture should be firm, not milky or stringy.

What the taste should be is a most elusive, if not impossible, thing to describe. The best description I know is that an oyster should have '*le goût de la mer*' (the taste of the sea). It is a description that will be understood at once by any oyster eater; it is likely to be incomprehensible to anyone who has never eaten an oyster. It does not mean that in a good oyster you should taste crude sea water but that you should taste what seems to be a nectar that the oyster has magically distilled from the sea. Sweetness and a slight nutty flavour should be perceptible when you chew a good oyster, two qualities which are usually more pronounced in the native than in the rock oyster.

The pleasure of eating oysters is not just in the taste. It is also in the unusual sensation of putting into your mouth something that is cool, wet, soft and sensuous. And you can also entertain the thought that oysters, which used to be recommended as an invalid diet, have nutritional virtues. A balanced appraisal of the food value of oysters was included in a report published by the Government in 1956:

Opinions which have been expressed regarding the food value of oysters vary from condemnation as 'very expensive seawater' to almost lyrical praise, as in the French expression '*l'huître, aliment complet, médicament précieux.*' In fact the composition of oysters is most easily compared with that of fresh milk… the percentage of water is about the same, while fats are less abundant in oysters, which are however substantially richer in both proteins and carbohydrates. Oysters, like fresh milk, contain several essential vitamins…. They also contain a variety of minerals including iodine, iron, copper, zinc, manganese and arsenic, in addition to the more commonly occurring calcium, magnesium, potassium, sodium, phosphorus and sulphur.

Oysters are therefore a well-balanced, easily digestible, nutritious food, rich in those elements – minerals and vitamins – which are most likely to be deficient in the highly processed foods which form the bulk of modern diets.[1]

Recently attention has been paid to more trendy aspects of the oyster's nutritional properties: they are rich in Omega 3, a fatty acid which helps lower cholesterol levels and is the key ingredient in those fish oil tablets that are eaten nowadays by people who worry about cholesterol; and they contain an amino-acid (taurin) which can help lower blood pressure.[2]

Taste and size

To think that 'big is better' is a mistake with oysters, as it is with most foods. It is an idea that has been fostered by a few expensive restaurants and oyster bars which offer only large native oysters. Large oysters look impressive and, since they are more expensive, a restaurant will make more money from them than from small ones. Fortunately for the consumer, London restaurants and oyster bars seem at last to be changing their ways and offering small natives.

With native oysters the smallest size you are likely to be offered in England (No. 3's or No. 4's) usually have the most taste. Go for them where you are offered a choice. Beware large coarse flat oysters with heavy shells that are sometimes offered as natives by slightly off-beat oyster establishments. They are the modern equivalent of the scuttle mouths (*pieds de cheval*) which were sold cheap on the streets of London in the nineteenth-century oyster boom (Chapter 3). They come direct from natural beds where native oysters that have grown to all sizes are still sometimes found. The true natives, which you will normally be offered, have been re-layed to fatten and finish in estuarine waters.

With rock oysters you are not often offered a choice of size in Britain (in contrast to France), and what is on offer can vary considerably from one supplier to another. Sometimes you will be offered rock oysters that are very large and whose flesh is too fatty or milky. At other extremes they may be small, perhaps misshapen and too lean and stringy inside. Avoid the extremes and choose those of moderate size. It is impossible to give more precise advice because of the lack in Britain of a standard grading system.

In France, you need to go for grades higher than the minimum. The French offer *Belons* (natives) down to such a small size that it is best to go for a medium grade. The same is true of rock oysters. Moreover because French rock oysters in important growing areas have for several years been suffering from poor growth (see Chapter 9), they are often of poor quality, meaning that there is little flesh in them and what there is is watery. It therefore pays to go for *fines* or *spéciales* so that you can be sure there will be flesh in your oysters. Or, better still, go for *fines de claires*: oysters are so much cheaper in France than in Britain that you can afford it.

Seasons

A good rule is that oysters are at their best from the end of October or later, depending on the weather, to the end of February. This applies with particular force to natives. They can be bought only when there is an R in the month. In the summer, their breeding season, they become disagreeably milky, or appear gritty if carrying larvae; and they take time to recover and reach prime condition.

The rock oyster, for which there is no close season, can be good to eat in the summer in Britain, since the waters are usually too cold for it to breed and become milky. But that is not always the case. In a warm English summer, they can become broody and milky, though it depends on the warmth of the water in the growing area from which they come. In the more southerly parts of France, where the waters are sufficiently warm for Pacific oysters to breed regularly, they are best avoided in the summer. In the north of France, where water conditions are much like those in Britain, Pacific oysters can be good in summer.

Keeping oysters

Oysters are not best eaten straight out of the water. Their taste is at its best after a day or two out of the water, during which time the seawater within them will have become less tangy. They can be kept for a week or more in a cool place. The ideal temperature is about 5 to 8 degrees C., which is to be found in the less cold part of a typical refrigerator. Do not expose oysters to a temperature around freezing point or you may kill them. Keep them covered with a damp cloth to prevent them drying out. *Never* put them back into water, salt or fresh. Before you use them, check that your oysters are alive by tapping those that are gaping open (see page 16).

You can keep oysters, like other fish, deep frozen for up to three months. The low temperature in a deep freeze kills them but also prevents them from going bad – which is not the case if they are exposed to temperatures around zero. Provided you cook deep-frozen oysters soon after thawing them, they will be good. They should not be eaten raw.

Opening oysters

To the uninitiated, opening oysters is a daunting task, but it is only a matter of learning the technique, which is essentially simple, and having a suitable oyster knife.

The mechanics of the operation

If oysters have mud and other dirt on the outside, first scrub them under the cold tap. Do not wash oysters in a basin, for the water will become muddy and may get into them.

Before attempting to open an oyster you must understand the mechanics of the operation. The object is to insert a knife between the upper and lower shells and then to move the knife across the oyster as close as possible to the upper shell so as to sever the muscle which holds the top and bottom shells together, where it is attached to the upper shell. If this is accomplished, the body of the oyster will be intact in the lower shell, still attached to it by the lower end of the muscle. If you fail to keep the knife against the upper shell and sever the muscle lower down , you will have cut through the body of the oyster leaving part of it attached to the top and part to the bottom, altogether a rather mangled mess.

A second, easy, operation is to sever the lower end of the muscle as close as possible to the lower shell. The body of the oyster is then free and can be picked up with an ordinary fork and eaten. In France this second operation is usually left to the eater, who is provided with a small oyster fork with blades in the recesses between its points with which to cut the oyster free from the lower shell. Oyster forks are a rarity in Britain. But the crucial question is how to get the knife between the upper and lower shells of the oyster when

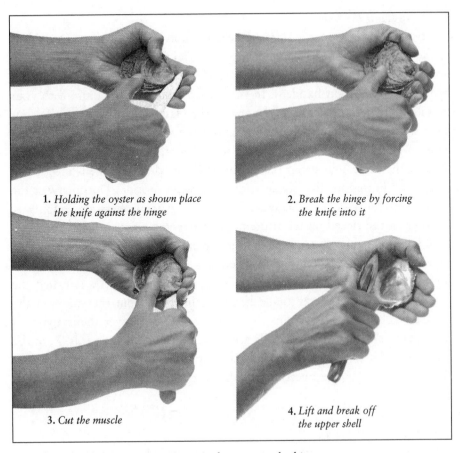

1. Holding the oyster as shown place the knife against the hinge

2. Break the hinge by forcing the knife into it

3. Cut the muscle

4. Lift and break off the upper shell

Opening a rock oyster at the hinge.

the oyster, resisting assault, will be holding its shells together with all its strength.

There are two methods – from the side and from the hinge. Opening from the side is more refined. It requires less brute force once you have mastered it. But, except in the hands of an expert, it is less well suited to the Pacific oyster than to the native because the shell of the Pacific is more crumbly and you risk ending up with fragments of shell in the open oysters which those who eat them will have to pick out – or remove as delicately as they can from their mouths when they bite on them. Moreover, entry from the side is more dangerous to the novice, since the risk of the knife slipping and wounding the hand that is holding the oyster is greater than when opening from the hinge.

Opening from the side

To open an oyster from the side you need to apply the knife about two-thirds of the way along the oyster from the hinge, so that it will enter the oyster just ahead of the muscle. Hold the oyster cushioned by a cloth in your left hand (if you are right-handed). In your right hand hold the knife with your thumb about 1 cm away from the end of the blade, so that if the knife slips your thumb may prevent it sliding across the shell and entering your left hand. With the knife, find the divide where the top and bottom shell meet, holding the knife almost flat (i.e. at the angle at which the shells meet), and wiggle the knife into the divide with a sideways motion. Do not twist the knife. A useful trick for a beginner is to take a pair of pliers and snip away the shell of the closed oyster at the point where you want to insert the knife until you expose the divide between the top and bottom shells. It is then easy to insert the knife into the divide. There is a gadget on the market designed for this technique which combines a snipper and a blade. It is called the 'Oyster-cracker'. Once the blade has been inserted from the side and the muscle has been cut, it remains to pull the upper and lower shells apart till the hinge snaps and the two shells are separate. While you do this, keep the lower shell flat so as not to spill the water in it, which is known as the liquor. We shall return to the question whether the oyster eater should drink the liquor.

Opening from the hinge

Opening from the hinge means forcing the knife into the oyster at the hinge or close to it and working the knife to and fro sideways or twisting it till you snap the strong ligament that holds the two shells together at the hinge. It requires a good deal of force. Although the risk of the knife slipping is less than with opening from the side, since you are from the start pushing the knife into a visible recess, the damage you may do yourself if it slips is greater, since you are using more force. An excellent gadget which reduces this risk is made in France, the *Clic d'Huître*. It consists of a little plastic block hollowed out to the shape of the lower side of a Pacific oyster. You place it on the edge of a table and put the oyster in the hollow. (The block has a lip to prevent it sliding away from the edge of the table.) Holding the oyster down with your fingers spread out away from the line of the knife, you then use your knife to attack the hinge or the side with little risk of damaging yourself.

Oyster knives

The novice opener would be well advised to start by learning to open oysters not with an oyster knife but with one of two gadgets which make oyster opening relatively safe and easy, the *Clic d'Huître* and the oyster-cracker. There is a lot to be said for starting with the oyster-cracker, the safest of all oyster-opening intruments, and then going on to use the *Clic d'Huître* which, if well used, makes less mess of the oyster than the oyster-cracker. Most people will want to move on to using a knife in the traditional way, or will at least want to try their hand at it. For that purpose you must get an oyster knife. If you use an ordinary knife, you may easily bend or break it, and you may hurt yourself badly if the knife slips. Oyster knives are available at smart kitchen shops, and are on offer from most of those oyster growers who sell direct to customers. Some have guards on them, like those on a carving fork, which are intended to protect your hand if the knife slips, but guards do not afford much protection. The blade should be short. If you open oysters at the hinge, the knife mainly

The pleasure of oysters – Le Capucin Gourmand.

23

serves as a lever and needs to be really strong; a clean screwdriver is a safe alternative for breaking the hinge, followed by a small kitchen knife for cutting the muscle. If you open from the side, a thinner less strong knife is suitable.

Unorthodox methods
There are two unorthodox methods of opening oysters. You can deep freeze them, after which they will open on being thawed; or you can put them singly under a microwave for 20 seconds, after which they will be easy to open. Since both methods

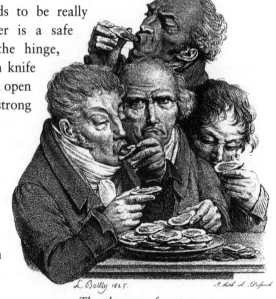

The pleasure of oysters –
Les Mangeurs d'Huîtres.

kill the oyster, it is important to eat oysters to which these techniques have been applied without delay.

Serving oysters

There used to be debate about whether it was best to serve oysters on the lower shell ('on the round'), in which case the liquor is retained, or on the upper shell ('on the flat') without the liquor. Nowadays oysters are almost always served in the lower shell, leaving the oyster eater to decide after eating the oyster whether he wants to raise the shell to his lips and drink the liquor. Some people hold that you want to taste the pure flavour of the oyster without the liquor, others that the liquor is delicious. In fact the liquor varies in flavour according to the characteristics of the water from which the oyster came, how long it has been out of the water and how long it has been open. The best advice is to try the liquor and see what you think of it.[3]

A refinement in the serving of oysters that used to be common is to cut off the beard, i.e the outer fringe of the oyster, which, being sometimes rather tough, may remain in your mouth like a small stringy bit of meat. This practice is almost unheard of nowadays.

Oysters are served, usually six to a plate laid in a circle, accompanied by thinly sliced brown bread with butter to hand. It is a mistake to butter the bread, both because it becomes soggy and because there are people, of whom I am one, who think that butter does not go well with oysters. Oysters are quite often served on a bed of crushed ice. Unless it is hot, there is no merit to this practice, except that crushed ice serves as a bed in which oysters can be made to lie on their backs without falling about spilling the liquor. Of course you want oysters to be cool, not warm, when you first put them into your mouth, but you do not want them to be cold; their taste only emerges if they reach a reasonable warmth in your mouth. They can be made to stand without tipping over by being served on an oyster plate which has indentations the shape of an oyster shell, or by by putting a bed of seaweed or salt on each plate.

People add all kinds of things to oysters – lemon juice, black pepper, red pepper, tabasco sauce, vinegar. The serious oyster lover is often shocked by the way he sees these additives applied, most of all if he sees them applied to natives. Natives have such a delicate flavour that many connoisseurs consider them best on their own, unadulterated. Try one or two that way before adding anything; then add only some drops of lemon and perhaps a little pepper to one oyster at a time before you eat it; and then go back to an unadulterated oyster as a reference point. The Pacific oyster, having a sharper flavour and sometimes being too fat, can better withstand strong additives, but if your Pacific oysters are of a moderate size, good texture and flavour, treat them with the same respect as natives. It is when they are too fat that sharp additives seem positively to be called for to help you get them down. But remember that you can refrain from eating fat oysters or cook them (see below).

What to drink with oysters

Dry white wine, slightly chilled, is the classic drink with oysters. Muscadet or Gros Plant, two quite cheap wines, both go well with Pacific oysters or with native oysters. Chablis, softer and more expensive, goes well with natives but is rather wasted on Pacific oysters; and so does Sancerre. Champagne with oysters is glamorous and festive, but not, to my mind, a particularly pleasing combination. Guinness, which goes very well with oysters in a cool climate, fits a particular Anglo-Irish mood. And so of course does Black Velvet (Guinness fortified with one part in seven – no more – of champagne). As with so many foods, wine does not complement the taste of oysters so closely that it is best to sip wine after every one or two oysters. There is a lot to be said for eating several oysters, exploring repeatedly their subtle taste, and then pausing for a little wine.

Cooked oysters

Good oysters, in particular natives, are so good raw that it is a shame to cook them. It is not such a shame to cook rock oysters or the types of oyster found in America, especially if they are too fat. But even then cooked oysters should be approached with great caution. In the first place people invent ghastly ways of cooking oysters. One example is the Carpetbag Steak, an Australian invention. You take a thick fillet steak, cut a pocket in the middle of it, stuff it with fresh oysters and grill it. The result is that both the steak and the oysters are ruined. Maybe this recipe has gone out of fashion since immigrants from southern Europe improved the Australian cuisine. But it is not only our rugged cousins in the Antipodes, poised over barbecues, who have savaged the oyster. That bird of a very different feather, Noel Coward, who fancied himself as a cook, invented a dish of oysters enveloped in mashed potato and deep fried. When he tried them on his friends they did not go down well. Oysters enveloped in potato were later found hidden in pot plants and down the sides of chairs.[4]

I recommend Oysters Mornay, Oyster Stew (as cooked and served on the east coast of the United States), Fried Oysters with Bacon (whether with the oysters wrapped in the bacon to form Angels on Horseback or served separately) and, for those who feel really extravagant and are good cooks, Oysters in Champagne. I also recommend using oysters instead of kidneys to produce Steak and Oyster Pie and, better still, Steak and Oyster Pudding. That is a majestic dish. Preceded by raw oysters, the pudding makes a wonderful winter feast for a gathering of oyster lovers. Recipes for cooked oysters can be found in cookery books.

CHAPTER THREE

The mid-19th century oyster boom in Britain

O YSTERS ARE SUCH a rarity in England today that they can scarcely be found outside a few oyster bars in London. Few English people know how to eat oysters, let alone how to open them. Most English people are afraid of oysters. Yet in Dickens's time they were eaten by the masses in London. And in France today you see them in abundance on stalls outside Paris restaurants; you find them in the markets and fish shops of provincial French towns; and at Christmas every French family eats them. If the French can enjoy oysters in abundance today, why cannot we? Why have they become so scarce here but not in France?

But first, is it really true that in the middle of the 19th century oysters were abundant and cheap in Britain? For an answer it is necessary to rely on bits and pieces of information, since statistics of the oyster trade were first produced only in the 1890's. Dickens is a good starting point.

Dickens

Dickens's best-known passage on oysters is in *Pickwick Papers*, written in 1836. It is a conversation precisely to the effect that oysters were a food of the poor. Mr Pickwick has just set off for Ipswich by coach, attended by Sam Weller and Sam's father, Mr Weller senior. They are going along Whitechapel, through the East End of London:

"Not a wery nice neighbourhood this, sir," said Sam, with a touch of the hat, which always preceded his entering into conversation with his master.

"It is not indeed, Sam," replied Mr Pickwick, surveying the crowded and filthy street through which they were passing.

Oysters, Sir, Illustrated London News, *1860's.*

"It's a wery remarkable circumstance, sir," said Sam, "that poverty and oysters always seems to go together."

"I don't understand you, Sam," said Mr Pickwick.

"What I mean, sir," said Sam, "is, that the poorer the place is, the greater call there seems to be for oysters. Look here, sir; here's a oyster stall to every half-dozen houses. The street's lined vith 'em. Blessed if I don't think that ven a man's wery poor, he rushes out of his lodgings, and eats oysters in reg'lar desperation."

"To be sure he does," said Mr Weller, senior; "and it's just the same vith pickled salmon!"

"Those are two very remarkable facts which never occurred to me before," said Mr Pickwick. "The very first place we stop at, I shall make a note of them."

By this time they had reached the turnpike at Mile End.[1]

Dickens also wrote a little moral tale, "The Misplaced Attachment of Mr John Dounce", originally called "Love and Oysters", in which he describes a superior oyster shop of the same period. He plays on the reputation of oysters as an aphrodisiac. It is the story of a retired glove and braces maker, a widower who, on his way home from an evening spent drinking with other 'old boys', is attracted by 'a newly-opened oyster shop, on a magnificent scale, with natives laid, one deep, in circular marble basins in the windows, together with little round barrels of oysters directed to Lords and Baronets, and Colonels and Captains, in every part of the habitable globe. Behind the natives were the barrels and behind the barrels was a young lady of about five-and-twenty, all in blue, and all alone – splendid creature, charming face and lovely figure!'. Ordering some of the oysters at eight pence a dozen and then more, John Dounce becomes besotted by the girl, so much so that in the days that follow he neglects his friends and his spinster daughters and woos her over many oysters. But she, 'having derived sufficient profit and emolument from John

Dounce's attachment' rejects him, and he 'having lost his old friends, alienated his relations, and rendered himself ridiculous to everybody, made offers successively to a school-mistress, a landlady, a feminine tobacconist, and a housekeeper; and being directly rejected by each and every one of them, was accepted by his cook with whom he now lives, a hen-pecked husband, a melancholy monument of antiquated misery, and a living warning to uxorious old boys.'[2]

In *Great Expectations*, published in 1861, by which time the price of oysters was rising, there is another reference to them. Pip, an orphan, having been brought up at the forge of his devoted uncle, Joe Gargery the blacksmith, comes into a generous allowance from an unknown benefactor and moves to London to be educated and made into a gentleman. When he revisits the neighbourhood where he grew up in order to call on Miss Haversham, whom he believes to be his benefactor, he fails through feelings of social superiority to call on Joe Gargery at his forge. Filled with remorse on his return to London, he at once sends Joe 'a penitential codfish and a barrel of oysters'.[3]

Mayhew

A more analytical view of the oyster in the mid 19th century, with particular emphasis on the role of the poor in peddling oysters and in consuming them, is to be found in Henry Mayhew's *London Labour and the London Poor: a Cyclopaedia of the Conditions and Earnings of Those That Will Work, Those That Cannot Work, and Those That Will Not Work*.[4] Mayhew is remarkable for having reported in a most lively style the condition and conversation of the poor and also for having made statistical estimates of what the poor of London lived on. His study, first published in 1851, was based on articles he wrote for the *Morning Chronicle* in the years immediately before that.

Mayhew tells how the coming of railways, which carried fish rapidly from distant parts of the coast, brought about a huge increase in the supply of fresh fish to London, causing it to be cheaper than before and to be conveyed by costermongers 'to every poor man's door, both in the thickly-crowded streets where the poor reside – a family at least in a room – in the vicinity of Drury-lane and of Whitechapel, in Westminster, Bethnal-green and St. Giles's, and through the long miles of the suburbs. For all low-priced fish the poor are the costermongers' best customers, and a fish diet seems to be becoming almost as common among the ill-paid classes of London, as is a potato diet among the peasants of Ireland.'[5]

Far and away the most important cheap fish were herrings, which constituted 'the great slop diet of the metropolis', but oysters were sold in astonishing numbers too: Mayhew estimates that nearly 500 million oysters and over 1,000 million herrings passed through Billingsgate in a year. These figures come from estimates he made of the quantities of fish of many kinds passing through Billingsgate. One hopes they are reasonably accurate, for there is no other figure for the supply of oysters in Britain of which the origins can be traced until official statistics were first published in the 1890's.

The evidence as to their accuracy is not altogether reassuring. Mayhew says they are based on 'facts… furnished me by the most eminent of the Billingsgate salesmen – gentlemen to whom I am under many obligations for their kindness, consideration, and assistance, at all times and seasons.' A contemporary described his methods of work in rather unflattering terms:

> He was largely paid, and, greatest joy of all, had an array of assistant writers, stenographers, and hansom cabmen constantly at his call. London labourers of special interest, with picturesque specimens of the London poor, were brought to the *Chronicle* office, where they told their stories to Mayhew, who redictated them, with an added colour of his own, to the shorthand writer in waiting. His younger brother, Augustus, helped him in his vivid descriptions, and an authority on political economy controlled his gay statistics.[6]

His figure implies that if all the oysters passing through Billingsgate were eaten in Greater London, of which the population was 2.7 million, average consumption was 185 oysters a year per man, woman and child. This is probably too high, since more oysters were probably sent from Billingsgate to destinations outside London than came into London by markets other than Billingsgate. By way of comparison, average consumption of oysters in France today, taking national output divided by population, is probably about 40 a year; in Britain it is now only a fraction of an oyster a year. In short, Mayhew's figure is an indication that an awful lot of oysters were eaten in London at this time; it does not look reliable, but it is the best figure we have.

By applying prices to his estimates of quantities Mayhew made estimates of the value of fish sold. The total comes to nearly £1.5 million, of which £900 thousand is for herrings and £156 thousand for shellfish; of the figure for shellfish, which 'can only be considered as luxuries', oysters account for £125 thousand: they are the principal luxury. In these calculations Mayhew takes the price of both herrings and oysters to be four for a penny, a price which makes herrings seem truly cheap and oysters a minor luxury. By comparison, cod is priced at 1½d. a pound and salmon at 6d. a pound.

The oysters came to market up the Thames on oyster boats that were moored close together at Billingsgate:

> The costermongers have nicknamed the long row of oyster boats moored close alongside the wharf "Oyster-street". On looking down the line of tangled ropes and masts, it seems as though the little boats would sink with the crowds of men and women thronged together on their decks. It is as busy a scene as one can well behold. Each boat has its black sign-board and salesman in his white apron walking up and down "his shop", and on each deck is a bright pewter pot and tin covered plate, the remains of the salesman's breakfast... the red cap of the man in the hold bobs up and down as he rattles the shells about with his spade. These holds are filled with oysters – a grey mass of shell and sand – on which is a bushel measure well piled up in the centre...[7]

The trade had changed since 1848 when large shelly oysters, called "scuttle-mouths" by the costermongers, were first introduced from the Sussex coast. The flesh inside these oysters, which were dredged up from natural deep oyster beds in the Channel, was small relative to the size of the shell, and it was coarse compared with that of native oysters bred and fattened on the coastal beds of the greater Thames estuary. The French term for them is '*pieds de cheval*' – horses' hooves.

Mayhew reports that the sale of the scuttle mouths was at first enormous; and that under the influence of this increase in the supply of oysters, prices had fallen. One street-seller told him that eighteen or twenty years before he sold oysters "oft enough at 1d a piece. Now I sell far finer at three a penny...". Since the general level of prices was nearly stable, his figures tell us that oysters became really cheap at this time; and so do his reports of what is said by those who sold oysters on the streets.

An old woman who had 'seen better days', but had been reduced to keeping an oyster stall, gave him an account of her customers.

> As to my customers, sir, she said, why, indeed, they're all sorts. It's not a very few times that gentlemen (I call them so because they're mostly so civil) will stop – just as it's getting darkish, perhaps – and look about

The oyster seller, H. Morland.

them, and then come to me and say very quick: 'Two penn'orth for a whet'. Ah! some of 'em will look, may be, like poor parsons down upon their luck, and swallow their oysters as if they was taking poison in a hurry.

I many a time think that two penn'orth is a poor gentleman's dinner. It's the same often – but only half as often, or not half – with a poor lady, with a veil that once was black, over a bonnet to match, and shivering through her shawl. She'll have the same. About two penn'orth is the mark still; it's mostly two penn'orth. My son says, it's because that's the price of a glass of gin, and some persons buy oysters instead – but that's only his joke, sir. It's not the vulgar poor that's our chief customers. There's many of them won't touch oysters, and I've heard some of them say: 'The sight of 'em makes me sick; it's like eating snails.' The poor girls that walk the streets often buy; some are brazen and vulgar, and often the finest dressed are the vulgarest.... One of them always says she must keep at least a penny for gin after her oysters.

My heartiest customers, that I serve with the most pleasure, are working people, on a Saturday night. One couple – I think the wife always goes to meet her husband on a Saturday night – has two, or three, or four penn'orth, as happens, and it's pleasant to hear them say, 'Won't you have another, John?' or, 'Do have one or two more, Mary Anne.' I've served them that way two or three years.

I send out a good many oysters, opened, for people's suppers, and sometimes for supper parties – at least, I suppose so, for there's five or six dozen often ordered. The maid-servants come for them then, and I give them two or three for themselves....[8]

The first day of oysters, Illustrated London News, *1861.*

Mayhew had a quaint view, apparently derived from pundits of the day, of the nutritional value of fish and the effects that eating so much of it might have on the poor of London.

If the diet of a people be a criterion, as has been asserted, of their character, it may be feared that the present extensive fish-diet of the working-people of London, is as indicative of degeneracy of character, as Cobbett insisted must result from the consumption of tea and 'the cursed root', the potato. The 'flesh of fish', says Pereira on Diet, 'is less satisfying than the flesh of either quadrupeds or birds. As it contains a larger proportion of water (about 80 per cent), it is obviously less nourishing.' Haller tells us that he found himself weakened by a fish-diet; and he states that Roman Catholics are generally debilitated during Lent. Pechlin also affirms that a mechanic, nourished merely by fish, has less muscular power than one who lives on the flesh of warm-blooded animals. Jockeys, who *waste themselves* in order to reduce their weight, live principally on fish.[9]

From the low price and the greatly expanded consumption of oysters described by Dickens and Mayhew we can infer that there was a great increase in the supply of them. How did this come about? Where did they come from?

First, a word about quantities. Apart from Mayhew's figure of nearly 500 million oysters sold at Billingsgate in about 1850, there is one other statistic for this period that one comes across. It is that 'according to calculation' in 1864 700 million oysters were consumed annually in London, and considerably more than that number in the provinces. This statement, which implies that total consumption in the provinces and London together was of the order of 1.5 billion, appeared in *The Times* on October 15 1867.[10] There is no indication who made the calculation. If you take from it the proposition that considerably more oysters were consumed in the provinces than in London and apply that to Mayhew's figure for London, you get a figure of rather more than 1 billion for total national consumption. None of these figures is worth much. It is possible that *The Times* figure of 700 million for London is derived by increasing Mayhew's figure for a decade earlier, in which case all the figures rest on one uncertain foundation stone, the words of "the most eminent of Billingsgate salesmen" from which Mayhew derived his figure.

To see the boom in perspective we need to look back at the previous history of the oyster industry. There are only morsels of history to go by.

Hore

One source of such morsels is J.P. Hore, who in the 1880's wrote a pamphlet arguing that restrictions to stop 'over-dredging' (the dredging of so many oysters that the oyster banks were denuded) and the enforcement of a close season were the right means of dealing with the oyster shortage that followed the oyster boom. As you would expect in pamphleteering, he dredged history for evidence that fitted his case and interpreted it with a slant. All the same what he has to say is interesting.

Way back in 1418, the Mayor of London in a formal proclamation fixed the price of oysters at 4d a bushel. From that date till the beginning of the 17th century, says Hore, 'I have found from time to time that these prices remained unaltered' – which, if true, is a remarkable case of price controls working for two centuries. Early in the 1600's the price rose to one shilling a bushel and by 1634 it had reached 2 shillings and 8 pence, an eightfold increase altogether. Over the same period, the price of superior oysters also rose eightfold, going from 1 shilling to 8 shillings a bushel.[11]

The high prices were attributed to excessive dredging and to inordinate exportation to foreigners, principally the Dutch. Measures were taken to forbid the export of oysters, but they were not effectively enforced. A difficulty was that at the instance of the King, Charles I, permission was accorded to export oysters for the use of his sister, the Queen of Bohemia, and her husband, the Prince of Orange, and their household. "Armed with this privilege, which was greatly abused, all the oysters that could be obtained were ostensibly shipped for these potentates, so that supervisors were at a loss how to act."[12] The high prices continued and the problem was referred to the Admiralty Court, which then had jurisdiction over all matters connected with our sea and coast fisheries. In July 1638, the judge of the court, Sir Henry Marten, wrote advising that the trouble was too much indiscriminate dredging of young and old oysters, the marketing of oysters that were too small, and that in Kent there was

> a greate extraordinary number of oystermen there more than in former times, and the moste parte of them beinge poore, unruly, and incorrigible, and violatinge all orders in dredginge in the sett groundes at prohibited times, and taking broode, have thereby in greate parte taken awaye the stocke and nurserye of oysters.

He concluded by saying that the taking of small oysters should be stopped and that the export embargo enforced, subject to the enforcement of limited exemptions for the Queen of Bohemia and the Prince of Orange.[13] In Hore's opinion the measures were the right ones but, he reports, they were ineffectual in restoring the prices and supplies that formerly prevailed.

In Hore, who must have been an energetic historian, there are anecdotes which suggest that in the 16th and early 17th century oysters were the food of kings and queens. When Henry VIII went to meet the King of France, Francis I, at the Field of Cloth of Gold in 1520, among the provisions sent to Calais were nine barrels of oysters costing 1 shilling and eightpence a barrel. In this he is slightly inaccurate. The meeting, lasting nearly a fortnight and for which the suites of Henry VIII and his queen came to over 5 thousand persons, must have been one of the greatest parties ever held. In the state papers of Henry VIII, the accounts for expenditure on provisions for the meeting include 506 geese, 632 herons, 92 cygnets, 78 storks and vast quantities of other food and drink. But there is no mention of Hore's oysters, the quantity of which anyway seems rather trivial compared with what else was bought. On further examination of the records, the entry for these oysters is to be found in the list of items bought for Henry VIII's meeting with the Emperor Charles V which took place at Calais after the Field of Cloth of Gold and was a relatively modest event.[14] Charles V apparently liked oysters. When, after abdicating his various thrones, he retreated in 1556 to a villa in the grounds of a monastery in Spain, oysters used to be sent up to him from the coast by special courier.[15]

When Queen Elizabeth visited Harefield in 1602, she received as presents: from Mr Doctor Harris, two firkins of oysters; from Sir Thomas Mildmay, two firkins ditto; from Sir Thomas Lucas, four firkins ditto; and from Mr George Hyre, four firkins of "greate" ditto and four firkins of "small" ditto.

Oysters were certainly given to Queen Elizabeth and her courtiers in the expectation of favours by the borough of Colchester:[16]

...on several occasions the Bailiffs despatched presents of oysters (generally a horse load at a time) to Sir Francis Walsingham, and Elizabeth's favourite, Lord Leicester. These presents were made, as was usually the case, to influence these powerful Courtiers to assist the Authorities in some difficulties affecting the borough, and from the replies which the Authorities received... they were not without effect. These replies were as follows:-

From Sir Francis Walsingham
After my hartie commendations. I have receaved your letter of the fourthe of this p'nt, and am verie glad therby to understand that all your controversies be so well appeaced and that you be grown to so good an unitie amonge your selfes; the continewance wherof I greatly wyshe, as the only thinge that shall make your towne to prosper, and to bee well thought of all men. Towching your liberties, for that in other Incorporations I have sometymes so much standying uppon Charters and

Privilidges, that hir Majesties necessarie service hathe thereby been hindred, I would not wishe you, except it be in some great poynt that may towche your town, deeply to stand uppon them. Notwithstanding I will be carefull for the preservation of the same as farre forth as conveniently I maye in the direction of the Commissions and all kynd of service from this place. So withe my hartie thanckes for your present of oysters I byd you farewell. From the Court at Greenwich the fyfte of September 1579.

Your verie loving frend,
Fra. Walsyngham

From the Earl of Leicester
After my right hartye commendacons. I have receyved yor l'res and the oisters you sent me, and do very hartilye thancke you for them, and for your often courteosies in visiting me many times with the lyke, which as occasion shall serve, I will not forget to requyte. Touching your towne my affection is and shall be as it hath bene allwayes, viz., very ready to do anything I may for it, And so shall you well percyve as any occasion shalbe offred wherein I may stand it in steade. In the mean tyme gladde to heare of your good quyet, whiche I wish longe to continewe, I thus bid you right hartily farewell. From the Court the VIth of September 1579.

Your very loving frende,
R. Leycester

That oysters were consumed by people of lesser rank is indicated in a dispatch by the Venetian ambassador, sent in 1554, about the state of England at that time, in which he speaks of the immense supply of oysters and says that occasionally as many as 20 smacks are seen filled with oysters in the Thames. And Hore, in explaining why people were so shocked by the rise in the price of oysters in the early 1600's, says he believes that in the shellfish taverns which our ancestors patronised in those days they were not charged for oysters eaten on the premises but paid only for what they drank: oysters, he implies, were the nuts and olives of that period.

At this time, Mr Hastings, a colourful fox-hunting squire who kept all manner of of hounds 'that ran buck, fox, hare, otter and badger', and who made all his neighbours welcome at his house where they found 'beef pudding and small beer in great plenty', kept at the lower end of his parlour an oyster table which was in constant use all the year round, since 'he never failed to eat oysters before dinner and supper through all seasons', a feat that is plausible since he lived near Poole, a traditional source of oysters. He is a possible example of the invigorating and nutritious properties of the oyster. According to the highly entertaining sketch of him by the first Lord Shaftesbury, he bestowed all his time in blood sports and fishing, 'but what he borrowed to caress his neighbours' wives and daughters, there being not a woman in all his walks of the degree of a yeoman's wife or under, and under the age of forty, but it was extremely her fault if he were not intimately acquainted with her'; and he lived to a hundred.[17]

During the Civil War and the Commonwealth the oyster beds enjoyed a respite as a result of the unsettled state of the country and the impressment of the majority of dredgers into the Channel Fleet during the wars against the Dutch. But with the Restoration, which brought in an oyster-loving court, and the re-opening of trade with the Dutch, there was again a shortage accompanied by high prices. Again there were remonstrations, in response to which measures were taken to enforce restrictions against over-dredging and the observance of the close-season. The result, Hore claims, was that "cheap supplies and cheap prices once more became the order of the day".[18]

After Hore's account of the early 17th century, there is a gap in British oyster history until the mid-19th century, apart from accounts of legal wrangles about titles to oyster beds, and references to oysters by diarists and other writers. In the 1660's Pepys often recorded eating oysters and receiving presents of them: there are more than 50 references to oysters in his diary.[19] Sir Aston Cokayne, the 17th century poet, playfully suggests that the oysters of Essex tempted Julius Caesar to cross to Britain from France, a suggestion in the making of which he may have been influenced by Suetonius, the Roman biographer who said that Caesar came to Britain in search of pearls.[20] In 1662, it was recorded that 'oysters, put up with care, and carried in the cool, were weekly brought fresh and good to Althrope, the house of Lord Spencer', which was eighty miles from the sea.[21] Later, Sir Robert Walpole was regularly sent a couple of barrels of oysters by a neighbour from Lynn, a very welcome gift, we are told, if Walpole's huge bill for oysters shown in his accounts for 1733 is any indication of his love of them.[22] The kindly Dr Johnson was so indulgent to his cat, Hodge, that he used to go out and buy oysters for it, 'lest the servants having that trouble should take a dislike to the poor creature'.[23]

Oyster smacks dredging off Herne Bay, Illustrated London News.

The Boom

The surge in oyster production which reached its peak around 1850 to 1860 seems to have begun some time after the ending of the Napoleonic Wars, probably in the 1830's. Industrial production then rose fast, railways spread rapidly and both population and income increased, generating a general growth in demand for food, which in the case of oysters was amplified by fashion. The Inspector of Irish Fisheries, who was probably not exempt from the gift of embellishing a yarn, tells that it became the fashion in Paris 'to introduce oysters at four meals: at breakfast, luncheon, dinner and supper; no entertainment was considered complete without oysters, and that fashion came into operation in England, and a vast demand for oysters arose'.[24]

There was much poverty at this time, which must have meant that there was no lack of men anxious to make a livelihood by scraping the sea-bed for oysters to be sent by rail to the cities; and fishing boats and dredging techniques were being improved. On the side of both demand and supply the conditions were thus present for a more intense exploitation of the oyster. And then came the discovery of the new deep beds of coarse oysters in the Channel, the scuttle mouths referred to by Mayhew.[25] As you might expect, this discovery of new untapped deposits open to all, like the discovery of a gold field, produced a rush. In the prosaic language of the Royal Commission of 1866 these deep Channel beds 'which have of late been so much worked' produced 'very large returns to the oyster dredgers'.[26]

We have some indications of the increase in fishing activity:

1. The number of men belonging to the Whitstable Oyster Company increased from 36 in 1793, when it was formally created out of an ancient corporation in the nature of a guild, to 408 in 1866, of whom about 300 were working.[27] At Colchester, the other famous centre of English oyster production, the number belonging to the Colne Oyster Fishery Company increased from 73 in 1807, when it was formed, to 280 in the early 1840's and over 400 in 1866.[28] Since the members of the companies were supported by apprentices, the total numbers engaged in oyster fishing at these places must substantially have exceeded these figures.

2. In a petition to Parliament in 1836 it was claimed that there were 2,500 dredgermen in the parishes adjoining Colchester who were dependent on seeking oysters around the coasts of England, France and the Channel Islands in the summer months.[29]

3. Hervey Benham, who wrote lovingly about the history of east-coast fishing boats and fisheries, tells us that, after rapid growth, the Colne Fishery in 1844 employed five hundred fishing smacks and two thousand men, and that there were probably as many more at work nearby in the Blackwater and out of Maldon. 'While hundreds of little cutters averaging from five to fifteen tons were kept busy on the cultivation of the Essex and Suffolk oyster beds, bigger craft ranged far afield to seek the large deep-sea varieties, and also to raid or find legitimate employment in other beds wherever they might be.'[30] Wherever oysters bred 'Essex men would seek them out, and unfortunately generally work them out'.[31]

4. In 1866, upwards of 300 vessels, mostly from Colchester, Rochester and Jersey, were employed in fishing the deep beds in the Channel.

5. Fights over oyster beds occurred in this period, though there was nothing very novel about that. Rights to sea fisheries are not easy to define and enforce, and today there are international quarrels over fishery rights. It is the ferocity of the oyster quarrels that is impressive.

Oyster dredging, E. Duncan, Illustrated London News, *1856.*

For example, in about 1870, when some Brightlingsea smacks went to the Firth of Forth to dredge oysters, the Scots fishermen attacked them in boats laden with stones for ammunition. The men had to sleep under police protection, armed with hatchets and pokers, and finally a gunboat was called in to restore order.[32] Such ferocity has a long history. In Edward III's time a fisherman was killed in a fight over oysters between men from neighbouring fishing villages on the east coast of England. In modern times there was still spectacular violence over oysters after the second world war at Chesapeake Bay in the United States. There had long been oyster wars in the bay where poachers took advantage of a dispute over titles between Maryland and Virginia, the two riparian States, and of rivalry between the oyster police forces of the two states. The end came in 1959 when a poacher called Berkeley Muse was killed in a blaze of gunfire from an oyster-police patrol boat. After that episode the two states got together and an act establishing a joint Potomac river fisheries commission was passed by Congress and signed by President Kennedy in 1962.[33]

Grenville Murray

A popular book, published in 1861, conveys the rumbustious spirit of the oyster boom. It is *The Oyster: Where, How and When to Find, Breed, Cook and Eat It*, with illustrations (only three) by George Cruikshank. It is anonymous.

The opening paragraph of the book gives its flavour:

> Of the Millions who live to eat and eat to live in this wide world of ours, how few are there who do not, at proper times and seasons, enjoy a good oyster. It may not be an ungrateful task, therefore, if I endeavour to inform them what species of animal the little succulent shell-fish is, that affords to man so much gastronomical enjoyment – how born and bred and nurtured; when, and where; and, lastly, how best it may be eaten, whether in its living and natural state, or having undergone the ordeal of cooking by the skill of a superior artist.[34]

The book tells the reader all kinds of things about oysters. The Romans had a weakness for them; at the time of Agricola they started importing them from England (though nobody knows how); according to Pliny, they invented the art of oyster farming; and rich Romans allegedly ate them in extraordinary quantities.

The physiology and reproductive mechanisms of the oyster are described; the places where oysters are produced in Britain and the methods used; how pearls are produced; the relative merits of the oysters of different countries – though the English are, of course, by far the best. Throughout, the virtues of the oyster are extolled, often with hyperbole, and never more so than with reference to their medicinal properties:

> Oysters taken before mid-day with a glass of wine produce a most salutary effect. The nerves and muscles regain their strength, and the body its mental and physical powers, bringing cheerfulness and energy to compete with the duties of the day. If not a cure, at all events, an oyster diet, under medical supervision, brings unquestionable relief to those who are suffering from pulmonary complaints, indigestion, or nervous disorders.[35]

The reader is told that you cannot eat an oyster in greater perfection than at a street stall, because, as the capital of the owner is small, so, too, is the stock;

and that in the Midland counties Christmas-eve would scarcely be Christmas-eve without an oyster supper. 'Let me,' says the author, 'sketch the scene.':

> In the centre of the table, covered with a clean white cloth up to the top hoop, stands the barrel of oysters, a kindly remembrance from a friend.... Each gentleman at table finds an oyster knife and a clean coarse towel by the side of his plate, and he is expected to open oysters for himself and the lady seated by his side, unless she is wise enough to open them for herself. By the side of every plate is the oyster-loaf made and baked purposely for the occasion, and all down the centre of the table, interspersed with vases of bright holly and evergreens, are plates filled with pats of butter, or lemons cut in half, and as many vinegar and pepper castors as the establishment can furnish. As the attendance of servants at such gatherings is usually dispensed with, bottled Bass or Guinness, or any equally unsophisticated pale ale or porter, is liberally provided; and where the means allow, light continental wines, such as Chablis, Sauterne, Mousseux, Meursault, Moselle, or any light Rhenish wine, and failing any of these, Madeira or Sherry, are placed upon the table.[36]

There is a list of 15 recipes for cooked oysters, starting with simple dishes such as Fried Oysters and Oyster Soup, but ending with Cabbage with Oysters and Fried Larks, and Fried Hind Legs of Frogs with Oysters; and, in the second edition published in 1863, there is a guide to where to buy and eat oysters in London. Fifteen places are named, usually with some comment, of which four still exist today: in Maiden Lane (where it still stands today) was Rule's oyster-shop, with two huge clam-shells in the window. 'Mr Rule and his two sons – they are a "rule of three" – are quaint priests at this *Temple of Ostrea Edulis*, who find a beauty in their business, and creating a rus in urbe, a pretty oasis, in a crowd of walls. The fish sold by them are excellent, as good as any in London.'; at Scott's in Coventry Street (where it remained until 1967) 'oysters are handed to you in perfection.'; Wilton's (then in Great Ryder Street) was a place 'where you may eat oysters as fine as anywhere in London, and with this advantage, that here they are always opened in the lower shell, without the trouble of asking, which is necessary at other places if you would preserve the tonic liquor which nature herself intended should be the only sauce for our favourite mollusk.'; and beyond St Paul's was Sweetings 'celebrated oyster warehouse – warehouse in every sense of the word; for though we may have our sixpenny-worth opened over the counter, as at any retail shop,' this is 'one of the great centres of London, from which barrels of oysters are continually travelling to all parts of the country.'[37] The book ends with a prescient warning, that 'Our immense consumption is exhausting our oyster-banks,' and a plea for a respite.[38]

The reviewers gave the book favourable notices but, though they praised the author highly, they revealed nothing of his identity. Almost certainly he was Eustace Clare Grenville Murray, commonly known as Grenville Murray, a most colourful and talented rogue, who is somehow representative of the spirit of the oyster boom in England. From Roman times onwards, the oyster has been written about as a festive object, a food for times of celebration and indulgence, but those who wrote about oysters in Victorian times seem to fall into two categories: those who are unable to mention enjoyment; and those who delight exaggeratedly in festivity, celebration and indulgence, who enjoy kicking over the traces. An example of the first category is John R. Philpots who in two fat volumes assembled every fact he could lay his hands on about oysters and their cultivation in Britain and abroad;[39] and another is T.H.Huxley, about whom I shall say more later. Murray is the leading specimen in the second category, to which Dickens perhaps belongs too.

Murray was the illegitimate son of the second Duke of Buckingham. Having entered the diplomatic service at the instigation of Lord Palmerston who had known him from an early age, he was posted in July 1851 to Vienna but soon got into trouble for acting on the side as the correspondent of the *Morning Post* and for lampooning his ambassador in print. Protected by Lord Palmerston, he was posted here and there until he behaved so badly as consul-general in Odessa, issuing birth and marriage certificates of questionable legality and charging extortionate fees, that he was dismissed after a long and acrimonious official enquiry had produced a report on his conduct of no less than 306 pages.[40] Undaunted by dismissal, Murray plunged into journalism but was soon in trouble again. He was horsewhipped by Lord Carrington 'at the door of the Conservative Club in St. James's' for slandering his father, the second Lord Carrington, in an article entitled 'Bob Coachington Lord Jarvey'. After taking Lord Carrington to court for assault but being caught out for perjury, Murray skipped to Paris where he lived in exile for the rest of his life calling himself the Comte de Rethel d'Aragon, a name he took from a Spanish lady he married.

CHAPTER FOUR

The biology, economics and terminology of oysters

B EFORE GOING FURTHER, it is useful to consider the nature of oysters
and the techniques and economics of oyster production.

The biology and breeding of oysters[1]

The oyster is a mollusc, a term applied by Linnaeus, the great classifier, to a mixed group of invertebrates; and amongst molluscs it is in the class of bivalves, meaning that it lives within two half shells, each known technically as a valve. The two half-shells of the oyster are held together in two places: by a hinge, in the form of a ligament attached to the two shells at their base; and secondly by a strong muscle between the middle of the two shells. By relaxing and contracting this muscle, the oyster causes the shells to open and close about the hinge. When open, the oyster pumps sea water through itself by means of gills and absorbs food from the water in the form of plankton, that is, in the form of floating micro-organisms. It does this at a remarkable rate – 10 litres (more than 2 gallons) an hour for a mature native oyster, and more for Pacific oysters.

The sex life of the oyster is odd. It is hermaphroditic, meaning that at one reproductive cycle it will be male and produce sperm, at another female and produce eggs, a point to which Ogden Nash applied his rhyming talents,

> The oyster's a confusing suitor
> It's masc., and fem., and even neuter.
> At times it wonders, may what come,
> Am I husband, wife or chum.[2]

For an oyster to breed, the temperature of the water must be right and so must the salinity of the water and the supply of food in it. When these conditions are right, oysters will usually breed and change sex once a year. Around the British Isles, relatively far north, only natives oysters will breed, and they do so more erratically than further south.

Rock oysters come from warmer climates and do not normally breed in British waters, but if young rock oysters, bred in warmer climates or in hatcheries, are laid down here, they grow and fatten well. They have a greater ability to live in muddy waters and to tolerate low salinity, and generally speaking they are hardier than flat oysters.

When they breed, oysters produce enormous numbers of eggs and sperm of which only a tiny number survive. Each female rock oyster when breeding releases tens of millions of eggs and each male several hundred million sperm into the surrounding water where, with luck, some meet and fertilisation takes place. With the native oyster what happens at this initial stage of breeding is slightly different. The eggs are retained within the female's shell and are fertilised by sperm entering with the flow of sea water, after which they are not released for a week or so, during which time the eggs go through the phases of incubation and initial development within the female shell. With this mechanism, the total number of eggs produced is less than with the rock oyster – a matter of anything up to a million, rather than tens of millions.

The fertilised eggs, once released from the female or, in the case of rock oysters, after being fertilised in the water, become larvae with a slight capability to swim, propelled by little hairs (*cilia*). Using this capability, but mostly carried by currents, the larvae float about gregariously for a week or more seeking a hard surface to which to attach themselves. That they do by means of a glue produced by a gland. Once attached to a suitable surface, oysters quickly grow shell. At this stage baby oysters are known as "spat" and the event as a "spatfall". Oystermen speak of a good or bad spatfall as farmers speak of a good or bad harvest.

The oyster grows seasonally, adding to itself circles of shell. These it produces by the interaction of an organic chemical that it secretes and calcium in the water. The same process produces pearls, but pearls of value come from oriental oysters. The pearls sometimes found in the oysters we eat are lustreless and of no value. The circles of shell are quickly formed as "shoots" and then thicken. After about 3 or 4 years an oyster will, in favourable conditions, be ready for the market.

The enemies of the oyster

Oysters face a great many threats to their lives. In the first place, they face many predators and competitors. There is the starfish which, if large, may open and eat grown oysters, and if small may feed greedily on young oyster spat; there is the boring sponge, *Cliona celata*, which may riddle the shells of mature oysters with holes; and there are indigenous whelk tingles and a more ferocious variety of whelk tingle imported from America in the late 1920's: these have a tongue like a gimlet with which they drill a hole in the shell of the oyster, killing it, but they are now in decline, having been killed off by TBT, an anti-fouling paint which, as we shall see, also did great damage to oysters. And then there is the slipper limpet, brought in with imported oysters from America in the 1890's. It is a competitor which displaces the oyster rather than a predator which attacks it directly. It grows in the same conditions as the oyster and in a similar way, but it is hardier. If left undisturbed it can smother an oyster bed, causing mud to accumulate and the settlement of oyster spat to decline. Unrestrained, it may oust the oyster.

Another hazard in northern waters, such as those around Britain and the north of France, is extreme cold. When in these climates there have been exceptionally hard winters in which there is much ice in the rivers and estuaries, oysters have suffered very high mortality rates. This has been caused directly through oysters being frozen and indirectly through the exceptional drop in the salinity of the water to which the oysters are exposed when the thaw brings a spate of sweet water down river into the estuaries.

Further hazards are oyster diseases, which include bacterial and viral infections. These can wipe out oysters – without harming humans.

Finally, there is industrial pollution which can kill off oysters and other shellfish. It needs to be distinguished from sewage pollution which will mostly injure not the oysters themselves but the eaters of oysters – if the polluted oysters have not been purified. As we shall see, both have been important problems since the end of the last century.

Oyster cultivation

Edible oysters grow naturally near the coast or on banks further off shore where the water temperature is right and the sea bottom firm. They do particularly well in estuaries where sea water mixed with sweet water nourishes the growth of the types of plankton that suit them.

Our ancestors originally gathered oysters by picking them up full-grown on the shore at low tide or lifting them from natural beds at sea. The coarse cheap oysters of the mid-19th century were a product of that kind of fishing, but they were fished out. A natural supply of mature oysters is rare in Europe nowadays.

Oyster cultivation consists of two stages, obtaining young oysters and tending them thereafter as they grow and are fattened.

Broadly speaking, there are two traditional methods of obtaining young oysters: by dredging a natural bed for spat and part-grown oysters; and by collecting on a private bed spat which may have been formed by larvae which have drifted to that bed from natural beds or by larvae generated within that private bed or others near it. When young oysters have grown to a diameter of half an inch or more they are known as brood and are bought and sold for laying down to grow and fatten.

Oyster fishing with rake and dredge, illustrated in l'Encyclopédie, France, 1771.

The key to the breeding of oysters, whether on public or private beds, is to have enough breeding stock in a suitable place and to maximise the area of sheltered clean hard surfaces on which larvae can settle to form spat. The traditional method of doing this is to provide a hard bed of 'cultch', meaning a mixture of the old shells of oysters, cockles, mussels and other shellfish, plus other suitable oddments, for example, bits of broken crockery. In the middle of the 19th century, man-made surfaces ('collectors') were introduced in France – a Roman practice re-discovered.

Before the spatting season the bed needs to be raked or harrowed so as to lift existing cultch out of the mud and remove weed; and new cultch may be added. Artificial collectors, the use of which has never caught on in Britain, have to be prepared and put out.

The oyster grower needs regularly to watch over his or her oysters to make sure they are neither smothered by silt, sand or weed, nor damaged by predators, pests or competitors for space and nutrients, nor stolen. Oyster layings, both for breeding and for later growth, may be on the foreshore i.e. the area between high and low tide, or further out to sea. With a laying on the shore, the object of the oyster farmer is to keep the oysters covered in sea water all or most of the time and yet be able to tend them on foot. This is achieved by placing the oysters between the level of normal low tide and the lower level to which the water recedes every month on the large spring tides. In this zone it is possible to inspect the oysters on foot during the days of the spring tide, and to use those days to rake them over or collect them for the market.

Where the shore is relatively flat you can enclose an area above the normal low tide level so that it will retain a few inches of water while the tide is out, and you can improve the surface of the bottom of the enclosure. Such enclosures are called parcs in French.

Oyster beds further out have to be tended from a boat with dredges and harrows. The aim of dredging is to skim off oysters, cultch and rubbish. What is brought up is sorted. Rubbish will be removed and oysters thrown back until they are ready to be marketed as brood or for consumption.

Before oysters are marketed they may be moved into areas known from experience to be good for fattening and imparting a good taste to them. In some areas of France a complex system of artificial beds has long been in use for this purpose. That is the system of *claires*. *Claires* are shallow basins with clay walls located in marshy areas at the level of high tide. Water is let into them at high spring tides and retained by a system of dykes and sluices until the next spring tide. In the summer the stagnant water in the *claires* develops a bloom of blue-green organisms which, besides fattening the oyster and giving them a good flavour, may make them a greenish colour, a characteristic that has been held in high esteem as evidence that the desired flavour should be present. This system was evolved at Marennes which, in the days when it was a major source of flat oysters, was renowned for its seasonal supply of *Marennes vertes*.

Finally oysters may be moved into storage pits near the high water mark into which sea water will flow when the tide is up. Here the oysters are accessible and can be fished out when needed to meet orders.

A variant of these traditional methods which has been adopted on a large scale in the Mediterranean since the end of the last century is to grow oysters, and mussels, suspended in the water.[3] They may be placed in perforated containers of wood and metal or plastic mesh suspended from frames that are

built up from the sea bed; or they may be suspended in the water in a variety of other ways. For example, part-grown oysters are nowadays stuck at close intervals to ropes that are then suspended from the frames. The sticking is done by laying the ropes horizontally on a long table, putting large blobs of cement round the ropes at intervals, then sticking three oysters round each blob. As soon as the cement is dry the ropes are taken out to the frames and hung in the water.

This technique is well suited to places where the absence of tides means that there is little flow of water carrying nutrients, with the result that oysters placed densely on the bottom will exhaust all the nutrients in the lower layer of water without gaining access to the nutrients in other layers. To suspend the oysters vertically gives them access to all layers of water and means that more oysters can be grown satisfactorily on a given area of the seabed. The technique is particularly well suited to those lagoons, such as the Étang de Thau near Sète, where a sand bar cuts off a lagoon from the sea. Here there is no movement of the water other than that caused by the wind, but the water is rich in nutrients; suspended oysters and mussels grow fast.

These are the methods of oyster cultivation that were practised for most of the period with which we are concerned. Since the middle of the 20th century, techniques have been developed for breeding oysters in hatcheries and placing them to grow on the foreshore in plastic mesh bags on trestles. These new methods, which are now very widely used, are described in Chapters 9 and 10.

From the latter part of the last century until the 1960's a further source of supply to the British market was the importation of oysters at an advanced stage of growth to be re-laid in British waters to fatten before they were sold. These oysters, which were mostly of kinds that will not normally breed in British waters, came from America and from the Continent. We shall describe this trade more fully later.

The Economics of Oyster Fishing

The essential economic problem which runs through the history of the oyster fisheries of Britain is whether oyster fishing should be left open to all as a common property right or should be restricted. It is a problem that is not

OPPOSITE: *The method of dredging oysters: a Whitstable yawl at work (the lower part of the drawing gives the water in section so as to show the dredge at work on the bottom),* Illustrated London News.

unique to oysters. It has long been familiar, for example, with respect to game; and in recent times it has become familiar with respect to species that are threatened with extinction, for example, elephants, whales and various kinds of seafish.

A common property right means that there is no exclusion of anyone from the use of a property; that there is no limit to what use they make of it; that there is no charge made for use. So long as there is no scarcity of the product yielded by a common property, so long, for example, as there are plenty of fish in the sea or oysters on the seabed, a common property right raises no problems: there is plenty for everyone and there is no case for any form of restriction or exclusion. But once increased demand or reduced supply causes scarcity of a resource, there is no automatic mechanism to prevent its over-exploitation and, in the case of a biological species, its extinction. On the contrary, it is predictable that several things will happen:

1. People will exploit the common property so long as they can gain more that way than they could in other occupations. In other words, the property will be exploited until the income that it yields is reduced to an unacceptable level. In the case of fisheries, the reduction in income will occur because more fishermen crowd in, because it is necessary to fish in increasingly deep and difficult waters, or, as in the case of an oyster bed, because it has been fished bare.

2. Exploitation will be pushed further the smaller is the income available from other occupations – the poorer is the community of potential fishermen and the worse their chances of employment in alternative jobs.

3. Each exploiter of the resource will know that if he holds back in order to conserve breeding stock for tomorrow, he cannot rely on others to follow his example. Rather, he will fear that if he holds back, others will push on and he will be left out of the spoils. For this reason, conservation will not occur unless access to the property is limited and those enjoying access are firmly restrained, by government regulation or by the creation of exclusive titles to the property.

Two implications of these propositions have long been well understood. First, in order to function, an economic system requires that any scarce natural resource, for example fertile land, instead of being open to all, must be in private ownership, or subject to a public regime for its orderly exploitation. Secondly, in the case of animals, fish or plants that reproduce themselves, a prime purpose of private ownership or a public regime is to conserve the breeding stock so that future produce is not sacrificed in a competitive rush for produce today: it is necessary to maintain breeding stock, as farmers have known since biblical times. The oyster is no exception.[4]

The doctrine of *laissez-faire* rests, implicitly if not explicitly, on the assumption that scarce natural resources, starting with land, will be in private hands or subject to public regulation. For that must be so if private individuals or companies are to be induced to invest in future production by the knowledge that the resulting produce will be theirs – if, in other words a market economy is to be given a chance of working. The opposite notion – that there should be common property rights to scarce natural resources so that they are open to unrestricted exploitation by all – may be part of the doctrine of anarchy; it has no place in the economic doctrine of *laissez-faire*. On the contrary, the doctrine of *laissez-faire* is about the beneficial results that will flow from competition in a society in which scarce property is in private ownership.

Terminology

In the history of the oyster, terminology has to be used that is different from that in use today (see page 12). The problem concerns the cupped oyster. In the last century a type of cupped oyster called the Portuguese began to be imported, mostly from France. Imports of these continued until the 1960's when the Portuguese oyster was hit by disease. Since then another type of cupped oyster, which to the consumer is indistinguishable from the Portuguese, has been introduced. That is the Pacific oyster which is now commonly called the 'rock oyster'. In describing the history of how all this happened, I shall use the terms Portuguese and Pacific, but readers should remember that what is being talked about is the rock oyster they are offered today or its almost identical precursor.

The meaning of native has not changed so much. It has always meant the same type of oyster (*Ostrea edulis*). Nevertheless a minor caveat is needed, for the word native has been used in two ways. Until late in the last century the only type of oyster known in Britain was the native. It originally grew wild on the seabed at many places around the coasts of Britain. But it was cultivated and put to fatten at places on the coast where the conditions were found to produce oysters of particularly good flavour, texture and body. The best of these places were on the east coast of England, notably Colchester and Whitstable, where the bed of blue London clay was said to foster plankton particularly well suited to the oyster.[5] In order to differentiate oysters from this area from others, the word natives came to be used, at least by purists, to describe only oysters that had been cultivated in the greater Thames estuary which, on the widest of various definitions on offer, was said to reach from Margate to Harwich.[6] Oysters of the same type which came from other parts of the coast or from natural beds in the sea used to be just plain 'oysters'. With the passage of time the east coast, as we shall see, has ceased to be much of a producer of natives, and the term natives has come to be applied to flat oysters (*edulis*) wherever they are produced. The result makes sense: the word natives has come to be applied, without geographical distinction, to the one type of oyster that is a native of these waters. But the change from the restricted to the general meaning of the word is a nuisance. My aim is to use it in its modern general sense, but it will crop up in its old restricted sense. I shall try to make sure that the reader knows when that is so.

The names for the various kinds of place where oysters breed and grow are another problem. I shall aim to use the word 'bed' for a place where oysters grow naturally (the French word is *un gisement*); and a 'laying' for a place where oysters are put by man to breed, grow or fatten. (The French distinguish layings of different kinds and so use several terms, *un parc*, *une claire*, and *un étalage*.)*There are ambiguous cases, for example, old natural beds that have been re-laid by man.

CHAPTER FIVE

Scarcity and the Royal Commission

FROM THE FEW statistics we possess it is clear that there was a precipitous fall in oyster production between the 1850's and the 1880's. For the beginning of the period, we have Mayhew's figure of 500 million oysters a year going through Billingsgate in about 1850. The end of the period is marked by the appearance of the first official oyster statistics. These are for 1886 and show that oyster production in that year was only 40 million. Even if you make every reasonable allowance for error in the figures, there is no question that there was a huge decline in oyster production in this period. The decline is confirmed by the cessation of talk about oysters being the food of the poor, and by a big increase in the price of oysters.

The price of oysters

In the 1850's, the wholesale price of natives declined to about 0.15p. each, or less, equivalent to about 0.25p. retail (prices expressed in modern pennies) – and much less for the coarse deep-sea oysters that were then flooding the market. In about 1860 the price began to rise. By 1865 the price of natives was two to three times above the level of the 1850's; by 1876 four times; and by 1889, seven or eight times. This increase in the price of oysters was not a result of inflation. On the contrary, the general level of prices fell by 20 per cent or so during the period 1860 to 1890, depressed by imports of cheap food. What we are observing therefore is a rise in the price of oysters by about ten times relative to other foods, a change likely to induce a major reduction in the consumption of oysters.

The question that presents itself is why oyster production collapsed like this: how important were man's activities compared with natural causes in reducing the oyster population, and what was government policy?

Government policy

The policy adopted by the Government was decisively shaped by a Royal Commission on Sea Fisheries which reported in 1886. To this day the oyster industry operates within legislation based on the Commission's recommendations.

Before the Royal Commission there was very little regulation of sea fishing of any kind. Since the 17th century there had been attempts to build up the British sea fisheries, meaning essentially herring fisheries. In the time of Charles I and Charles II, companies were formed and various forms of protection were provided, but without success; the British fisheries could not compete with the Dutch who, with government support, had created a most efficient fisheries industry. A bounty was introduced in Britain in 1749 after a committee appointed by the House of Commons had conducted an inquiry into the herring and white fisheries. The bounty was given, presumably for simplicity of administration, with respect not to the quantity of fish caught but to fishing boats. Initially it was 36 shillings per ton, but it was raised to 56 shillings in 1757 and then to 80 shillings in 1759, when a bounty on fish was added of nearly 3 shillings per barrel. The policy was criticised by Adam Smith, on the grounds that it was too common for vessels to fit out for the sole purpose of catching not the fish but the bounty.[1] It proved to be no more successful than earlier policies, and the bounties were cut back.

In 1808, however, when the Dutch fisheries were crippled by the Napoleonic wars, the British Government seized the opportunity to try to build up the British fisheries and wrest trade from the Dutch. Bounties were stepped up; a board of seven commissioners of the herring fisheries was created; the inspection and branding of herrings was introduced with rules copied from the Dutch. The aim was to induce the fisheries, which commonly used 'the rudest and most imperfect methods of curing herrings' to improve their product. It was laid down that fish were to be gutted and packed in barrels within 24 hours of being caught; the fisheries were given exemption from the salt tax; and government agents were appointed to inspect and brand the barrels of herrings to certify that they were of good quality, rather than leaving it to buyers to discover which seller offered good herrings, which bad.

Fraud proved such a problem in administering the bounties that many restrictions were imposed and eventually all the measures to support the industry were repealed in 1830. The herring fisheries subsequently boomed as the railways opened up the new urban market for fish. There was one exception to the abolition of restrictions: the Scottish commission for inspection was kept on. It was still in existence administering the herring brand when the Royal Commission on Sea Fisheries was appointed in 1863 – though the trade now paid a charge for this service rather than relying on the Government to finance it. In England and Wales the brand was gone and no commission or body of inspectors for sea fisheries remained.

With respect to oysters, there was a long-standing custom here and abroad that there should be a close season for oysters in months without an R, that is to say, oysters should not be fished in the summer months of May, June, July and August. There are four traditional arguments for this convention: in the summer when oysters are breeding they are milky with eggs or sperm and do not taste good; their breeding should not be disturbed; when the sea water is warm it is more likely than at other seasons to contain organisms harmful to human beings; and it is difficult to transport and distribute oysters in good condition in hot weather, an argument that has lost force since the introduction of man-made ice and, later, the introduction of refrigerated storage and transport. But the close season was not actively enforced by British Governments in the first half of the 19th century and was observed voluntarily only in parts of the trade. Its enforcement, and also the imposition of a limit of 2½ inches width on the size of oysters fished, was recommended by a Select Committee of the House of Commons in 1833, after it had heard complaints of over-fishing, but nothing was done until some years later when a convention was negotiated with France to stop disputes and regulate fishing of all kinds in the waters between France and Britain. 'For some years previously French fishermen had complained bitterly against the English practice of dredging for oysters in the vicinity of the French coast; while large fleets of French fishing vessels from Calais, Boulogne and Dieppe were in the habit of fishing off the coasts of Kent and Essex, in many cases within half a league (about three miles) of the shore.'[2] The convention, which was passed into British law by an act of 1843, included a provision that there should be a close season in the four summer months during which there should be no fishing for oysters and no boat should have on board any dredge or other equipment for catching oysters. The convention was for the guidance of fishermen of Britain and France with respect to the seas lying between the coasts of the two countries; it included a general provision that fishermen of each nation should not fish within three miles of the other nation, where fishing of all kinds was reserved to the subjects of that nation.

There was a difference in the French and British approaches to the enforcement of the close season which provides a foretaste of differences in policy to come. The French wanted a close season in the Channel both so as to help conserve the stock of oysters in the Channel and so as to make it impossible for oystermen evading the French close season in French territorial waters to claim that oysters they brought ashore out of season had been caught legally in the Channel. A report made later describes what the problem had been:

> With a view of competing with English fishermen in the working of the open sea, fishermen living near the Granville and Cancale banks were authorised to break the rule which restrained them from ever staying out at night with their boats. It resulted that under pretence of dredging concurrently with the English on the common grounds, they worked in preference upon the oyster-beds reserved in the territorial waters and ruined them.[3]

In Britain, where a close season was not being imposed by the Government, the attitude to the close season, if not negative, was certainly far from positive. There were complaints from the oysterman that enforcement of the Convention Act would prevent them from moving their oysters from one bed to another within the 3-mile limit; and that the Act would force them to give up their habitual practice of dredging for young oysters in the summer (which is what one would suppose it was intended to do). The Board of Trade, after consulting the Government law officers, gave instructions that the Act should not be enforced within the 3-mile limit for the present; and little or no attempt was made to enforce it beyond the 3-mile limit until 1852, when the French called upon the British Government to do so. Then it was found that the Customs and Admiralty officers lacked adequate powers to perform their task. At last in 1855 an Act was passed that gave them the power to seize the oysters and dredges of offenders; but the Convention was still not enforced within the 3-mile limit. Such was the position when the Royal Commission began its work.

The other main means by which the Government could influence the conservation of the stock of oysters and perhaps induce improvements in oyster cultivation was by limiting the public right of access to oyster beds through new arrangements for their ownership or for public regulation of their exploitation – in short, by modifying, locally, the common property right applicable to oyster beds. In this respect the position in Britain was – and is – far from straightforward.

The law of the foreshore

To the eye of the layman, the law of titles to the seabed, like so much of English law, is a tangle. It is best to go back to Blackstone, the great authority on the laws of England, and start from the laws relating to the tenure of land. He tells us that after the Norman Conquest, at the Great Council convened by the King to enquire into the state of the nation which led to the compiling of the Doomsday Book, oaths were taken and commitments made by the landowners by which the feudal system was adopted nationally and freely. The landowners achieved security, after a period of troubles, by making oaths of fealty and committing themselves to perform military service for the King. In so doing, they became vassals or servants of the King, holding their land by feudal tenure. In consequence of this change, says Blackstone

> ...it became a fundamental maxim and necessary principle (though in reality a mere fiction) of our English tenures, 'that the King is the universal lord and original proprietor of all the lands in his kingdom; and that no man doth or can possess any part of it, but what has mediately or immediately been derived as a gift from him to be held upon feudal services.'[4]

The same law applied to the foreshore, i.e. the area between high and low water and the territorial waters. The Crown was the ultimate owner; it had the right to grant a several fishery (meaning that a fishing area is severed and not shared with others) to a subject; and it had the power to bar fishing or fowling in any river so as to reserve it for the pleasure of the King. But these royal rights to exclude people from fishing were stopped in 1215 when the barons became so aggrieved by the increasing feudal impositions imposed on them that they rose up against King John and forced through Magna Carta.

A second element telling against the granting of exclusive rights of fishery is the common law, according to which the public has a right to fish in the tidal reaches of rivers and estuaries and in the sea within the limits of territorial waters – except where the Crown or some subject has acquired a property exclusive of the public right or where Parliament has restricted the common law rights of the public.[5]

So effective was the stop on the granting of exclusive fisheries in Magna Carta and the force of common law that the Royal Commission in its report (1866) found that

...any exclusive fisheries which now exist are held either under charters from the Crown of an earlier date than Magna Carta, or by immemorial user [meaning the use had gone on for as long as could be remembered] from which such grants may by law be presumed. The result is that, with the exception of the estuary of the Thames, where a considerable number of such grants were made in early times, there are very few places along the coast where exclusive rights of oyster dredging exist; and the beds we have spoken of are in general only beds lying between high and low water mark, where oysters which have been dredged up elsewhere, and have become private property by appropriation, are laid down upon ground under leave from the owner of the foreshore. Such beds are not suitable for breeding oysters, and are in general used only to keep a supply of oysters for the market. In some few cases, as in the River Stour, oyster beds have been formed under a lease of the soil from the Crown, and oysters laid there even below low water are considered as private property, and possibly even the brood of such oysters may at law be considered the property of persons who laid down the parent oysters; but no such case could be maintained where at any previous time oysters have been dredged by the public, nor could the public be prevented fishing on the grounds for any other fish.[6]

The Commission noted that in 1864, while it was undertaking its enquiry, an Act of Parliament was passed which granted the newly-formed Herne Bay Company the exclusive right of fishing over an area seven miles in length and one mile in depth lying between Whitstable and Margate. The bill had been strongly opposed by the Whitstable Company on the grounds that it appropriated a considerable extent of ground on which the public generally, and especially their members, had been in the habit of dredging for brood. The Commission noted that similar bills were before Parliament for converting into private property certain portions of the flats and of the estuaries of the Essex rivers. In short, the long period in which there was a stoppage on the granting of oyster concessions was coming to an end through the granting by Parliament of new concessions in response to private initiatives, stimulated no doubt by the high price of oysters. Such was the position the Commission found and reviewed.

There was a further complication scarcely touched upon by the Commission, namely that the loss of the ancient records of the realm meant that

Oyster cultivation in Brittany: English visitors at the oyster beds at Cancale,
Illustrated London News, *1893.*

it was impossible to say with respect to many places whether the Crown had parted with the fishery rights before Magna Carta, or with general rights to the foreshore, including, for example, the right to take gravel. This meant that there was much scope for appeal to immemorial usage. Further, one finds the argument that where the Crown has granted a title to a manor or estate adjacent to the shore, that manor or estate extends to the low-water mark and includes the foreshore; therefore it is wrong to accept the theory that, unless proved otherwise, the foreshore belongs to the Crown. This argument was eloquently expounded in the 1880's by a lawyer, Stuart A. Moore, who claimed that the correct starting point was that *prima facie* the foreshore belongs to the adjoining land. He showed how over the centuries the argument went to and fro, with some monarchs, in particular Queen Elizabeth and Charles I, asserting the claims of the Crown, while at other times, in particular during the Commonwealth and in the reign of Charles II, the opposite view prevailed.[7]

The report of the Royal Commission

The appointment of a Royal Commission on Sea Fisheries was proposed in a motion by members of the House of Commons who feared that the seas were being depleted of fish as a result of the great increase in its consumption and the increasing use by fishermen of trawls and seine nets, two new methods of fishing that were indiscriminate, and hence destructive of young fish and spawn, compared with traditional fishing by line and hook.[8] The motion was passed. On 8 June, 1863, the Queen replied:

> I have received your Address, praying that a Royal Commission of Inquiry into our Sea Fisheries may be issued, with the view of increasing the supply of a favourite and nutritious article of Food for the benefit of the Public. And I have given directions that a Commission shall issue for the purpose which you have requested.[9]

The Commission, which had only three members, Mr James Caird, Professor T. H. Huxley and Mr G. Shaw Lefevre, reported in just over two years, having taken evidence at 86 places in England, Wales, Scotland, Ireland and the Isle of Man.

On opening the leather-bound volume of evidence taken by the Royal Commission it is impossible not to be favourably impressed. Here, on huge pages beautifully printed, are verbatim records of the questions asked by the members of the Commission and the answers they received from a great number of fishermen and fish merchants. The volume runs to more than 1,300 pages and includes a superb index. It is all so correct and stately, suffused with Victorian formality of style and address.

But when you start to read the impression weakens. The fishermen describe their customary ways of fishing and their beliefs about the habits of fish; they put up arguments, understandably in favour of their present methods. Those who use seine nets deny that they do any harm, while those who use hook and line accuse seine nets of causing awful damage to the fish population. Similarly, oystermen argue against any close season on dredging on the public oyster beds. The result is a muddled mass of tales from fishermen. And necessarily so, for in the 1860's there was little scientific knowledge of the dynamics of fish populations, and little or nothing in the way of an education system that could have conveyed such knowledge to fishermen.

The Commission concluded that there was no general shortage of sea fish or prospect of it; that trawling and netting should be allowed because they increased the supply of fish and did no permanent harm; and that all existing restrictions on sea fisheries should be removed. In England it was already the case that the sea fisheries were under no restriction, or next to none, apart from the oyster fisheries. In Scotland, there was a Fishery Board to help and supervise the fishery industries, and in Ireland the Board of Works had almost unlimited powers over fisheries (chapter 7); the work of both these boards with respect to sea fish might cease, the Commission concluded, without any injurious effect upon the fisheries. The system of inspecting and branding herrings as a mark of quality, which still continued in Scotland, should be abolished.

Oysters were an exception to the general proposition that there was no evidence of shortage. The report found that "The oyster fisheries in the bays and shallow waters along the coast have everywhere been represented to us as in a state of great depression, owing to the scarcity of oysters. In many places, the oysters have within the last three years almost entirely disappeared";[10] and there is a section headed "Regulations relating to Oysters; and Oyster fishing in general".[11] It plunges straight into consideration of the Convention Act with France and starts by describing the uncertainties of the law and its enforcement. The description is rather tendentious: it is strongly suggested that the Convention Act did not apply within the three-mile limit. The question is addressed whether a close season had good or bad effects on the stock of oysters. Many witnesses had alleged that the close season, which had been enforced with some effect since 1852, had done more injury than good because it prevented dredging which kept the ground clean of weeds and mud. The authors reaction is cautious: 'We feel great difficulty in expressing an opinion on this point', because for several years there had been a widespread failure of the spat. It was 'not therefore surprising that there should be generally a complaint of the falling off of full-grown oysters; and where such a falling off is observed, it is difficult to trace whether the decline is, wholly or partially, due to over dredging and to the taking of young oysters; or whether it is due to the neglect of dredging during the summer months; or whether it is caused neither by one or the other, but solely by the failure of spat'.[12]

The report then considers the evidence as regards oyster fishing with respect to three geographical areas, as follows:

1. Beyond the 3-mile limit. Recently discovered deep Channel beds are being intensively fished and 'show no sign at present of giving way'. They produce large coarse oysters which, improved by being laid for a time on inshore beds, are in great demand at fairs and races throughout the country during the summer, when supplies are drawn from stocks accumulated at the inshore beds. Everywhere fishermen who are engaged in this deep-sea dredging favoured adding May, or even June, to the open season.

2. The Thames Estuary. It has been the custom to dredge the open or public grounds for brood (young oysters) regardless of the season in order to lay it down to grow on private beds along the coast. 'In consequence of a succession of bad breeding seasons' there has been little or no brood found for some time past and full-sized oysters are very scarce. Some witnesses said you could not so completely clear ground of its oysters as not to leave sufficient to supply spat in a good breeding season. Another view was that the ground was so completely denuded of the parent oyster that the spat which settles on it must have come from the oysters lying in the private grounds, such as the Colne and Burnham rivers, and the Whitstable and Faversham grounds. They found it to be 'the universal opinion of the fishermen on all these parts of the coast, that if the Convention Act were strictly enforced, a close-time adhered to, and a limitation enforced as to the size of oysters, it would be fatal to the general prosperity of the dredgerman and to the interests of the private companies.' The principal reasons given are that vermin might set in; that dredging to prepare the ground for spat would be prevented; that in the summer, which is the best time to dredge, they would be forbidden to dredge; and that where the prosperity of the oyster bed requires a halt to dredging after the spat has fallen, the fishermen themselves refrain from working.

As for the private companies, it is said that those at Whitstable and Colchester, the two places that really matter, voluntarily refrain from sending oysters to market in the summer; they observe a limit on the size of oysters they sell; they restrict the quantity they sell and they care for their oyster beds. Although they thus regulate themselves, they have had a succession of bad breeding seasons. No comment is made on figures given in the report for the membership of the two companies which show a very marked increase, indicating an increase in fishing.

3. Areas within the 3-mile limit other than in the Thames Estuary. Local fishermen in these areas were, "with few exceptions, in favour of the maintenance of a close season".[13]

Having thus summarised the evidence about the close season the report draws conclusions with respect first to private oyster beds, meaning principally Colchester and Whitstable. It says:

> We conceive it to be satisfactorily proved that any interference with the working of the private oyster beds during the close-time would be highly injurious. It is conclusively shown that it is only by very careful working and superintendence that the injury resulting from the deposit of mud and the growth of weeds can be repaired, and that the destruction of the oysters on the great scale by inroads of mussels which choke them, or five-fingers [starfish] which devour them, can be prevented.[14]

The report then emphasises '...the great complexity of the conditions upon which the prosperity of an oyster bed depends...' and again urges caution: 'Nor is it possible to be other than impressed by the necessity of extreme caution in concluding that any observed increase or diminution in the supply of oysters has arisen from any one cause'. But in the following section on the effect of the close season on the public beds, which were the vital source of young oysters, caution is cast aside in a remarkable manner.

The report lists the arguments in favour of a close season and knocks them down as if they were Aunt Sallies. First there is the argument that oysters are unfit for consumption in the summer when they are spawning. This is dismissed on the grounds that not more than 20 per cent are ever spawning (and therefore nasty) at one time. Who, one wonders, wants to risk 20 per cent of nasty oysters?

Secondly, there is the argument that to disturb baby oysters will crush and destroy them. This they dismiss by pointing to the hardiness of two other species (Corallines and Ascidians), but they do not address the question whether the hardiness of these other two species tells you anything about the hardiness of baby oysters.

Finally, the report attacks the question whether restraints are needed to preserve a sufficient breeding stock of oysters. Two propositions are laid down:

1. It will be unprofitable for fishermen to dredge a public oyster bed quite clean: they will always leave some oysters behind.
2. 'Every spawning oyster may be calculated upon to produce 800,000 young. Reduce that estimate to 1/80th of what it is, and it is obvious that no oyster bed is in the smallest danger of exhaustion from over-

working alone, if only one per cent of the breeding oysters are left. For suppose that of every 500 oysters only 100 breed during the season, and the spat of only one of them is shed, that one will, by the supposition, yield 10,000 young oysters, or twenty times as many as the original stock.'[15]

The first proposition is acceptable, but the second is not. It is little better than saying that, since every man in his prime can frequently produce a million sperm, we could safely get rid of all but one or a few men in a million and still maintain the population. It is a worthless proposition because it is made without knowledge, which to this day is slender, of the biological mechanisms which obviously prevent the vast majority of the 800,000 offspring of one mother oyster growing up. There is no basis for the figure of 1/80th or for the one per cent. They are numbers plucked from the air. Yet it is on the basis of those numbers that the Commission, having earlier preached caution and emphasised the uncertainty of the evidence, arrives at its crucial conclusion that the oyster shortage could not have been been caused by over-fishing. Indeed the argument is stated in general terms and implies that no oyster shortage could ever be caused by over-fishing.

The rest of the report discusses the need to encourage the formation of private beds. Only if exclusive rights of ownership of oysters in an area are possessed by a person (or company) will that owner have an economic incentive to keep oyster beds in good order and tend the oysters in them; since in England the power of the Crown to grant exclusive rights of fishery in the sea and tidal rivers was abridged by Magna Carta, and there were consequently few private beds outside the Thames estuary (where a considerable number of grants were made in early times), new powers are needed.

The conclusions of the report with respect to oysters are as follows:

We have made diligent inquiry into the condition of the oyster fisheries, and have devoted a large section of our report to the discussion of the evidence which we have obtained. We find:

That the supply of oyster has very greatly fallen off during the last three or four years.

That this decrease has not arisen from overfishing, nor from any causes over which man has direct control, but from the very general failure of the spat, or young of the oyster; which appears, during the years in question, to have been destroyed soon after it was produced. A similar failure of the spat has frequently happened before, and probably will often happen again.

That the best mode of providing against the effects of these periodical failures of the spat is to facilitate the proceedings of those individuals, or companies, who may desire to acquire so much property in favourably situated portions of the sea bottom, as may suffice to enable them safely to invest capital, in preparing and preserving these portions of the sea bottom for oyster culture. By which term "oyster culture" is implied, not the artificial breeding of oysters, in the manner in which salmon are bred artificially; but, the collection of the brood in years when that brood is plentiful, and its preservation by the application of due skill and care, as a source of supply during the years when the spat fails – a practice in vogue among British fishermen from time immemorial.

That no regulations, or restrictions, upon oyster fishing, beyond such as may be needed for the object just defined, have had, or are likely to have, any beneficial effect upon the supply of oysters.[16]

Thus the problem of the oyster was not allowed to disturb the grand sweep of the Commission's conclusion that all restrictions on sea fishing should be removed, a proposition they expressed with fine formality at the start of their recommendations:

In consonance with the conclusions enumerated above we humbly submit the following Recommendations to Your Majesty:

I. We advise that all Acts of Parliament which profess to regulate, or restrict, the modes of fishing pursued in the open sea be repealed; and that unrestricted freedom of fishing be permitted hereafter.

The recommendation that the Government should legislate for more enclosure of the foreshore and seabed in order to encourage private oyster beds is a secondary theme. Given the Commission's main conclusion about oysters, this recommendation could not be put forward on the grounds that because man had probably helped cause the scarcity by over-fishing, new property rights were needed to induce men to preserve the stock of oysters.

To sum up, the Commission's position with respect to oyster policy is dominated by the proposition that there was no over-fishing and could be no over-fishing of oysters, a proposition that does not follow from the evidence and for which the argumentation offered is jejune. This is not to say that the evidence shows that over-fishing was the cause of the scarcity, or that the evidence shows anything conclusively. Scientific knowledge of the oyster was far too limited for that. What the evidence with all its imperfections suggests is that the poor breeding seasons and the resulting scarcity of oysters were caused by some combination of over-fishing and natural causes, and that it would have been prudent to take steps to conserve an adequate breeding stock. That is the view people came to later.

What caused the Royal Commission to take this position? What caused them to abandon the caution appropriate to the poverty of their evidence?

The character of the Royal Commission

The Royal Commission was appointed in the heyday of free trade and *laissez-faire*, a time when economic doctrine was more prominent in British politics than it had ever been before. The Corn Laws had been abolished in 1846 after fierce and long debate. In Britain the idea was victorious that restraints on trade were anachronistic, a relic of the medieval world of guilds, monopolies and protection; that to remove restraints on economic activity at home and restraints on trade abroad would be beneficial to the British economy and people. At a time when Britain, having experienced a spontaneous industrial revolution, was the world's industrial leader, when people had confidence, rightly or wrongly, in the continued vitality of the economy, and confidence in its ability to compete in world trade, these *laissez-faire* beliefs were eminently reasonable.

In this ethos the Royal Commission on Sea Fisheries was appointed by a Liberal Government under Lord Palmerston. On appointment, the members were apparently instructed to adopt a *laissez-faire* approach in some supplementary terms of reference the origins of which are obscure. The terms of reference given to the Commission by the Queen and announced in Parliament had been to conduct an enquiry 'with the view of increasing the supply of a favourite and nutritious article of Food for the benefit of the Public.' But in the opening paragraph of their report the Commissioners say they were appointed

> to inquire into the condition of the Sea Fisheries of the United Kingdom of Great Britain and Ireland, and especially instructed, by the terms of Your Majesty's Commission, to ascertain firstly, whether the supply of fish is increasing, stationary, or decreasing; secondly, whether any modes

of fishing which are practised are wasteful, or otherwise injurious to the supply of fish; and, thirdly, whether the said fisheries are injuriously affected by any legislative restrictions, ...

The difference between these two versions of the terms of reference is remarkable. The first conveys a paternalistic, or rather maternalistic, approach; it suggests that if there was a problem the Queen's government would do something about it. The second suggests that legislative action could only do harm and should be rooted out. It is conceivable that the members of the Commission themselves put this interpretation on the task they had been set, but it seems most unlikely that they would have done that without approval from the Government. The wording strongly implies that they received supplementary instructions, but I have been unable to find any trace of them.

In their report, the Commissioners make a powerful declaration of their belief in the principle of *laissez-faire*. Surprisingly, it is made with reference to the branding of herrings in Scotland. This system for certifying the quality of herrings, described earlier, was now paid for by the trade, not the government, and seems innocuous enough. A number of foreign importers of Scottish herrings had given evidence in favour of its retention.[17] But to the Commissioners the branding of herrings was a red rag to a bull. They were intent on rooting out government intervention and this was the only significant instance of it they could find, apart from the close season for oysters. They charged at it breathing fire:

> But we conceive that ... a violation of a great principle of public policy is involved in the very existence of the brand and its concomitant system of regulation and inspection. It is a direct violation of the greatest of all economical principles, and of that which is now adopted as the commercial policy of this country – the principle of Free Trade and the policy of removing every description of restriction and protection from commerce.[18]

The strength of their words reminds one of the politician who wrote in large letters in the margin of his speech, 'very loud – weak point'. But it is the dogmatic flavour not just of this statement but of the whole report that is so striking. No other report on fisheries in this era was anything like it. The explanation seems to lie in the composition of the Royal Commission, not just in the *laissez-faire* spirit of the times, though the two are closely connected. The chairman, Mr Caird (later Sir James Caird), a member of Parliament, was 'an ardent free trader' who first attracted attention in the free trade versus protection debate which continued after the repeal of the Corn Laws.[19] Mr George Shaw Lefevre, another member of Parliament, had grown up in political society where he had 'rapidly developed strong liberal, and even radical, leanings'.[20] But the person who must have dominated the Commission was T. H. Huxley, a man who possessed an extraordinary combination of brilliance, belligerence, charm and arrogance. From modest origins, Huxley by the 1860's had risen to a position of great eminence in British science, and he had achieved popular fame, indeed notoriety, for having championed Darwinism in debates with churchmen and other believers who could not the face the notion that man was descended from apes, not created in the Garden of Eden. That he was the most distinguished member of the Royal Commission on Sea Fisheries and the only one versed in marine biology is not the only ground for supposing that he was responsible for the argument against restraints on oyster fishing.

In the first place, Darwinism, of which Huxley was the leading evangelist, was, and often still is, carried over to economics so as to reinforce by analogy the notion that economic competition is natural and, by selecting the best, beneficial; it produces faith in a natural, immutable, competitive order; faith in leaving things to competition. One can see this approach in Huxley's essays and in the Report when, for example, it says, '...we are of the opinion that any tendency to over-fishing will meet with its natural check...'. Secondly, the Report often has the overbearing tone of someone who is convinced he knows the truth, has a duty to put others right and enjoys doing so pugnaciously. Thirdly, the same lines of argument and examples that were used in the Report are to be found in two papers that Huxley wrote about the oyster question some twenty years later.

In the later papers Huxley totally changed his position, presumably because the oyster population had not recovered as it should have done if the Royal Commission had been right. In one paper he now said, 'It is probable, in fact, that, unless conditions are unusually favourable, not more than two or three out of every million of fry of the oyster ever reach maturity'; and he went on to say, 'I must confess myself unable to arrive at a conclusion on the question of whether what is called "overdredging" – that is dredging to the extreme limit that it is commercially profitable to dredge – is alone competent permanently to destroy an oyster bed or not'.[21] In the other paper he went all the way and conceded that 'oyster fisheries may be exhaustible'.[22]

That would seem at a stroke to demolish the policy advocated by the Royal Commission, but Huxley clung to that policy and still opposed restraints on oyster fishing. To do so he shifted his ground. He now argued that restraints were desirable but could not be enforced. Previously over-fishing was impossible, now it was possible; previously regulation was unnecessary, now it was impossible. Nor is that all. Instead of acknowledging his change of position, he claimed, in a passage which makes one gasp and stretch one's eyes, that he and his colleagues on the Royal Commission had held this position all along. His precise words are these:

> When, nearly twenty years ago, my colleagues, Sir James Caird, Mr. Shaw Lefevre, and I, had to deal with the oyster question, I am not aware that any of us doubted the value of protection of public oysterbeds in the open sea, if it could only be made efficient.[23]

It seems that Huxley was amply endowed with the human tendency to select and amend what one remembers until one can live comfortably with what remains.

To his credit, he acknowledged in the first of these papers that the French system, whereby an estimate is made of the quantity of oysters in a bed and fishing is allowed only to the extent justified by the estimate, was the 'only protection of oysters which can possibly be efficient'; and he concluded the second paper with prescience

> I for my part believe that the only hope for the oyster consumer lies first in oyster culture, and secondly, in discovering a means of breeding oysters under such conditions that the spat shall be safely deposited. And I have no doubt that when those who undertake the business are provided with a proper knowledge of the conditions under which they have to work both these objects will be attained.[24]

After his triumphs in the Darwinian battle, Huxley's appetite for laying down the law and striking down those with different beliefs caused him increasingly to address political and philosophical subjects which were far beyond the realms of the physical sciences and hard evidence. For example, by 1890 he was writing on 'Natural rights and Political rights', 'Government: Anarchy or Regimentation' and 'On the Inequality of Man', offering dogmatic opinions charged with emotion. William Irvine, in his admirable comparative biography of Darwin and Huxley, put the point vividly:

Huxley began as an industrious scientific caterpillar chewing the prosaic vegetables of fact and creeping cautiously on the solid ground of empiricism. In certain fleeting but extra-lepidopteral phases, he became suddenly aquatic and roamed the seas, preying fruitfully on salps and medusae. At length, returning to his former habitat, he retired briefly into an academic cocoon and then burst miraculously forth, a gorgeous literary and philosophic butterfly, sipping innumerable sweet and unscientific nectars and describing all sorts of wayward arabesques in the soft, balmy airs of speculation.[25]

When in mid-career he addressed the oyster question, it seems that Huxley could not resist expressing an uncompromising opinion as to what was the right policy, using scientific formulations and lending the weight of his authority when the scientific evidence needed to support that opinion was lacking. It is the misfortune of the British oyster that it fell foul of him at that stage in his career, as well as meeting the high tide of *laissez-faire*. We shall see in the next chapter how very different were the views of his French counterpart, Monsieur Coste, another man of conviction.

The Reception of the Report

"A welcome New Year's gift is just presented to the public in the Report on the Sea Fisheries of the kingdom," said *The Times* on 2 January 1866. "More opportune assurances could never be given than are here offered us by the Commissioners… it is something to learn that there is no danger of a scarcity of fish… their recommendations point rather to the repeal than the enactment of fishery laws, which appear for the most part to be injurious instead of beneficial. Such is the substance of the results obtained by a diligent and impartial inquiry. There are exceptional conclusions, but they do not affect the main question. The oyster fishery has suffered of late, but only from natural causes, as it has often suffered before."

Less than two years later *The Times* had changed its tune. On 15 October 1867, it wrote 'The fact is that a wild Oyster has become pretty well as rare as a wild horse…. Our fishermen, French and British between them, have cleared the bottom of the sea out… we have only our own recklessness to thank for the fact that Oysters cost five times what they used to cost, but the lesson will be well worth its price if we do but apply the moral to all such rapacious and wasteful dealing with the bountiful gifts of Nature.' *The Times* was referring here to the oyster beds in the Channel which the Royal Commission had confidently said 'show no sign at present of giving way'.

In April 1866 Mr Milner Gibson for the Government promised in the House of Commons soon to introduce a bill giving broad effect to the Commission's recommendations for oyster fisheries. He said,

> Great caution would be required to be observed before any Department of the State should take on itself to grant exclusive rights of property in those cases in which rights were now possessed by the public. The question of enclosure of waste lands and public commons, was one which at the present day excited considerable attention; and if persons could easily enclose and appropriate to themselves portions of the coast where humble fishermen obtained a scanty livelihood, without fitting compensation and proper consideration, a general ground of complaint might be furnished.[26]

A little later the Marquess of Clanricarde told the House of Lords that there were 3 or 4 Private Bills before Parliament for the creation of private oyster beds, and suggested that these ought to be suspended while the Government speedily introduced a Public Bill. For the Government, Lord Stanley of Alderley replied that a Bill was already in preparation, and in June 1866 a Bill to give effect to the Royal Commission's recommendations with respect to the enclosure of the seabed was tabled and passed. In the following year, 1867, the provisions in the new Act for the protection of enclosures against theft and interference were extended to private oyster beds; and in the same year a Commission was appointed to renegotiate with France the close season for oyster fishing in the Channel.

After this preliminary activity, a Sea Fisheries Act was passed in 1868 which repealed all existing legislation with respect to sea fisheries in Great Britain (fisheries legislation for Ireland had been reformed in the 1840's) and enacted the only two bits of law for sea fisheries that were deemed to be necessary after the adoption of the policy recommended by the Royal Commission – a new convention with France and the new powers for the enclosure of the seabed for the purposes of farming oysters.

The new convention with France contained some general rules for the conduct of fishing boats from the two countries and introduced a shortened close season for oyster fishing in the Channel. The British, who favoured total abolition of the close season, had managed to get the French to agree to a reduction of the period of closure by six weeks – to start only on June 15th – despite the importance attached by the French to the close season in the Channel as a means of enforcing the summer closure in their own waters.[27]

As regards the enclosure of oyster beds in British waters, the Act, which incorporated the provisions of the Acts of 1866 and 1867 with some additions, provided for two kinds of enclosure.

First, there was the introduction of the 'several order' which gives an individual, cooperative or company the exclusive right to fish for oysters (or mussels) in the area specified in the order. Potential applicants for a several order had to 'make application by a memorial' to the Board of Trade; if the Board of Trade thought fit to proceed with the case, the applicant had to give notice to possible owners of the portion of the seashore he wanted to use and to owners of the adjoining land; for a month the Board of Trade would receive objections; if there were any objections, it would then appoint an inspector to make an enquiry and hold hearings in the area; the inspector would report in writing; the Board of Trade would decide whether to make an order; the applicant had to advertise the order in the vicinity of the concession; the order would be sent to be confirmed by Parliament, which, if the order was opposed, would send it to a Select Committee. All expenses incurred by the Board of Trade, including the pay of the inspector, the costs of the enquiry and advertising, were to be borne by the applicant; and the Board of Trade was given power, if it thought fit, to call upon the applicant to put up an advance against the costs.

Secondly, there was the introduction in 1868 of the 'regulating order', under which powers could be given to regulate an oyster fishery by restricting dredging and the size of oyster to be taken, and also by licensing fishing and levying charges. To obtain a regulating order the applicant had to go through the same Byzantine procedure as the applicant for a several order. The applicants for regulating orders typically have been local authorities or sea fisheries committees formed by them.

The Government's object in devising such a complex system for obtaining several or regulating orders was to appease all those whose interests could be affected. Nevertheless the House of Lords introduced two amendments to enhance the protection of property rights. Both were described and commented upon by Mr Farrer, the Permanent Secretary of the Board of Trade, some years later. The first of these amendments provided that the power to obtain land above high watermark so as to have access to a fishery, which had been written into the Bill, should not be operative where there were any existing rights below low watermark, for example rights to take gravel. Since, said Mr Farrer, there exist a number of rights, some very clear and some very shadowy, over the foreshore and bed of the sea, under all sorts of feudal grants and charters, and prescriptions, 'it is a question to say whether that restriction may not have had a very injurious effect both in preventing people from applying for orders and in preventing the grant or due operation of such orders.'[28]

The second amendment was a safeguard to a position that already seemed safe. It was already provided that orders made under the Act had no effect unless confirmed by Parliament, so that, in the words of Mr Farrer, 'after having passed the ordeal of the inspector and of the Board of Trade, they can be taken before a Select Committee just in the same way as a Private Bill'; yet the House of Lords had inserted a clause saying, 'No order made by the Board of Trade under this part of this Act shall take away or abridge any right of several fishery, or any right on, to or over any portion of the seashore, which right is enjoyed by any person under any local or special Act of Parliament, or any royal charter, letters patent, prescription, or immemorial usage, without the consent of such person.'[29]

With hindsight one would think it should have been obvious from the start that the complications and costs of the procedure, and the uncertainty whether an application would be successful, would be a formidable deterrent to potential applicants, in particular to traditional oystermen who generally had very limited means and limited education; and that the system would discourage the making of applications for small concessions, in relation to which the costs would be high as compared with large concessions.

The system has had a lasting effect on Britain's oyster fisheries. To this day it remains in force essentially unchanged, cumbersome, costly, slow and unpredictable. Nowadays the department of government that handles applications is MAFF (the Ministry of Agriculture, Fisheries and Food). Fortunately there is now, by accident of history, another way of getting concessions that is not quite so cumbersome. This is described in Chapter 11.

To sum up, the legacy of the Royal Commission and the Government's reactions to it was that almost all public regulation of oyster fisheries, such as it was, was swept away. A system of private enclosure was introduced but it was so complex and so costly that one might almost suppose it had been devised to prevent any enclosure being achieved. Yet obviously the new system of enclosure was not the product of a scheming mind with a perverse intent.

Rather it was the natural child of British property law, with its rich inheritance of complexity and ambiguity, and of a Government attempting to create powers to enclose property without injuring existing property rights.

Ten years after the Royal Commission had reported, a Select Committee was appointed in 1876 to inquire into the continuing scarcity of oysters. It rejected the opinion of the Royal Commission and found that '... the principal cause of the shortage of oysters was to be found in...the continual and constantly increasing habit of over-dredging for them in open waters...'[30] At the end of the century, a Select Committee on Sea Fisheries, having reported that without possibility of doubt there had been extensive depletion of the oyster beds, feebly offered the old view that the cause was 'repeated and continued failure of the spatting seasons'.[31] Neither report led to any significant action. The unrestrained exploitation of the declining British oyster population continued. What is perhaps most remarkable is that the scarcity of oysters was regarded in 1876 as a matter of sufficient political concern to merit the appointment of a Select Committee devoted to oyster fisheries and nothing else.

How unrestrained were the fishermen in pursuit of any oysters they could find was well conveyed by a witness who described to the Select Committee of 1876 what had happened when a new bed was found on the Whitstable Flats:

> ... within 48 hours of that fishery being discovered, I counted, I think it was, 75 boats upon this one little spot. I went there myself; it was quite a narrow limit, about 30 yards long and 10 broad, and upon this I dredged. The boats were jammed close together. You went up and down with boats on each side touching....[32]

CHAPTER SIX

France in the 19th century

FRANCE, LIKE ENGLAND, suffered an oyster shortage in the middle of the 19th century. The causes were the same as in England, but the response of government was very different. Where the English removed all restraints on fishing, the French acted powerfully to restrict fishing and restore the oyster population. What the French did, and why, is the subject of this chapter. But first a look at the earlier history of the French oyster industry.

French writers on oysters, like their English counterparts, start by telling the reader how the Romans ate oysters hugely, imported them from the shores of the Channel and thought oysters from their country the best; and they go on to tell you legends about oyster eating by their compatriots. Napoleon, it seems, ate several dozen before each of his great battles; Voltaire, Diderot and Jean-Jacques Rousseau drew inspiration for their creative spirits by frequently eating several dozen oysters; the revolutionary leaders, Danton, Camille Desmoulin and Robespierre found that eating oysters renewed their determination (*volonté*) and energy.

Cancale

An excellent history of the oyster industry of Cancale, not far from Mont St. Michel on the north coast of Brittany, written by a local oyster grower, gives an account of the evolution of the local oyster industry and the national policies applied to it.[1]

Cancale was a very important source for the supply of oysters to Paris before the railway era. It was near enough to Paris for it to be possible to ship fresh oysters to the capital by boat along the coast and up the Seine, or overland by horse transport; and Cancale oysters were highly esteemed. In 1545, Francis I rewarded Cancale with the title of 'ville' and other privileges for supplying oysters to his table, and further rewards were given to Cancale by later kings.

There was no restraint on fishing until the 18th century. Regulations for mussel fishing had been introduced in 1681, but it was then considered that oyster fishing need not be regulated because the natural oyster beds were inexhaustible. From about 1720 onwards, however, there appears to have been pressure, interrupted by wars, on the supply of oysters in France. In 1750 all oyster fishing was forbidden at Arcachon for 3 years, and in 1759 a close season of six months, from the end of April to the end of October, was introduced in the whole of France; during those months there was to be no fishing, trading or peddling of oysters. Pressure on supplies continued, aggravated on the north coast of France by the intrusion of English fishing boats which annoyed the local fishermen and gave rise to strong accusations, including the suggestion by one le Sieur Hélie (le Sieur is equivalent to Esquire) that the English were out to ruin the French oyster fisheries in order to force the French to buy from them at exorbitant prices. The English from time to time became similarly enraged with French fishermen who crossed the Channel in the other direction.

In 1766 the shortage of oysters in the area of Cancale became so severe that a local enquiry was conducted by the French Admiralty, following which it was ruled that fishing was to be permitted only on beds declared open for the year; small oysters were to be put back on the seabed. There followed a temporary easing of the oyster shortage, but the fishing regulations, as distinct from those for marketing, were not adequately enforced. In the early years of the reign of Louis XVI there was a renewed scarcity, in response to which an inspector was appointed to visit the Cancale area.

After he had reported, a new set of regulations was introduced in July 1787. These regulations, which built on the Admiralty regulations of 1766, were very detailed and were clearly designed with an eye to better enforcement. A striking innovation is that responsibility for the application of the regulations was placed largely in the hands of persons chosen by the local fishermen. The Admiralty was to appoint an inspector at Cancale, and the masters of the local fishing boats were to elect every year four of their number to take part in the enforcement of the regulations. The authority of these elected men, known as *gardes jurés*, depended on their having been elected and then sworn into office by the inspector; they did not enjoy the powers of the police, but their evidence carried greater weight than that of ordinary citizens. They were rather like water bailiffs on a river; they were not just guards; they had to decide where and when fishing would take place.

Transport of oysters by express carrier from Cancale to Paris.

The main regulations were these:

1. A close season for oyster fishing from 1 April to 15 October;

2. Each year in late September the *gardes jurés* together with their predecessors from the previous year, will assess all the oyster beds in the bay by dredging to discover the condition of the beds and the quality of the oysters on them. On the first Sunday in October there will be a meeting of all the masters of the boats in the presence of the inspector at which the *gardes jurés* will report on the state of the beds and it will be decided by a majority vote which beds will be open to fishing during the year.

3. The King expressly forbids fishing on other beds on pain of a fine of 60 livres and the confiscation of the miscreant's boat and dredges. If it is found during the year that a bed is becoming excessively denuded of oysters an extraordinary meeting will be called to decide in the presence of the inspector and the *gardes jurés* whether the bed should be closed and whether another should be opened.

4. Boats from other ports can apply for permission to fish for oysters at Cancale but the local officers of the Admiralty will set a quota for the total number of permitted boats; and in the allocation of that quota fishermen from Cancale have precedence over outsiders.

La Caravane.

5. The *gardes jurés* will decide when (on which tides) fishing will take place; all the boats will then go out together, led by the boat of the *gardes jurés*; they will return when the guard boat returns; and anyone who fishes at night or during the day at times not approved by the *gardes jurés* will be fined and have his boat and dredges confiscated. The procession of boats that went out to fish together came to be known as the 'Caravane'.

6. The catch must be sorted at sea and all under-sized oysters and cultch must be thrown back into the sea at the place where they were fished up; the catch will be inspected by the guards on the shore to make sure that under-sized oysters have not been taken; and fishermen are forbidden to take small oysters and put them to grow on their private layings (*parcs*), or to sell them to be exported.

The French Revolution soon intervened, but these regulations, introduced by royal declaration in 1787, were maintained in acts passed in 1790, 1791 and 1795. In practice, however, the Napoleonic Wars and the activities of the British fleet made fishing almost impossible; the oyster beds enjoyed a respite from fishing. When fishing was resumed, the close season was reduced by three weeks, but otherwise the regulations continued in force with the oyster boats going out together under supervision in the *Caravane*. Indeed the *Caravane*

Sorting oysters on the beach at Cancale at low tide.

went on into the 20th century; pictures of it can be seen today on old postcards of Cancale.

The number of boats and the intensity of oyster fishing increased. From 1823 to 1835 production at Cancale averaged 31 million oysters a year; from 1836 to 1847 56 million a year. In this period production reached its peak, encouraged, as in England, by improvements in the means of transport by which to send oysters to the expanding towns, and by rising demand. But in the mid-40's production began to decline and the price to rise.

In 1845 there was a fierce dispute between the fishermen and the authorities at Cancale over the enforcement of the regulations. The potato harvest, on which the local people, like the Irish, were highly dependent, failed; the following winter, when the effects of the potato shortage were acute, the fishermen asked for an extra day's oyster fishing, which the authorities at first promised and then refused, since no official would take responsibility for varying the rules; the fishermen, frustrated, went to sea in 200 boats and came back in the evening laden with oysters. They were forbidden to unload the oysters but paid no attention, an act of revolt which was not allowed to go unpunished. At dawn a formidable military force arrived at Cancale, consisting of two brigades of gendarmerie on land led by senior officials (the *sous-préfet*, the *procureur du roi* and the *commissaire de la marine*) and two naval cutters

Le Restaurant du Parc, Cancale: Oysters being taken from the water at the edge of the terrace where they are served.

at sea. Daunted, the fishermen reluctantly obeyed orders to take the oysters back and deposit them on the beds where they had caught them.

The oyster shortage was a national phenomenon, but there are no national statistics for this period with which we can assess its severity. All we know is that there was a shortage, that prices rose and that the French Government reacted energetically.

National policy

Three things help to explain why the French reaction to the oyster shortage was so very different from the British: the general approach to economic policy-making and public administration instituted by Colbert; the French law relating to the foreshore and to the granting of concessions; and, thirdly, the work of one remarkably influential French scientist and his political master.

The legacy of Colbert

An Englishman looking at French oyster policy soon sees how important was the mercantilist belief that it was the task of the French Government to protect French industries and support them actively for the sake of the strength and welfare of the nation. It is that economic philosophy which largely explains why a policy of active regulation of the oyster industry was followed without question in France, just as it was belief in *laissez-faire* that explains why a policy of *laissez-faire* was applied without question to the oyster industry in Britain. That is not to say that Britain's policy of *laissez-faire* was disadvantageous when applied to the general run of British industry and agriculture. Rather, the misfortune was that in Britain, *laissez-faire*, the national economic credo, was applied to the oyster, an extinguishable species to which, exceptionally but rather obviously, it was inappropriate. The French had the good fortune that their general economic approach – mercantilism – was appropriate to the special needs of the oyster industry.

The person primarily responsible for France's mercantilist approach to economic policy-making was Colbert, Louis XIV's brilliant economic administrator who set out to make France a dominant commercial and military power. Obedient to mercantilist principles, he used the power of the state in an active, participatory manner to build up France's capacity to produce high quality goods and works of art so as to gain a competitive advantage over other nations. As a part of that policy, the spirit of which still permeates French economic policy-making (including policy towards the oyster industry), he sought to make France a dominant naval power so as to be able to expand French commerce and acquire colonies. So persuasive and effective was he that Louis XIV entrusted him with responsibility for finance, manufactures, arts, commerce, maritime affairs and colonies.

In building up the French navy, Colbert introduced a system for manning the ships that served later to help the Government regulate oyster fishing. In place of impressment by force, on which the French navy had relied previously, Colbert introduced a more civilised system which included economic incentives. This was *l'Inscription Maritime*. It applied to the Atlantic Fleet, not to the Mediterranean Fleet which consisted of galleys, manned by a mixture of criminals who had been sentenced to the galleys, recalcitrant Protestants and slaves from Africa and Canada. (Galleys were used in the Mediterranean by the French navy until the middle of the 19th century, when they were abolished by Napoleon III; the ex-galley slaves were transported to a penal colony at Cayenne, on the coast of French Guiana.)

Under the *Inscription Maritime* all sailors and fishermen were registered compulsorily and were called up by rotation – except in war when a general call-up could become necessary. Civilian ships were forbidden to take on *inscrits maritimes* (sailors registered under the system) who were due to serve

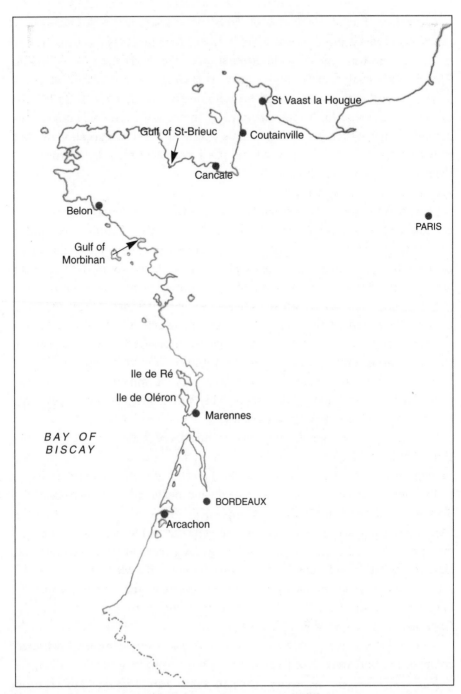

Important oyster centres in France.

with the navy. There was a wage for those on military service, paid to their families while they were away; there was a retainer for those not called; and there were benefits for the wounded and for pensioners.[2] As an additional incentive, the *inscrits maritimes* were given priority in the allocation of oyster concessions by the Government.

Colbert's third legacy to the oyster industry was the creation of an integrated administrative hierarchy. At the top was the Ministry of Marine and Colonies, responsible for the navy, the merchant navy, sea fisheries and colonies, a combination of functions which reflected Colbert's belief that the way to achieve prosperity and national greatness was by the promotion of the export trade, the creation of a strong navy to protect that trade, a merchant navy to carry it, and the acquisition of colonies with which to exchange goods and in which to have bases. Sea fisheries fitted naturally into the ministry, the more so since the *Inscription Maritime* made fishermen part-time members of the navy. Within the Ministry of Marine, fisheries and the *Inscription Maritime* were administered together by a hierarchy that reached down to each part of the coast.

The French Law of the Foreshore

Before 1544 there were some privately owned fisheries in France, but in that year Francis I promulgated 'the inalienability of the maritime domain', meaning that no one was entitled to enclose the foreshore or seabed within territorial waters; they belonged to the Crown which held them for public usage. In 1584 Henry III reinforced that ruling by ordering the destruction of all exclusive fisheries, unless the owners could justify them by producing authentic titles. Subsequently the practice of making enclosures on the foreshore appears to have grown up, no doubt encouraged by the mid-19th century oyster shortage. In 1852 a law came into force requiring that all enclosures on the shore for the purpose of growing oysters be authorised. Since then it has been true to say that oyster layings in France are almost invariably concessions granted by the Government.[3] Some private beds under ancient titles survive, for example at St Vaast la Hougue, but they are few. On this legal foundation a system was built which ensures, as we shall see, that fishermen of modest means can get concessions and which provides one of the levers by means of which the state regulates the oyster fisheries.

The way public rights of fishery were established in France may seem very similar to the way they were established in England, but there is an important difference. In France the King stopped the private enclosure of the shore and seabed in order to make it a public domain where he – and the governments which succeeded the monarchy – were able to grant concessions and take other steps to conserve and develop the supply of oysters. In England it was the other way round: the barons in Magna Carta forced the King to stop enclosing the shore and seabed for his own purposes and in doing so effectively prevented future monarchs and governments from making concessions to fishermen for many centuries. Thus the authoritarian actions of the French monarchy providentially furthered the interests of the producers and consumers of oysters better than the anti-authoritarian actions of the English barons.

Coste and Napoleon III

The man who almost single-handed shaped the French Government's response to the oyster scarcity was Monsieur Coste – in full, Jean Jacques Marie Cyprien Victor Coste, Member of the French Institute and Professor of Embryology at the *Collège de France*. He had been working on the artificial breeding of freshwater fish, the technique whereby, for example, the eggs are squeezed out of a female salmon and mixed with sperm similarly 'stripped' from a male salmon, so as to obtain fertile eggs which are then put to hatch and grow in controlled conditions. At the instigation of the French Government, he went on a journey along the coasts of France and Italy in order to explore the possibility of extending to sea fish the artificial means of fish culture developed for freshwater fish. Near Naples he came upon methods of oyster farming that had been in use since Roman times, of which he wrote a fascinating account in his *Voyage d'Exploration sur le Littoral de la France et de l'Italie*, first published in 1855. He describes two lakes, the Lake Lucrino and Lake Averno, at the bottom of the Gulf of Baia. In lyrical terms he recalls the classical associations of these *'bassins tranquilles où la mer semblait venir se reposer'* and goes on to tell the story, most of which can be traced back to Pliny the Elder,[4] of Crassius Orata, the inventor of oyster cultivation (meaning the placing of oysters in man-made enclosures favourable to breeding, within or around which surfaces are provided on which the larvae can settle).

Crassius Orata was a thrusting Roman businessman and innovator who made a great deal of money, according to Pliny, by inventing shower baths and selling country villas that were fitted out with them. He started importing oysters from Brindisi, fattening them in Lake Lucrino and claiming they had a better flavour than oysters from other places. His oyster business expanded and

Coste's drawings of Roman methods of oyster culture used at Fusaro
RIGHT: *rocks surrounded by stakes*
BELOW: *faggots suspended on ropes*
BOTTOM: *baskets of oysters ready for sale suspended on ropes.*

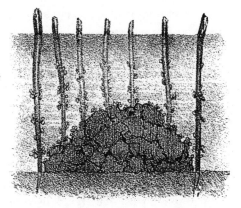

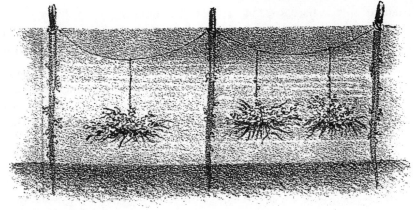

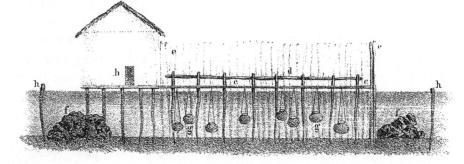

took up so much space that his neighbours complained, in response to which he devised the system of putting oysters to fatten in containers suspended in the water. In Lake Fusaro, a shallow lagoon lying between Lake Lucrino and Cape Miseno, Coste saw in use a method of breeding oysters which had been depicted, he found, on Roman vases. Rocks had been stacked in the water to form mounds which were encircled by stakes of wood driven into the sea bed. Parent oysters were placed amongst the rocks so that their larvae might settle on the rocks or on the stakes. In addition, faggots were suspended on ropes strung between stakes in the lagoon to provide further surfaces on which the larvae could settle. Coste summarised the technique by saying that the stakes and faggots with which the artificial banks of rock were surrounded served the purpose of stopping the loss of larvae by offering them surfaces to which they could attach themselves, like a swarm of bees meeting some branches after they have left their hive.[5] Coste fiercely condemned the over-fishing of oysters in France and recommended that the methods used in the Gulf of Naples be adopted to replenish the French oyster beds. But he emphasised that this could be achieved only if the Government took the initiative: since the sea was a public domain, it was the responsibility of the Government to supervise the conservation and development of this source of nourishment; the French marine administration had in its hands all the powers needed to undertake the task; he had no hesitation in advising it to embark on that course. He added that he did not think it feasible artificially to fertilise oysters like salmon; oyster growers must be recommended to rely on natural fertilisation and use the Roman methods to catch as many as possible of the larvae so produced.

As often happens with innovations, Coste was not alone in proposing steps along these lines. At St. Servan, near St Malo, the local commissioner for fisheries, Monsieur de Bon, was experimenting in 1853, while Coste was on his journey to Italy, with methods of reviving the local oyster beds. He found that oysters would breed after being moved from one part of the coast to another, and also that they would do so when placed on the foreshore, i.e. in places that were not always covered with sea water at low tide. He began experimenting with collectors designed to provide surfaces to which oyster larvae would attach themselves. He achieved success with platforms of planks mounted about 20 centimetres above parent oysters laid on the shore.[6] In August 1857, Coste, while touring the French coast on the instructions of the Emperor, saw what de Bon had achieved and seized upon it. In the words of a later French report on oyster culture in France, 'His lively imagination grasped with enthusiasm the discoveries of M. de Bon; to popularise them he consecrated his high situation in the *Collège de France*, his reputation and experience as a scientific man, and the declared support of the head of State.[7]

In February 1858 Coste wrote a report – one of many – addressed directly to Napoleon III. He asked for six to eight thousand francs to try restocking the

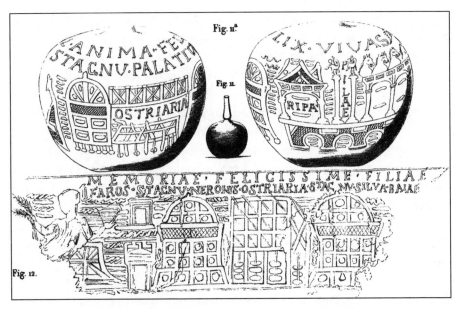

Coste's drawing of Roman vases depicting oyster culture.

Bay of St. Brieuc, to the west of St Malo on the north coast of Brittany. He set out in detail how he proposed to proceed. The oysters to be brought there must be kept out of the water for as short a time as possible; they must be carefully guarded; a staff with a boat was needed; faggots would be used as collectors, held down by weights on the bottom. He called for much closer general regulation of the dredging of public oyster beds, based on the system in force at Cancale, where each bed was opened only in years when it had been established that there were mature oysters ready to be harvested and sufficient mature oysters were left on the bed as breeding stock. And he also called for the establishment of a plan of the oyster growing areas of the coast which should record how each part was used, what condition it was in and what was produced.[8] With an exuberant confidence and enthusiasm that pervades all his reports, he declared that if the job was done in the manner that he had the honour to propose to His Majesty, he dared to assert that the coast of France would soon be one long chain of oyster beds, interrupted only by stretches where there was too much mud.

Coste, having apparently got all he asked for at once from the Emperor, reported to him a year later, in January 1859, that the experiment at St Brieuc had been a triumphant success. There had been a rich harvest of spat with as many as 20 thousand spat deposited on a single submerged faggot which took no more space than a sheaf of corn in a field. Coste 'felt it his duty' to recommend to the Emperor the immediate restocking of the whole French coast, the Mediterranean as well as the Atlantic coast and the north coast of France; Algeria as well as Corsica.[9] In another report, in November 1859, he recommended the restocking of the Bay of Arcachon; the Government should establish two 'model farms', initially stocked with one million local oysters, where young oysters would be gathered on collectors and fattened. The farms would be divided into lots granted to the most energetic seamen; the project would serve to restore the stock of oysters in the whole bay, into which would flow the surplus larvae not caught on the collectors at the farms.[10]

Other Frenchmen were making innovations. At the Ile de Ré, near La Rochelle, a stonemason named Boeuf found a way of using the muddy shore to grow oysters. He had observed that oysters had accumulated on a sea wall and sought to replicate those conditions. He enclosed an area of hitherto useless shore that was exposed at low tide by making a wall that would act as a boundary line and retain some water at low tide, and he put stones on the bottom as collectors. The experiment worked; oysters placed in his *parc* bred excellently. Other people copied his method and soon miles of muddy shore, as far out as possible, were producing oysters. A variety of materials was placed on the bottom of the *parcs* to act as collectors, including broken pottery. Faggots of wood were found unsuitable. Another development was the use of tiles as collectors. At Arcachon it was found that everyday pan tiles made good collectors; larvae would collect to form spat on the underside of the tiles if they were placed concave side down; and at the Ile de Ré a Doctor Kemmerer invented a technique for covering the tiles with lime cement and a layer of paper so that it was easier to detach the spat undamaged.[11]

Coste was important because he formulated, in the most persuasive manner, what French oyster policy should be. But it was Napoleon III who adopted that policy and put it into effect. That Coste was able so directly and powerfully to influence the Emperor must have been partly the result of his powers of persuasion. Monsieur de Bon, who became Director of Administration at the Ministry of Marine, wrote that Coste gained the support of Napoleon III 'by the eloquent ardour of his convictions'.[12] But that is not all. Coste was a medical adviser of the Empress Eugénie, a position which gave him access to the Emperor and helped gain him his support.[13]

That the Emperor was sympathetic to Coste's recommendations is not

The use of tiles as collectors, Illustrated London News, *1881.*

surprising. He was a supremely pragmatic politician who, having embraced socialist ideas in his youth, fought the Reds and went on to advocate and practise dictatorship. He intervened to help the poor when there was a food scarcity; he summoned Haussman to rebuild Paris and turn it into a magnificent city; he created banks and undertook public works to help the economic development of the country; in the tradition of Colbert he took for granted that the state should support economic enterprises. On general grounds, it is understandable that he should have supported the oyster industry, or any industry.

While Coste comes out with flying colours for having advocated the right policy for oysters, it has to be said that his scientific reputation is blemished, particularly in English eyes. In 1838, when he was 31, long before he became concerned with fish culture, he was accused by Richard Owen, FRS, a leading zoologist, of having misunderstood some evidence that Owen had shown him and, worse, of having wrongly laid claim to a discovery of Owen's, accusations he refused to admit. The substance of the dispute, which was about the reproductive mechanisms of the kangaroo, is pretty impenetrable to the layman, who is told, for example, that Coste's false dogma was 'that the *chorion* of the mammiferous *ovum* is the analogue of the vitelline membrane'. But the tone in which the row was conducted as it gained heat is another matter. Huxley was not alone amongst Victorian scientists in being pugnacious when roused in verbal combat, and the reader of the exchanges in this row feels as if he is in a ringside seat at a prize-fight. In the second and final round, some of Owen's sharper jabs are:

'The blunder into which M. Coste falls in his first step ....;
With the same taste which pervades the whole of his work on Embryogénie M. Coste observes ....;

> In this paragraph M. Coste spoke more truths than he intended, in confessing his ignorance ....;
> I shall leave M. Coste in the state of ignorance in which he confesses himself to be .....[14]

Owen, let it be said at once, did not confine himself to abusive remarks. On the contrary, he deployed his scientific case against Coste majestically. Later he fought a long and bitter battle with Huxley over the validity of Darwinism.[15] What is remarkable is that his scientific argument is embellished with such hot personal stuff. As for Coste, it was not the only row in his career. He came into conflict with various people in France, including a water and forest engineer called Millet.[16]

Coste's career seems not to have been damaged by his row with Owen. Five years later, in 1843, he was appointed to the newly-created chair of embryology at the *Collège de France,* and in 1851 he was elected to the Academy of Sciences.[17]

The execution of government policy

To implement Coste's policies, the Government could bring into play the Colbertian machinery of the Ministry of Marine. In 1868 the branch of the ministry responsible for the *Inscription Maritime* and fisheries, no doubt enlarged by the endeavours of M. Coste, had a staff of nearly 700, if one includes 300 *gardes-maritimes*.[18] (The English Government at this time resisted paying for one inspector for the whole country.) The primary task of this staff was the administration of the *Inscription Maritime;* on the fishery side, it was responsible for the supervision and regulation of the fisheries, the enforcement of fishery laws and the collection of fishery statistics. At the top of the hierarchy was the minister, advised by a permanent Fishery Commission, presided over by M. Coste. The country was divided and sub-divided into 5 *arrondissements*, 13 *sous-arrondissements* and 60 *quartiers*. With respect to oyster fisheries, the two main tasks of this machine were to regulate on a local basis how and when public and private beds should be worked; and to allocate concessions. At the national level a decree forbade the sale of oysters for consumption in the four summer months – the months without an R – and there was a limit on the minimum size of oysters that could be sold for consumption.

The exploitation of public oyster beds was closely regulated in a manner derived from the system at Cancale. In each of the 60 *quartiers*, a local commission inspected all the public beds every year and directed which beds or parts of beds would be open for fishing and when. The *inscrits maritimes* of a *quartier*, as well as being given priority in the allocation of concessions, were given priority in the right to fish on the public beds, sometimes to the exclusion of all others, with the result that many or all of those who fished the public beds were dependent on the local branch of the Ministry of the Marine for rulings as regards their military service, reserve pay and other benefits and also their access to oyster beds, private and public. The local administrators had several levers in their hands.

The system of granting concessions, which was set out formally in a law of 1852, was simple compared with that in England. There were no arguments about whether the ownership of the foreshore belonged to the Government. The general type of concession was a lease which could be revoked by the Government at any time but normally was allowed to run on. It could be granted for areas above or below high water and could apply to natural beds, man-made enclosures (*parcs* and *claires*) and other facilities on the shore. The procedure for obtaining concessions was rather complex and could be slow, but since the aim of the policy was to encourage the oyster industry, the decisions were likely to be positive, and the cost to the applicant was minimal: it was a system designed to help men of modest means – the *inscrits maritimes*. Moreover those who obtained concessions were often given assistance in the form of supplies of oysters and collectors from the 'Imperial Parcs', the state stations where oysters were bred for the combined purposes of experiment, the education of the local oystermen and the supply of young oysters to growers, to whom assistance was 'very liberally dispensed'.[19]

French techniques

Following the introduction of the techniques spread by Coste, two methods of oyster cultivation could now be distinguished, the traditional method and the new French method. Both were now practised in France. With the traditional system, which was mainly confined to natural beds that were never uncovered by the tide, fishing was principally by dredge. Cultivation consisted in cleaning the beds, throwing down enough cultch for the larvae to adhere to and conserving a breeding stock of oysters. The young oysters were moved to man-made layings to grow and fatten; or they were left on the natural beds where they were dredged up from time to time so that they could be sorted and predators could be removed.

The new French system was confined to shallow waters. Cultivation consisted in placing in these areas collectors (tiles, stones, faggots etc.) on which might settle the larvae produced by breeding oysters laid down amongst the collectors, or larvae that were carried by the tide from neighbouring natural beds. The spat formed by the larvae were usually left on the collectors until they were about a centimetre across. Then came *détroquage,* the scraping of the spat from the collectors, followed by *élevage* when the spat were often put into mesh containers on legs (*ambulances*) until they had hardened, after which they were put into man-made layings to grow and fatten.

Essentially the same methods continue today, though the productivity and certainty of oyster farming have been transformed in the past thirty years by the advent of hatcheries in which limitless spat of Pacific oysters can be bred and by the introduction of the practice of keeping the growing oysters in plastic mesh bags placed on trestles on the foreshore (see chapters 9 and 10).

The results of Coste's policy

Monsieur Coste's policy met with initial success and euphoria, followed by a period of disastrous failure in many areas in the 1860's. After this turbulent beginning and the interruption caused by the Franco-Prussian war, progress was made again in the 1870's by which time oyster breeding was concentrated in a few proven areas. But Coste, who died in 1873, saw little of this.

An eloquent summary of his achievements is to be found in a report made to the French Minister of Marine in 1881 by M. Brocchi, a French zoologist, after he had visited the principal centres of oyster culture before beginning his work:

> I feel it my duty to render you an account of what I have had the opportunity of observing during my trip, and to lay before you the actual state of oyster-culture in our country. This industry, which is so new and so essentially French, has made rapid strides.... It was not till after the publications and the experiments of M. Coste (1856-58) that the attention of the inhabitants of our coasts was attracted to the possibility of rearing oysters artificially. These experiments, to which the State devoted considerable sums, produced great effect. M. Coste, with an enthusiasm perhaps somewhat exaggerated, but productive of definite and happy results, announced that a new source of wealth opened up to France. The experiments, conducted simultaneously in the Ocean and the

Mediterranean, proved for the most part failures. On the other hand, and this has been too much overlooked, the experiments in the basin of Arcachon were crowned with success. Since then the stimulus has been given, and the industry of oyster-culture has not failed to make rapid progress.[20]

A year later Brocchi published a more personal and touching tribute to Coste:

If he made some mistakes, he suffered cruelly for them. He died blind, disowned and, what is perhaps more terrible, doubting himself and his life's work. Nevertheless I am convinced that without him *l'ostréiculture* would not exist, not only in France but also abroad.[21]

In 1891 an American oyster expert who examined French oyster growing wrote that it was Coste who had furnished the ideas, ideas which with improvement had made the industry practicable and profitable; what Coste did was now well recognised.[22]

The two places where oyster breeding flourished after 1870 were Arcachon, south of Bordeaux, and the Gulf of Morbihan on the Atlantic coast of Brittany. Accounts of how extremely tight were the regulations that were found necessary in order to restore the breeding stock in these two places make one marvel at the negligence and folly of governments in Britain, where all this was reported, in allowing dredging on our public beds to go on unrestricted.

Arcachon and Morbihan

Oyster fishing at Arcachon was unrestricted, apart from the close season in the summer and prohibition of the taking of oysters of less than 5 cm, until 1860-61 when the oyster population was found to be at risk as the local people scrambled to benefit from the expanded market opened up by the railway. Since the beds at Arcachon were 'ebb-dry' (meaning exposed at low water) they were fished by hand and could easily be picked almost bare. In 1860-61 extremely tight restrictions were introduced. Only a few hours fishing were allowed each year on the public beds. For example, in 1865-66 fishing was allowed on December 1st for 2 hours, and on 4 other days during one tide; and 123 acres were totally closed. In some years no fishing was allowed on the public beds; in the eight years 1870-77 the time permitted for fishing averaged one hour a year. What could happen in an hour was described by Major Hayes, the Irish inspector of fisheries:

The public fishing by hand, picking and with small rakes on all the public beds, began on the 2nd December, 1877, upon a flag being hoisted as a signal about one hour before low water of spring tide. The fishing lasted only about one hour, as the incoming tide forced the fishers to leave about that time, some 5,000 persons being engaged; and on the 4th December about 2,000 boats dredged in the channels for the same period. The take amounted to 22,000,000 of oysters, of the value of 185,000 francs, or £ 7,400 in, it may be said, one hour's fishing.[23]

It was not until about 1873, the year of Coste's death, that the oyster population began to recover at Arcachon as a result of several years of heavy spatfall. It then did so dramatically: the number of oysters shipped from Arcachon, which had fluctuated between 5 and 10 million oysters between 1865 and 1872, rose to 112 million by 1875 and to 195 million by 1880; the number of concessions rose from 485 in 1870 to 4,239 in 1880. Portuguese oysters had been introduced into the Bay of Arcachon earlier, but the increase in oyster production at Arcachon in the 1870's appears to have consisted predominantly of natives.[24]

The success of the conservation policy applied to the public beds at Arcachon seems to imply that the local people, unlike those of Cancale, were not so dependent on income from oyster fishing as to make severe temporary restriction of fishing unenforceable. But measures to protect the oyster beds from law-breakers were clearly most necessary. The state employed an inspector and 12 *gardes maritimes* at Arcachon, and the individual concession holders in 1877 maintained about 700 covered boats in which guards lived on watch over their beds.

In the Gulf of Morbihan the story was much the same. Before the railway, the beds had been used only to satisfy the modest local demand; the only restriction on oyster fishing was a close season; no limit was applied to dredging at other times or to the size of oysters taken. In 1864-65 a conservation policy was introduced. Part of the natural beds were made a state reserve upon which no dredging was permitted and from which oysters were taken when necessary to restock the public beds. Fishing on the public beds was strictly limited by rules that were decided locally each year. For example, in the year 1876-77, when there were 700 boats, each was allowed 12 outings of one hour using one dredge.

Statistical uncertainties

Once France had recovered from the Franco-Prussian war and its aftermath, production of oysters, for which figures were by then collected, showed a respectable upward trend, subject to considerable year to year fluctuations. But it is hard to know what was the true quantity of oysters produced for the market, since the official statistics appear to be seriously defective. The chief problem is double-counting. For example, in the late 19th century oysters appear to have been counted when they were sold by one oysterman to another for re-laying, and then counted again when they were sold by the second oysterman for distribution to consumers – or possibly were sold to be re-laid yet again. Another problem, which one can identify in 1896, is that dead oysters brought in with the catch were counted as production. The work of one French expert suggests that the figures have been improved since that time, but in 1987 another wrote that the lack of an adequate statistical system meant that the published figures were bound to be imprecise or even totally erroneous.[25]

As they stand, the figures show production running at over 500 million a year in the years 1877 to 1887, and at more than 1,500 million in the years 1910-14. The increase was caused by a surge in production of Portuguese oysters. These began to be imported from Portugal in the 1860's to make up for the shortage of native oysters in France. In 1865, following a storm in which a cargo of Portuguese oysters was jettisoned in the Gironde estuary, they began to grow naturally on the west coast of France later. Subsequently they were cultivated in the south-west of France on an increasing scale.

It looks as if the removal of double-counting might reduce these figures by as much as two-thirds. If that is right, French production was about 150 million a year in the period 1877-87 and about 500 million a year in the period 1910-14. The range of uncertainty is great. Nevertheless it is clear that oyster production showed a very healthy recovery in France compared with what was happening in Britain at this time. British figures show production running at only about 40 million a year in the period 1877-87, followed by a decline to an average of about 25 million in the years 1910-14.

CHAPTER SEVEN

Oyster policy in Ireland

IN THE 19TH century the British introduced a regulatory regime for oyster fisheries in Ireland. This regime was nothing like as formidable as the French, but it is remarkable that the British, who rejected any regulatory regime at home, should have introduced it. That they did so was a result of the semi-colonial way in which Ireland was then ruled.

After the Act of Union of Ireland with England, which was introduced in 1801 in the wake of attempted revolution, the English custom of leaving responsibility for government as far as possible to local institutions and local landowners could not prudently be applied to Ireland. In such a divided and rebellious country, it would have been dangerous to rely heavily on local self-government. Nor could an economic policy of *laissez-faire* be applied uncompromisingly to Ireland, a country where the infrastructure and other preconditions for economic development did not exist. Yet economic improvement was seen to be needed for the sake of political stability.

In these conditions, law and order was imposed from the centre. (To this day the police of Ireland and Northern Ireland, the Garda and the Royal Ulster Constabulary, are centrally-organised on a national basis, not locally-organised like the police in Britain.) And some action was taken by the centre to promote economic development. An important mechanism for applying this semi-colonial approach to government was the creation by Parliament of permanent Irish boards, subject to Treasury control from London – for example, boards for health and for education. One of these was a new Board of Public Works created in 1831. This could finance not just public works but also fisheries, mines and communal resettlements.[1]

Broadly speaking, fisheries policies until the 1830's had been much the same in Ireland as in England. There had been bounties which were stepped up during the Napoleonic wars and, having earned a bad name, were swept away, along with the herring brand, in 1830.[2] In 1835, however, a commission was appointed to examine the state of the Irish fisheries and consider means of extending and improving them. The commissioners, when they reported in 1836, took a jaundiced view of government support for the industry. They were not swayed by the pleadings for protection of the witnesses they heard, who were sometimes charmingly ingenuous. One group of witnesses, for example, delivered a paper arguing for 'a small Tonnage Bounty, just sufficient to afford protection against a ruinous loss, and yet not large enough to operate as an inducement to fraud.[3]

The commissioners concluded that they could not recommend the Government to take a part in any remedial measures other than replacing the existing tangle of laws with a single new statute, putting control of fisheries into the hands of a single public department which should report annually, improving law enforcement and doing a few other limited things. They discussed the desirability of re-introducing the brand, a proposal put to them on the grounds that if the brand be good for Scotland (where alone it had been continued after 1830) it must be good for Ireland. Nothing, they said, could be more slovenly than the general manner in which herrings were cured in Ireland, 'they are stowed away in stores, or in decked boats, piled in enormous masses; and, in many instances, the process is not commenced till the fish have ceased to be fresh – the curers standing out for prices with the fishermen.' But they doubted whether the brand could be made to work efficiently, and ended up by suggesting that the matter be referred to the Board of Trade 'with a view to rendering the law uniform in all parts of the empire'.

The general view of the commission was that only gradual improvement could be hoped for and it could 'only be effected by the hearty endeavours of individuals and bodies, locally interested, who, from good motives or trading enterprize, may seize favourable opportunities, and apply means for the purpose'. But the report seems to have led to little or no immediate government action; the fisheries of all kinds declined; and the hearty endeavours of private citizens seem to have been applied extensively to breaking the law and to fighting and bloodshed, which was particularly pronounced over salmon fishing, where there was a conflict of interest between traditional fishermen and those who were introducing stake weirs, a type of 'fixed engine' for trapping salmon.[4]

Aroused more by the bloodshed, it seems, than by the decline in the fisheries, the Government finally passed an Irish Fisheries Act in 1842 which followed the recommendations of the 1836 Report and replaced all previous Irish fisheries statutes. The most significant feature of the Act was that it gave the commissioners of public works almost absolute authority to make regulations with respect to the different kinds of fishing carried on in Ireland; and it empowered them to appoint inspectors of fisheries who, under a subsequent Act, were made members of the board as inspecting commissioners.[5] There was nothing comparable in England.

Salmon fisheries

Salmon was now the fish that received most attention in Irish fishery policy and the same was soon to be true in Great Britain. The salmon is anadromous: it ascends rivers to spawn and to live the early stages of its life but otherwise lives and feeds in the sea; it normally returns to breed in the river where it was born. The consequences of these characteristics are several: the salmon is unusually vulnerable to over-fishing since it can be caught at any convenient point on its journey along the river in which it breeds, including the estuary; there is much scope for conflict between those who have fishing rights, or practise fishing without them, at different points on a salmon river, including the estuary; and the breeding of salmon as well as immediate fishing will be stopped if dams, weirs or other obstructions are put across rivers, a problem that became severe in England during the industrial revolution when there was much building of water mills, canals and railways.

The problem for policy-makers in Ireland and Great Britain was to limit the use of fixed engines for catching salmon without causing too much upset to landlords on whose waters they stood and who as a class were powerful; to introduce close seasons; and somehow to enforce the regulations as regards fixed engines, close seasons and poaching at a time when there was much poverty and lawlessness.

After some false starts, the solution found in Ireland, which was in place by 1848, was to enact that all fixed engines and other fishing devices should be licensed and a fee charged for them. Simultaneously, responsibility for collecting the fee and for spending it was put into local hands. This was done by creating fishery districts to be supervised by boards of conservators appointed by the licensees themselves. These conservators were given the task of collecting not only the licence fees but also an annual rate on several fisheries and penalties for illegal fishing; and they were empowered to use the money they collected for the maintenance of the fisheries in their district. The system was designed to

*How a plate of oysters
should look. Two versions
from Scotland, one from
Loch Fyne* (right), *the other
from Kishorn* (below).

ABOVE: *Dutch still life of oysters by Osias Beert 'who loved the grey tones of oysters',
from the Prado Madrid.*

BELOW: Huîtres, *Edouard Manet, from the National Gallery, Washington D.C.*

Oysters for sale on the streets of Paris.

RIGHT: *A small oyster shop.*

BELOW: *A big oyster bistro.*

OVERLEAF: *The most exuberant of all oyster paintings,* Le Déjeuner d'Huîtres, *by Jean-François de Troy, which was commissioned by Louis XV for a dining room at Versailles used after hunting expeditions. It shows young bloods eating oysters and drinking champagne while the servants gaze upwards in amazement as a champagne cork, visible against a marble column, sails up into the air. It was painted in 1734, just after Dom Pérignon had invented champagne, and is believed to be the first painting of champagne.*

induce cooperation and make those who gained most from fishing pay most for its preservation. The father of it was William Ffennell, who was to make an important contribution to fishery policy in Britain.

In Scotland, salmon fishery laws based on these principles were introduced for two of the principal rivers, the Tay and the Tweed, in 1857. When, shortly after that, a Royal Commission of three persons was appointed to enquire into the salmon fisheries of England and Wales, Mr Ffennell was made one of its members. In their report, published in 1861, the commissioners found that the existing laws caused confusion and uncertainty; that the fisheries of Ireland 'had exhibited a gradual and steady improvement' under the new system which had been established there and had then been adopted for the Tay and Tweed; they recommended that a system along those lines should be adopted in England and Wales.[6] There followed the Salmon Fisheries Amendment Act of 1861 and the appointment of Mr Ffennell to fill one of the two posts of Inspector of Fisheries established under the Act.

Irish oyster policy

In the period of 'legislative frenzy' that followed the Irish Fisheries Act of 1842, new measures were introduced for oyster fisheries.[7] Already private beds existed whose owners, with exclusive rights under old titles, fished for the oysters that grew naturally on them; and Irish fishermen had established the practice of making artificial enclosures on the public shore or seabed where they stocked oysters caught on the public beds; but there was no oyster cultivation and there was little or no legal protection against theft of oysters from the beds.

Between 1842 and 1850 Acts were passed which provided that the fishery commissioners could grant to any owner or occupier of land by the sea the right to create a private oyster bed on the shore or on the sea bed beyond the shore. Theft was made an offence, subject to the proviso that the person taking the oysters had not acted 'under a fair and reasonable supposition' that he or the public at large had a right to take the oysters, a caveat which was a forceful reminder of the public right of fishery and was to prove a boon to poachers defending themselves before the magistrates.

These measures did not lead to great results. They were introduced at the time of the potato famine. Even thereafter, in the 1850's, the oyster fisheries suffered greatly from lawlessness, a phenomenon from which no one seems to have been immune. Wilkins tells the story of how in 1865 a licence for a private oyster bed at Achill Sound on the west coast of Ireland was granted to Archbishop McHale of Tuam, who delegated its management to the local curate, the Rev. E. Thomas. After spending £75 on buying oysters to stock the bed, the curate opined that 'very little artificial aid will be required to make it productive and beneficial to the poor'. The latter opinion indeed proved right, since 45 boats 'all of them poor and few of them legal' plundered the beds, usually by night. The archbishop suggested to the fishery commissioners that something should be done 'to check the daring outrages of those who are forever plundering or attempting to plunder the private oyster beds'. 'To his credit,' says Wilkins, 'he himself did nothing to check those who, after all, were his own flock'.[8]

But whatever the difficulties of enforcing the new policy in Ireland, its introduction was a notable step. It was the first attempt in Britain or Ireland to provide in modern times for the enclosure of the shore or seabed for the purpose of oyster farming – or indeed for the purposes of aquaculture of any kind. It was a precedent and, more important, it meant that from 1845 onwards there were Irish fishery commissioners who were granting licences for private oyster beds, examining the problems of oyster fisheries and seeking ways forward for the industry. True, their attention was divided between salmon and oysters, but the job of observing and analysing the problems of the oyster industry was being done. In England, Scotland and Wales it was not being done; and the principal advance later was with respect not to oysters but to salmon, when inspectors were appointed under the Salmon Fisheries Acts of 1857 and 1861. One is tempted to wonder how far the attention paid to the salmon and the neglect of the oyster is related to the difference in the social esteem accorded to the pursuit of the two species. Would things have been the same if oyster fishing, like salmon fishing, had been a sport of gentlemen?

In the records of the various official enquiries into the English oyster fisheries that were held in the second half of the 19th century, one finds that the Irish inspectors were commonly called to give evidence and that when they did so they displayed a depth and range of knowledge that was seldom matched by British witnesses.

It can perhaps be said of Irish oyster policy that in the last century disorder and poverty brought into existence the kind of central framework that is required for a positive approach but also made any policy largely unenforceable at that time. At the end of the century the high price paid for oysters in England

and the poverty of Ireland led to the depletion of the Irish oyster stocks. In the early years of this century annual production of oysters in Ireland was estimated to be only about 3 million a year, but Irish oyster beds were being used extensively for the re-laying of American and French oysters destined for England.

CHAPTER EIGHT

Health scares in England and France

AT THE END of the century a new problem hit the oyster industry in both England and France – scares over infected oysters. What is remarkable is not that there should have been a crisis of this kind but that it did not happen earlier. In the mid 19th century when sanitary conditions were primitive, hundreds of millions of oysters were eaten each year, many of them peddled on the streets of Paris and London, but people do not seem to have been put off oysters by the risk of infection. Probably everyone was unwell so often and the understanding of the causes of illness was so limited that the oyster was not identified as the cause of sickness as often as it should have been. Moreover the sea must still have been clean in most places.

By the end of the century conditions had changed. The growth of towns meant that human excrement, which previously had been deposited in the ground in a dispersed manner by a rural population, now had to be disposed of in large quantities from densely populated towns. The cheapest and simplest method was to discharge it into the sea or a river. Since estuaries, which are the ideal habitat for oysters, usually offered the advantage of having sheltered harbours and therefore had towns built on them, sewage was commonly discharged into the very places where oysters were likely to be. In France the problem was probably not as bad as in England, since the main centres of the French oyster industry are on the Channel and Atlantic coasts of France where there are not many substantial towns. In England, however, the most important oyster-growing area was the greater Thames estuary into which London and other towns poured sewage and industrial effluent and tipped garbage. There was a greater likelihood than before that oysters would be infected.

The oyster scare in England

That there was a connection between typhoid fever and the consumption of polluted oysters had long been suspected and was established in one country after another in the 1890's. In England the demand for oysters fell quite sharply in 1894 after it had been reported that cases of typhoid fever had been traced to the eating of oysters contaminated with sewage. The producers of oysters were sufficiently concerned to join with consumers in asking for an enquiry.[1] The Local Government Board responded by appointing their medical inspector to investigate. His name, which Dickens might have been proud to have invented, was Dr H. Timbrell Bulstrode. Having visited all the oyster-growing areas on the coast of England and Wales, he reported in unpalatable detail that in many cases oysters were laid in dangerous proximity to the mouths of drains. That was in 1896.

In response to Dr Timbrell Bulstrode's report, some action was taken by owners of oyster beds and by those in the oyster trade, but while demand for the 'inferior kinds of oyster' recovered quickly, demand for the better kinds of oysters remained depressed for some time.[2] In May 1899, however, the Government, having been 'urged by an extremely powerful deputation representative of twenty-eight of the largest towns in the kingdom', introduced an Oysters Bill that would empower the county and borough councils to test the water in which oysters were laid, and to prohibit the removal of oysters if contamination was discovered.[3] But a Select Committee of the House of Lords to which the Bill was referred so changed the Bill that the Government decided to withdraw it. The Select Committee felt that if responsibility for testing the water and taking action was given to the local councils, they would be inclined, when they found that the water was polluted, to close the oyster fisheries, an action that would cost them little or nothing, rather than clean up their sewage systems, which would cost them a lot. The Select Committee therefore amended the Bill to give the responsibility for its execution to the local fisheries committees which the local authorities had been given the power to create under an Act passed in 1888. But the Board of Trade found this solution impracticable since in many cases these fisheries committees had no authority in the estuaries where the oyster beds were situated and if their authority was extended to those estuaries it would conflict with other authorities who had jurisdiction there. What the 'other authorities' were and why they could not act is obscure. The Government proposed to go back to their original plan and give the responsibility to the local and borough councils, but they then decided to withdraw the Bill for lack of Parliamentary time.[4] They did not revive the Bill in the next Parliament. Nothing was done.

By the turn of the century demand for oysters had recovered from the setback of 1894, but in 1902 there was a much more dramatic typhoid scandal. On November 10th of that year, mayoral banquets were held at Southampton and Winchester. At both banquets oysters were served. A large proportion of the guests was attacked by illness; many of them afterwards developed enteric fever; four who had been at the Winchester banquet died. Dr Timbrell Bulstrode was called upon to investigate and established the strongest possible presumption that the cause of the disaster was the oysters, which for both banquets had been supplied from the same place, Emsworth, near Portsmouth. The mayor of Winchester survived, thank goodness, to become father of June Evans, née Bowker, who added so much spark to life in Cambridge when we all came back in 1945 and who now lives in France, so youthful that it is hard to believe her father was a mayor 93 years ago.

This scandal dealt the oyster trade in Britain a severe blow with lasting effects. The Fishmongers' Company later claimed that the industry lost 75 per cent of its trade and that recovery was prevented by frequent irresponsible reports of shellfish poisoning, based very often on quite insufficient evidence. The official statistics show that trade in home grown oysters and imports taken together was halved: production of oysters fell from 37 million in 1901 to 28 million in 1903 while imports fell from 121 million to 53 million. The figures

Oyster pits at Emsworth, Hants: whence came the oysters which poisoned the guests at the Winchester Dinner, Illustrated London News, *1903.*

stayed at these reduced levels till war broke out in 1914, when new troubles were to follow.

The problem of sewage pollution and its possible remedies were by now clear. They were admirably set out in the Annual Fisheries Report for 1903 by the Inspector of Fisheries, Mr Charles Fryer. He emphasised that what happened in one place had effects beyond its boundaries. In particular, infected oysters from one place could cause an oyster scare that hit the industry nation-wide, and pollution from one area could flow into another. He saw the need for central action in the common interest. He suggested that local authorities should not bear all the cost of stopping pollution. He discussed the case for compensation payments by local authorities to oystermen whose beds had to be closed. And, knowing that oysters quickly rid themselves of typhoid bacilli if placed in unpolluted sea water, he proposed that it be made easier for oystermen to establish storage pits in unpolluted waters where oysters could be put to clean themselves.[5] Under existing law, it was impossible for them to do that without going through the rigmarole of applying for a concession under the 1868 Act.

But far from causing the Government urgently to revive its old legislation or bring forth new, the 1902 oyster scandal was followed by remarkable inaction on the part of the Government and by action on the part of the trade. There was a triangle of forces that produced this result. There were the local authorities, now quite well equipped with medical officers responsible for public health.[6] They were interested in stopping people eating polluted oysters, but they rarely had any interest in the oyster industry or in spending money in preventing pollution. There was a Royal Commission on Sewage Disposal which wanted pollution to be reduced, an operation for which governments showed no signs of being willing to pay.[7] And there was the oyster trade which understandably liked the anti-pollution policy proposed by the Royal Commission but had two motives for taking action themselves to keep infected oysters off the market: the need urgently to save the reputation of the oyster and the desire to prevent the local authorities being given powers to close oyster beds.

The body that spoke for the industry was the Fishmongers' Company. Under a charter from James II and the Fisheries Act of 1877 it had the responsibility for preventing the sale of fish unfit for human consumption in the London markets. After Dr Timbrell Bulstrode had established that oysters were to blame for what happened at Southampton and Winchester, the Company

TOP: *The effect of the Fishmongers' Company's embargo on tainted oysters: idle oyster boats at Bosham.* ABOVE: *The condemned oyster pits at Bosham with oyster boats lying idle. Both from* Illustrated London News, *1903.*

decided 'in the interests of public health and the oyster industry' to commission an inspection of oyster and shellfish layings to see if they were polluted. Professor Klein, F.R.S., a bacteriologist whom they appointed to do the job, reported that many of the layings were polluted with sewage and that the shellfish thereon were unfit for human consumption. The company prohibited the sale of oysters from these places in the London markets and asked the local authorities to take action in all ascertained cases of serious pollution to prevent the sale of contaminated shellfish in their areas.[8]

The effect of the pollution 'scare' at Whitstable: a closed storage tank, Illustrated London News, *1903.*

The oyster merchants and planters, having started to meet at the Fishmongers' Company in 1902 as a committee representing the industry, formed the Oyster Merchants and Planters Association in 1906. By their own account they made every effort to ascertain that supplies came only from beds known to be pure, to render every possible facility to inspectors of the Fishmongers' Company to overhaul and examine all consignments of shellfish to the London markets and to investigate the shellfish layings. They gave evidence to the Royal Commission on Sewage Disposal, urging that pollution by sewage should be stopped, that the task of control should not be given to local authorities and that compensation should be paid to owners of oyster layings that had to be closed.

Meanwhile the Government appears to have done nothing much, other than prevent things happening. It did not follow the recommendation of the Royal Commission on Sewage Disposal, which proposed that rivers boards should be created, each responsible for the whole of a river system and all of them under a central authority; and that the central authority should have power to compel local authorities to restrict pollution and to decide when oysters beds should be closed. Nor did the Government back the local authorities.

A *Times* leader shortly after the fatal banquets at Southampton and Winchester took a lofty position against the pleas of the oyster trade for intervention by the central government to stop pollution:

> The meeting convened yesterday at the Fishmongers' Hall by the general committee of the oyster trade shows the depth of the impression made on the public mind by the typhoid epidemic in Hampshire, which has been shown to have been caused by the consumption of Emsworth oysters at mayoral banquets. Oysters are a highly appreciated delicacy, for which people are willing to pay a very high price so long as they can settle the bill by a cheque to the fishmonger. But when the account cannot be squared except by a tedious and dangerous illness, in addition to indefinite expense, the public not unnaturally conclude that it is wiser on the whole to practise a little self-denial, and to make shift as well as they can without oysters.
>
> ...the oyster trade is evidently not without apprehension that a regrettable falling off in the demand for oysters may have to be faced unless something is promptly done to reassure the public.
>
> ...Various well-intended resolutions were passed at the meeting yesterday....Every possible facility is to be given to the inspectors of the Fishmongers' Company to overhaul the consignments of shellfish to the London market....But the committee went further than mere protective measures on the part of the trade. It demanded nothing less than immediate legislation to prohibit altogether the discharge of sewage into rivers, estuaries or even the sea itself. This rather reminds one of the Chinaman who burnt down his house in order to enjoy roast pig. Oysters are fine things, and there are persons to whom cockles and mussels are dear, yet we might more easily sacrifice the whole lot than face the gigantic task of revolutionising the sewage disposal of the whole coastline of the country.
>
> ...Why do people almost invariably demand the very biggest and most ambitious remedies, without trying obvious and simple ones? We have some demanding the stoppage of all sewage that now finds it way into the sea. Others cry out for putting all oyster beds under municipal control, although some of our correspondents point out that

municipalities cannot be got to use their powers on the coast any more than upon insanitary houses in towns. Others want a new authority created – a general fishery board for the whole country – by way of adding to the existing chaos of overlapping jurisdictions.

...How would it be in these circumstances to begin with the modest measure of slightly enlarging the powers of the Local Government Board? Suppose it was enabled to enforce its inspection by declaring a polluted oyster bed to be an "insanitary area", and peremptorily shutting it up? That is all that is wanted for the protection of the oyster-eating public, and it is not more than the public may fairly demand. All the local questions that would arise might be left to local treatment. The owner of the oyster bed would have his remedy against those who had ruined his property, and when a man has his remedy, English law usually conceives that full justice has been done to him. It is not the affair of the public at large to settle these local squabbles, but it is the right of the public at large to prevent poisonous comestibles from being put on the market by anybody.[9]

This *Times* leader of 1903 tells us something about conventional English attitudes at that time towards the oyster and the policy issues surrounding it, attitudes so different from those of the French. It speaks of oysters as 'a highly appreciated delicacy for which people are willing to pay a very high price so long as they can settle the bill by a cheque to the fishmonger', thus portraying oysters as being by this time a luxury, typically consumed by the those who had cheque books, then a very small class, not a food bought at street corners by the working class. This is not surprising given what we know about the decline in production and the increase in the price of oysters since Dickens's time, but it is one of those comments, so hard to find, that tell us something of the social aspects of the decline of the English oyster.

In suggesting that it might be better to sacrifice the oyster altogether than clean up pollution *The Times* displays a philistine contempt for gastronomy.

The article is suffused by dogma. Common sense is cast aside, just as it had been in the 1860's by the Royal Commission on Sea Fisheries whose members were so reluctant to consider action to save the breeding stock of oysters from the threat of over-fishing that they managed to persuade themselves that such a threat simply could not exist. In this case, common sense tells you that if a person, firm or other institution causes pollution with costs that fall upon the surrounding community, rather than wholly upon that person, firm or institution, the arguments for refraining from intervention and leaving economic activity to be guided only by the market cease to be valid; some form of restraint is appropriate. It is a case that scarcely needs to be argued today. It was put forward by Mr Fryer in his Fisheries Report for 1903, but he was not heeded. It has to be said that economists must carry much of the blame for the dominance of economic dogma over common sense. The mainstream of English economics was devoted to exploring and extolling the merits of *laissez-faire*, to describing the beneficial effects of casting off medieval restraints on trade; the first leading English economist to discuss the case for state action in exceptional cases such as pollution was A.C. Pigou, in his *Wealth and Welfare*, published in 1912, and then he was rather brief and tentative.

The attitude of *The Times* to the untidy structure of internal government inherited from the past and to the law is complacent. Any new legislation, so runs the argument, would be bad because it would add to the 'existing chaos of overlapping jurisdictions'. There is no mention of the rather obvious idea that the chaos should be tidied up by reform. And then it is confidently suggested that the owner of a polluted oyster bed could satisfactorily seek remedy against those who had ruined his property by taking proceedings under English law. Yet many oyster beds were public, not private; the oyster fishermen who still worked the depleted public beds were usually poor; and where there were private beds under an ancient charter or under a several order, they would rarely be owned by people who could afford to fight a battle with a local municipality for whom a great deal of expenditure on lawyers would be less than the cost of introducing a sewage purification system.

A few days after this leader appeared, the state of affairs at Emsworth, the source of the infected oysters, and the difficulties of an owner of an oyster bed seeking redress under existing English law, were eloquently described in a letter to *The Times* by a local landowner, Lord Gifford:

> Sir, The events which have happened in connexion with the poisoning by the local authority at Emsworth of Mr Foster's oysters, stored in his beds, over which the sanitary authority have, I understand, been pouring a gradually increasing volume of sewage for some years past, are so intimately connected with the action which I brought some two years ago against the Chichester Corporation that I venture to trouble you with a communication on the subject. On that occasion I obtained an injunction restraining the corporation of Chichester from causing or permitting to

flow into the Fishbourne Creek any effluent polluted with sewage or containing sewage matter in such a state as to be, or to cause, a nuisance or become injurious to me as the owner of the Old Park residence and estate, which residence is situated exactly opposite the outfall, or from otherwise using or permitting their sewage works to be used so as to cause a nuisance to me. Such injunction was, however, to be suspended for six months, and, if at the expiration of such six months the defendants were proceeding diligently with the execution of remedial works and should continue so to proceed, the operation of the said restraint was to be suspended for a further period of six months. Among the other injuries of which I complained was the absolute destruction of the shellfish in the Fishbourne Creek, which, like Emsworth and Bosham Creeks, forms part of Chichester Harbour.

My immediate predecessor in title had constructed large oyster beds in the Fishbourne Creek; but at the time when I took over the estate in 1898 these beds and the shellfish industry – a very large one – had been rendered absolutely useless by the action of the Chichester Corporation; and the Bosham fishermen, most of whom are my copyhold tenants or live on my estate, have repeatedly complained to me, as well as to the Local Government Board and the Fisheries Board, of the injury done to their fish by the Chichester Corporation, and they have addressed a very numerously signed petition, which I also signed, to the Fisheries Board, who took about as much notice of it as if it had been addressed to them by someone in Ireland. I am now informed that the very extensive oyster fishery established in the Bosham Creek of the harbour, and leading into the main creek of Chichester Harbour, in both of which creeks there are very extensive oyster beds, has been entirely ruined from the fact that in consequence of the oyster scare the Fishmongers' Company has prohibited the sale of Bosham oysters.

No doubt the Fisheries Board, who, I believe, sent an inspector to Bosham, obtained some very definite information about the Bosham oysters before they took such a drastic step. I can only say that, if it is a fact that the oysters in the breeding grounds have been found to contain within them those interesting organisms which, although harmless to the oyster, are fatal to the human being who eats the oyster, the only possible source of pollution which could have contaminated the Bosham oysters proceeds from the outfall of the Chichester sewerage works.

When I obtained my injunction on June 27, 1901, I waited patiently until the end of the six months, and even gave a little extra time, with the result that, although a great deal of conversation took place between the Chichester Corporation, the Local Government Board, and various sanitary experts, nothing was done beyond the consideration of a scheme, which fell through about March 1902. I then, after further correspondence, applied in April for a writ of sequestration; and a two months' peremptory order was made by Mr. Justice Channell requiring the defendants to produce a new scheme. At the expiration of this time I again went before the Court, and Mr. Justice Channell made a further order requiring that the proposed works, after they had obtained the sanction of the Local Government Board, should be carried into effect within a further period of six months from June 27, 1902. The defendants commenced their works about six weeks ago, but when December 27 arrived I need not say that the works were not nearly completed, and are still not completed, and I am about to take further steps for the protection of my interests.

During the whole of this period, from the date of the injunction (June 27, 1901) to the present time, the defendants have been pouring their sewage into the Fishbourne Creek, opposite my residence, in ever-increasing volume, and the horrible smells which arise from it when the wind is in the right direction have been, if I may say so, infinitely worse than they were before I brought my action; I believe because an increased quantity of chemicals have been used which putrefies the sewage and makes it smell worse than it did before, or that occasions arose when the sewage had to be let go into the creek without proper – if any – treatment. It is, therefore, a moral certainty that this sewage has poisoned the Bosham oysters.

To prove that a most insanitary condition of things exists in consequence of the Chichester drainage system, I would ask how many cases of diphtheria and typhoid have occurred in Chichester in the last year; whether these two diseases cannot almost be termed epidemic; whether about 100 cases have not occurred?

This brings me to the proceedings the other day of the Fishmongers' Company and the committee of oyster merchants. I need not say I heartily approve of what they have done. They have taken the right step in urging upon the Government to give more extensive powers to the Local Government Board and also to accelerate the movements of that body. Any one who has had anything to do with the Local Government Board knows perfectly well that it is useless to apply to them for assistance, because the red tape and the circumlocution is so great that many months elapse before any result comes therefrom beyond voluminous reports, which nobody cares to peruse. I do not wish to attach blame to that body, but I blame the successive Governments who have not clothed them with sufficiently drastic powers.

As regards the Sussex branch of the Fisheries Board, I regard this body as absolutely useless, and I scarcely know for what purpose they were called into existence. They have practically turned a deaf ear to everything I have said to them, as well as to the complaints of the fishermen, and they seem to have been content to sit and fold their hands while I was fighting to a very large extent their battle at my own expense.

If these bodies are to be of any use, they must be a great deal more active than they are. They are too ponderous and unwieldy, and the local committees have not sufficient power. I am aware of course of the difficulties which surround the matter, especially the difficulty of proving that a particular nuisance affects breeding grounds for fish which may be situate at some distance; but I am convinced that everything that has happened is caused by the sanitary bodies not being entrusted by Government with sufficient powers and their being too cumbrous to attend to all the small cases of sanitary improvement which are required, either at the time when necessary or with the care which they deserve.

My only object in writing to you is to give the widest publicity to the fact that at the present moment the Government, by sanctioning all sorts of sewage outfalls into the sea and into tidal estuaries and creeks, have done enormous injury to the fisheries all round the country, and have given many kinds of fish which formerly were a staple food a very doubtful reputation; and I need not point to the enormous loss to the oyster trade caused by the recent scare, developed and intensified as it is by that portion of the Press which magnifies every sanitary mishap which occurs, particularly when it affects one or two prominent individuals, without regard to the effect which the promulgation of such matters as news to a sensation-loving public may have upon the trade of the country and the food-stuffs of the people.

I remain, your obedient servant,

GIFFORD

Old Park, Chichester, Jan. 8.[10]

In the long period of inaction that followed, the local authorities, increasingly sensitive to their responsibility if they permitted bad oysters to be sold or produced in the areas for which they were responsible, became restive and, predictably, sought powers to close oyster beds. In 1912 a senior civil servant from the Board of Agriculture and Fisheries said that a large number of local authorities were proposing to take powers by means of Private Bills in Parliament to close shellfish beds; in the interests of the shellfish trade, the Board of Agriculture and Fisheries was, he said, opposed to the granting of powers of this kind by means of local bills; if regulations were to be carried out on these lines they ought to be carried out by a central authority; the board therefore tried to prevent sporadic legislation and asked the Local Government Board 'at any rate pending any further legislation, to frame regulations in consultation with us, with a view to arranging that where it was necessary to close shell-fish beds it should not be done until after such enquiry, with such authority, and under such uniform regulations as would not prejudice fishery interests'. The words 'pending any further legislation' look like a non-committal allusion to a possibility that the recommendations of the Royal Commission on Sewage Pollution might be implemented. In any event, the Government was as good as its word in not supporting local authority Bills: in 1913-14 private Bills failed to get through Parliament that would have given the Corporations of three towns, Derby, Bolton and Preston, powers to prohibit the sale of oysters and other shellfish.[11]

The stalemate lasted until February 1915 when the Government did what the industry feared. In the authoritarian atmosphere of war, the Board of Local Government issued regulations under a Public Health Act that gave the local authorities sweeping powers to close oyster beds and other shellfish layings. In taking this action in 1915, the Board pleaded that opportunity had not yet arisen to alter the law in the way that had been recommended by the Royal Commission on Sewage Pollution in 1904.[12]

The product of this action in 1915 was a two part system. The inspectors of Fishmongers' Company continued to be responsible, as they still are, for the purity of oysters passing through London. The local authorities had the power, as part of their responsibility for public health, to prevent the sale of bad oysters to the public. The prevention of pollution, the radical solution to the problem, went by default. The work of the Fishmongers' Company was preventive in the restricted sense that its purpose was to prevent oysters infected by pollution reaching the consumer; the company had no power to prevent the pollution that caused the infection. The job given to the local authorities was reactive i.e. to take action after the event of human infection, not before. Moreover the local authorities could take action only after a good deal of delay, since a medical officer in an area which produced oysters that were infected could act only when he had been alerted that oysters from his area were suspect; and that could happen only after it had been established in the area where they were consumed, which could be far away, that infected oysters had apparently caused illness and the suspect oysters had been traced back to the supplying area.

Matters remained in this unsatisfactory condition, essentially unchanged, until 1 January 1993 when new and much better European regulations came into force in Britain as an adjunct of the single market. These are described in Chapter 12. Under the old system there were improvements. The local authorities were able to induce producers to install purification plant by imposing closure orders and lifting them on condition that purification took place in an approved manner, or by threatening closure. But it was still a reactive and leaky system in which there was no emphasis on preventing pollution, no systematic monitoring of water and little attention to the maintenance of cleanliness in the handling and distribution of oysters – except at Billingsgate where the Fishmongers' Company kept watch. Over the years there have been recurrent troubles with bad oysters. At the end of the 1950's there was an outbreak of typhoid fever among consumers of oysters from West Mersea after which 'a move was made to encourage the erection of privately owned oyster purification plants'.[13] Later there were several large outbreaks of gastro-enteritis caused by eating oysters.[14] In Cambridge colleges alone, considerable numbers of people have been taken taken ill in recent years after feasts at which oysters were served. In the late 1980's nearly all the guests at a feast at King's College were ill after eating oysters that were later found not to have been put through a purification plant as they should have been. The reputation of the oyster in Cambridge has suffered.

The oyster scare in France

In France, as in England, there was a major scare over infected oysters at the end of the 19th century, followed by a collapse in the demand for oysters: sales were approximately halved between 1898 and 1901. But demand for oysters recovered far better in France than in England; by 1914 production and sales in France look as if they had surpassed the 1898 level.

In response to the crisis, the Ministry of Marine in 1898 appointed an expert, Dr Mosny, to investigate. He found that the great majority of oyster layings in France were clean but that a minority, in particular those in ports, in the flow of effluents from old towns and in polluted estuaries, were not clean and ought to be closed immediately. A similar conclusion was reached by another French expert, Professor Giard, in 1904.[15] Nobody, however, was prepared to act. Legislation to deal with the problem came little by little and only in response to pressure from the industry. In 1913 a group of Parisian oyster merchants, concerned for the prosperity of their trade, established a *contrôle sanitaire* in the principal producing areas, a system that was valuable but, being voluntary, could not stop unscrupulous producers from selling dirty oysters and so damaging the reputation of the industry. In the following year the trade therefore requested the Government to establish an official body to control the whole industry; and they urged that the body should have sufficient independence to resist the pressures and special pleading which hitherto had nullified such efforts as had been made by the public authorities. Progress then began to be made by the public authorities. Decrees in 1915, 1919 and 1923, and later steps to strengthen inspection and enforcement of sanitary standards, improved the system. Moreover in the 1930's steps began to be taken to go to the root of the problem and stop pollution.

Nothing, however, was done until 1939 to ensure cleanliness in the handling of oysters by the distributive trades, where accidents were principally caused by attempts to 'refresh' stale oysters by sprinkling them with water or soaking them. A comprehensive system for the control of the production and distribution of oysters and mussels was then worked out in heated discussions on the eve of the war and introduced by decree. The wartime conditions that followed, in which the public were more fearful than usual of infection and more ready than usual to accept regulations, made it possible to enforce the new rules rigorously. Some notorious places, for example, the mussel beds at Marseilles and the oyster layings at Concarneau, were finally closed; their owners appealed in vain to the German occupation authorities, but they cared no less than the French for the purity of the oysters and mussels they consumed.

The comprehensive system established in 1939 continued little changed until it was adopted, with considerable modification, as the basis of the EU regulations that came into force in January 1993. Consistently with the French tradition of government, what was established in 1939 was an hierarchical system with power radiating from the headquarters in Paris of the *Service du Contrôle Sanitaire des Coquillages* under the Ministry of Merchant Marine. There were regional inspectorates, each supported by a laboratory. In 1950, the total staff on the coast and in big towns came to about 100.

As regards production, the producing areas on the coast were all tested. Dispatch of oysters was allowed only from listed establishments which were authorised to attach to each package of oysters a label (*étiquette sanitaire*) issued by the ministry. The label signified that the oysters came from an approved establishment and it carried the identity number of that establishment and the date of dispatch; only baskets and packaging of approved kinds might be used; and the label had to stay on the package right up to the point of sale to the public. In the chain of production and distribution there was inspection not only by the officers of the *Service du Contrôle Sanitaire des Coquillages* but also by veterinary inspectors (who in France are responsible for the inspection of the processing and distribution of livestock produce and fish), market inspectors and others. If oysters came from waters found not to be clean, they had to be purified by being re-laid in clean water or in purification tanks where they were subject to close surveillance; and then they had to be sold to distributors who were authorised to issue *étiquettes sanitaires*: a producer of oysters in dirty or suspect waters could not sell direct to the public or the trade. The aim of the policy was to get rid of pollution and ensure that all oysters came from clean waters. As regards natural oyster beds, which, unlike layings on the shore, are self-perpetuating and cannot be closed, the elimination of pollution is of particular importance; all natural beds were tested for cleanliness before fishing on them was allowed; and where some natural beds in a vicinity were found to be clean and others dirty, the two were never opened for fishing at the same time so as to avoid the mixing of clean and dirty oysters.

The system, much of which has been incorporated into the new single market regime, is impressive. The key to it has been the *étiquette sanitaire*, though that label would have been useless without the regime of inspection and the powers of enforcement which were built up in the first half of this century.

In the peroration to an article on this subject published in 1950 a French expert paid tribute to the system with that combination of eloquence and national pride which is so characteristic of the French and which seems to flow forth particularly freely when they write about oysters:

> *Les coquillages si nombreux sur nos côtes constituent une de nos richesses nationales. Leur pêche et leur élevage occupent plus de trois cent milles personnes qui fournissent à la consommation des aliments complets, riches en vitamines, sains et fort agréables a déguster, dont l'origine et la fraîcheur sont faciles a contrôler, grâce a l'étiquette sanitaire dont tous les paniers sont munis, étiquette qu'il faut toujours exiger.*[16]

France in the 20th century

IN THIS CENTURY French oyster production has advanced in great cycles: peaks in production have been followed by collapses as problems have hit the industry, and then by recoveries.

The record

Since the French historical statistics for oyster production may be highly misleading (Chapter 6), we shall not reproduce them. But the big ups and downs shown by the imperfect figures are significant: the magnitude of double-counting and other errors is most unlikely to have changed violently in alternating directions to produce big cycles; moreover there are convincing historical descriptions and explanations of the cycles. All we can say about absolute quantities is that recorded production has reached 130-150 thousand tons in recent years.[1] Assuming that double-counting is not now very extensive, this would mean that French oyster production is now around 2 billion. This figure is so vastly in excess of that for Britain (about 10 million) that the possible margin of error is unimportant for our purposes.

The main phases in French oyster production since 1900 have been these:

Before 1914: Production rose with Portuguese oysters now making up half the total.

The 1920's: Having been checked during the war, production was hit by massive mortalities of native oysters in France, as in the rest of Europe. But the loss of natives was more than offset by a surge in the production of Portuguese oysters. The result was a peak at the end of the 1920's.

The 1930's: Production in the early 1930's fell sharply following a series of poor spatting seasons for Portuguese oysters. Production of natives was recovering but was still relatively small.

1945 to 1971: After the war, production of Portuguese oysters soared to a peak in 1949 and then came down, at first gradually, then precipitately as a viral infection commonly called the *maladie des branchies* (gill disease) destroyed the Portuguese oyster in France. In these years the production of natives was good, though erratic from year to year: on average recorded production of natives was 200 or 300 million oysters a year.

Since 1971: Production of the Pacific oyster, the successor to the Portuguese, has soared to around 2 billlion. Meanwhile two diseases, *Marteilia refringens* which started in the early 1970's and *Bonamia ostreae* which started in 1979, have reduced production of natives to a low level.

Because oyster production has been restored to high levels after each crisis, the taste for oysters has never been lost in France. On the contrary, the existence, subject to periodic scarcities, of a copious supply of oysters has permitted the oyster to be a food for all classes, eaten by everyone at Christmas and New Year, – festive seasons which coincide with the time when oysters are usually at their best. Seventy-five per cent of French oyster consumption takes place around the turn of the year.

What is most striking about this history is the way that French oyster production was restored after a series of disasters. In Britain, production languished and fell away. The two physical advantages of France compared with Britain – warmer waters for oyster breeding and less pollution near the main areas of oyster production – are not a sufficient explanation why French oyster production was so resilient. They mean only that there was a setting in which recoveries could physically be achieved if the right human actions were forthcoming. That there were such remarkable recoveries means that those actions were forthcoming. The interesting question is how this came about. What is there about the economic, social and political setting, and about the behaviour of French oyster producers and about the relationship of the French Government to them that produced this resilience?

In France, oysters are nearly all produced by family enterprises. There are now about ten thousand enterprises producing oysters and mussels; the greater proportion of these are oyster producers. These small producers are like peasant farmers. They mainly live in communities where, with government encouragement, production of oysters is concentrated and in which, like traditional mining communities, most of the people are engaged in one occupation. The producers are individualistic. There are considerable differences in economic status amongst them. The biggest act as merchants, selling oysters bought from small growers as well as those grown on their own concessions; and they use wage labour. The smallest enterprises consist of members of a family who breed and grow oysters and sell to merchants. In between are enterprises that are big enough to have their own packing and dispatch facilities but normally handle only oysters grown on their own concessions.

The fact that the oyster industry is large means that there is a substantial number of manufacturers and suppliers of machinery, equipment and other items needed by the industry. Each year there is a fair, like an agricultural fair in Britain, at which the manufacturers and suppliers display their wares and the oyster growers get together. While they are far from subservient to the state, the French oyster growers have strong links with it as a result of government policies designed with that purpose.

The relationship with government

We have seen how Colbert in the 18th century established a single ministry for the navy, merchant navy, fisheries, and colonies, and how he made priority in the granting of oyster concessions a reward for service in the *Inscription-Maritime* (the naval reserve); we have seen how Coste in the 19th century saw that the close link between the ministry of marine and the *inscrits maritimes* could be used to help enforce his policies for the conservation of oyster stocks and the introduction of new methods of oyster production; and we have seen how the local regulation of oyster fishing was put into the hands of a combination of centrally-appointed officials and elected representatives of the local oyster growers.

Over the years much has been changed but not the strong link between local oyster producers and the Government hierarchy which reaches down from Paris through the *préfecture* to each locality. The most important changes have been the decline in the importance of the *inscrits-maritimes*; the formal creation of new consultative bodies; the growth of professional training in oyster farming; the modernisation of the system of granting concessions; and the development of a research organisation that is close to the industry and has a hand in the development and application of government policy.

The *Inscription-Maritime* declined in importance once peacetime conscription was introduced in France in the last century, but it was not abolished until after the second world war; and former *inscrits-maritimes* continued to get priority in the allocation of oyster concessions until 1983. In place of priority for the *inscrits-maritimes*, priority is now given to applicants who have had professional training in oyster farming. By this means, and by establishing training courses, the French Government has been raising the professional standards of the industry.

Concessions for professionals

The change in priorities in the granting of concessions has not been informal or vague. The old system was set out in decrees which contained detailed rules for the qualifications to be taken into account by the authorities in the granting of concessions. The new system is set out similarly. It is all very precise and logical, typically French and quite alien to the English. It is worth a moment's attention. A description of the old system, written in 1950, tells us that by a decree made in 1919 applicants were divided into four categories:

1. naval reservists *(inscrits-maritimes)* who have never had concessions;
2. oyster farmers *(ostréiculteurs)* who have never had concessions;
3. naval reservists who have possessed or do possess concessions;
4. oyster farmers who have possessed or do possess concessions;
5. others.

The categories were ranked in this order, but there was then the question how to rank applicants within each category. This was settled by laying down more rules, which were circulated in 1929 and 1934. Applicants were to be given positive and negative points and then ranked according to their score. Five positive points were accorded to an applicant for each child under sixteen (a reminder of the French concern at that time to increase the population), one for each year of military service, one-quarter of a point for each year spent at sea in the merchant navy or as fishermen. Negative points were given according to the area of concession already held by the applicant and these were scaled according to the quality of the concessions, which were classified very good, good, or average. After all this, the regional commissions which advised on the granting of concessions had overall discretion to override the rankings produced by these formulae. The commissions were made up of a mixture of Government officials and members drawn from the industry; they could recommend the elimination or demotion of applicants they considered unsatisfactory; they could promote those they thought deserving a favour – in both cases they had to give their reasons.

In circulars in 1945, 1946 and 1947 the regional commissions were instructed to take note if, during the second world war, an applicant had been taken prisoner, had served with the Free French Forces, or done forced labour. The tradition continued that oyster concessions were rewards for service to the nation.

The new system was set out in a decree in 1983, modified in 1987. It lays down that in each district *(circonscription)* there will be a *commission des cultures marines*, consisting of six officials representing different branches of government (two representing the maritime side and one each representing fiscal, health, consumer affairs and fisheries research); two mayors or elected members of the departmental council (the approximate equivalent of our county council); and eight professional members drawn from shellfish growers, other fishermen and persons engaged in related activities.[2]

The applicant for a concession, who must be French or come from a member state of the EU, must have followed a course of professional training that has given him a qualification at least equivalent to the *brevet d'études professionnelles maritimes de conchyculture* (a diploma of professional training in shellfish farming); or he must commit himself to go on such a course within two years of getting a concession. One way or another professional training is insisted upon for all applicants, apart from old hands, defined as those born before September 1958 who have worked in the industry for more than five years. Military service, the number of children and considerations of that kind no longer count.

All applications are subjected to an administrative enquiry and a public enquiry, for which purpose the applications are sent to the Government offices that deal with taxation, health and social affairs, competition and consumer affairs, as well as to IFREMER, the government research establishment for sea fisheries. These agencies have a month in which to offer comments.

The procedure for the public enquiry is that the local professional organisation of shellfish farmers and other kinds of fishermen, is informed of all applications; public notices are posted and the comments of the public and local councils invited. The *commission des cultures marines* for the area considers the evidence and advises the prefect, who makes the decision whether to grant a concession. The costs of the enquiry are borne by the state not the applicant. And rents are low: 1,200 French francs per hectare per year all over

France. The sale of concessions is now permitted, provided the buyer can satisfy the authorities that he has the professional qualifications required by the regulations. The maximum term of a concession remains at thirty-five years, renewable.

Besides advising on the granting of concessions, the *commission des cultures maritimes* has powers to recommend the adoption of plans for its area drawn up by the professional bodies, to restore and improve areas for shellfish cultivation, and they are expected to advise on what should be the size of concessions.

The producers organised

The French oyster producers are highly organised. This is the result of actions taken by French governments, notably in the time of General de Gaulle, to make effective the co-operation between the Government and producers which, in the tradition of France, has been regarded as the natural way to promote the interests of the national economy. True, there has recently been a political reaction against this general approach on the grounds that it is 'corporatist' and gives too much power to technocrats in the bureaucracy, but so far the reaction seems to have found expression principally in general political debate and, for example, in promises to privatise nationalised industries, not in the dismantling of institutional links between government and industry.

The arrangements for the organisation of the shellfish producers are laid down by the Government in a formal manner. In 1991 they were modernised and given a new form. The new law created an inter-professional organisation of shellfish growers (*une organisation interprofessionnelle de la conchyculture*) to which all members of the professions which engage in the production, distribution and processing of shellfish are obliged to belong. The organisation has a national committee and regional committees in each producing area (*bassin de production*). The tasks given to the organisation by the new law are listed under five heads. The first is to represent and promote the general interests of the industry, in which capacity it is represented on the local commissions, described earlier, which grant concessions for oyster beds and which have a hand in the management of shellfish cultivation in their localities. The remainder are tasks such as promoting a balanced management of resources, improving conditions of production and promoting economic and social measures to the benefit of the members of the profession.

All these arrangements, plus the French mechanism for regional planning, mean that in France, in contrast to Britain, oyster growing is geographically concentrated and that within each producing area there is a process whereby the Government, in co-operation with representatives of the producers, can frame a strategy for the best use of the local resources. And it means that a would-be oyster grower who has passed a training course knows where concessions are granted and how to apply for one. Added to which it is the case that in each main producing area training courses are available in state schools. There are two-year courses for the *Brevet d'Études Professionnelles Maritimes de Conchyculture* and three-year courses for the *Certificat d'Aptitude Professionnelle Maritime de Conchyculture*. The content of the courses is an impressive mixture of general and technical subjects. For the two-year *brevet* the curriculum is: French, knowledge of the contemporary world, household and social economics, English, maths, physics, the biology and technology of shellfish culture, legislation, accounting, commercial economics, the handling of shellfish, seamanship, the handling of boats, coastal navigation; the handling and maintenance of motors, machinery and land vehicles; first aid and sports. It is the possession of this qualification that is required of an applicant for a concession.

IFREMER

Another element in the supportive relationship between the Government and the shellfish industry in France is IFREMER, the French Institute for Research into the Exploitation of the Sea. It was created in 1984 by merging two institutes, the relatively young *Centre Nationale de l'Éxploitation des Oceans* which was created in 1967 to look at new fields, such as the deep ocean in which M. Cousteau had excited interest, and the farming of sea fish; and the relatively old *Institut Scientifique et Technique des Pêches Maritimes*, which had a more administrative tradition, having been responsible for advising the Government, inspecting the coastal waters and inspecting the standards of produce, as well as undertaking research.

IFREMER in 1990 had a budget of about 900 million francs (£100 million) comprised mainly of a state subsidy but partly of funds obtained on a commercial basis. It has research centres and smaller branch stations in more than fifteen places on the coast of France, as well as research outposts in other continents. On the French coast IFREMER is 'involved in research that is often related to regional management and economic development' and it 'has quite naturally established close relations with local authorities and with the regional structures in particular'.[3] It is responsible for keeping the quality of the water at oyster fisheries under regular observation, for classifying shellfish-producing areas according to water purity, and for giving warning in the event of dangerous pollution. It is one of the official agencies represented on the local commissions which grant concessions. Until recently it was responsible for issuing *étiquettes sanitaires* and for the inspection of produce on shore, but with the advent of the Single Market, those tasks were handed over to the state veterinary service, which also inspects animal foodstuffs. At the same time, responsibility for fisheries was moved to a newly-created Ministry of Agriculture and Fisheries (*Ministère de l'Agriculture et de la Pêche*), a change that finally brought to an end the last relics of Colbert's 18th-century administrative design.

Individualism and indiscipline

It would be a mistake to think that within this logical and coherent system of government and representation French oyster growers all behave like perfect little ladies and gentlemen. On the contrary, they are not always the most law-abiding of people; they are individualistic and, like French farmers and fishermen, they can become rebellious. This is the result not just of national character but also of national institutions. The paternalistic national regime within which the French oyster growers work means that, even though their representatives take part in running the system, it is natural for them to blame the state – and their representatives – when things go wrong. The tradition of *laissez-faire* within which British oyster growers operate means that the state does less and is blamed less; perhaps it should be blamed for inaction, but inaction attracts blame less than action.

The history of Cancale provides examples of turbulent behaviour in this century, as it did in the last. In 1908, when the local oyster stocks were severely depleted, an attempt by one grower to import oysters from other areas to be laid down at Cancale provoked an outcry from oyster growers who believed that the alien oysters would corrupt the special quality of their local oysters. There was a violent row in which the local oystermen boarded the boat bringing the alien oysters and pitched them into the sea; two brigades of *gendarmerie*, a fishery boat and a torpedo boat were sent to restore order; the owner of the offending oysters went to court and the town was fined. The townspeople made representations to the minister, who responded by forbidding the import of oysters from other areas to Cancale, a decision which, in the view of M. Pichot-Louvet, the historian of Cancale, was devoid of all sense and ensured the decline of the oyster industry at Cancale in the following years. A year later, in 1909, a new minister responded to representations from oyster growers of the neighbouring town of Granville, who wished to be able to sell their oysters to Cancale, by deciding to reverse the ban on imports. But so great was the consequent uproar that the mayor of Cancale assured the town that the new ministerial decision would remain a dead letter. Eventually things calmed down. The Government, though it had the powers of an autocratic bureaucracy, had bowed to local feelings. Eventually a decree permitting the import of oysters from other areas was accepted without trouble in 1930. The imports had to be native oysters, for in 1923 the growing of Portuguese oysters, which were gaining hold up the Atlantic coast of France, was forbidden north of the River Vilaine on the coast of Brittany, just south of the Gulf of Morbihan; only in 1959 was this restriction on Portuguese oyster-growing lifted.

At the end of 1993 there was some rough behaviour at Marennes-Oléron in protest against imports of foreign oysters, as we shall see later in this chapter.

Rapid innovation

An important aspect of the large size and strength of the French oyster-producing community is that it has been quick to seize upon innovations and exploit them. On the other hand, the individualism and disregard for restraints

An expanse of oyster trestles on the foreshore at Marennes-Oléron.

A punt loaded with bags of oysters, Marennes-Oléron.

of the French oyster growers, together with their power as an organised lobby, has meant that in thrusting to exploit every new technical opportunity as fast as it comes along they may short-sightedly have damaged the industry. There have been three important innovations since 1945 – the use of plastic mesh bags on trestles to contain and protect oysters as they grow and fatten, the introduction of the Pacific oyster and the successful breeding of oysters in hatcheries.[4]

The plastic mesh bag mounted on a trestle was introduced in France in 1963.[5] It is a development of the practice, established in the last century in France, of putting young oysters into mesh box containers on legs (*ambulances*) to grow for a while in protected conditions before being laid out on the sea bed. There are considerable advantages in keeping oysters permanently in containers that are above the sea bed but, being meshed, will allow the passage of sea water: the risk that they will be smothered by silt is greatly diminished, if not eliminated; their vulnerability to predators such as the crab is reduced; and the flow of sea water reaching them, which is the vital factor in their nutrition and growth, may be improved.

Working on the oyster beds with tractor and trailer, Cancale.

Meshed containers still are to be found in the form of trays that may be hung below rafts where there is a good flow of water, or placed in stacks on the sea bed; but it is plastic bags placed on trestles that are most widely used. The trestles are typically placed on the lower foreshore or on banks where they will be exposed by the spring tides twice a month, at which time they can be reached by tractor and trailer, or by boat. Periodically, the bags need to be inspected, shaken and turned to prevent the oysters becoming deformed through growing crowded tightly together in one part of the bag. Less frequently the bags of oysters are brought to a shed and emptied out so that the oysters can be individually inspected; predators, dead oysters and weed are removed; oysters that have stuck together are separated; they are graded by size; and they are put into bags again at a density that leaves space for growth. Bags of larger mesh are used as the oysters are larger, so as to allow them the maximum flow of water from which to derive nourishment. When they are young, the growing oysters need to be inspected and re-bagged in this way quite often; as they grow older, less often. When they are young, they are kept as far from shore as possible so that they will be covered in sea water as much of the time as possible.

The rush into Pacific oysters

It is with respect to the introduction of the Pacific oyster that impetuous uncontrolled action and lobbying by the oyster growers may have caused long-run damage to the industry. The possible damage – there can be no certainty about it – is that oyster disease may have been brought into France with the Pacific oyster. The evidence was well set out in 1991 by two French experts, Messrs Grizel and Héral, both on the staff of IFREMER.[6]

In about 1966, when the production of Portuguese oysters was weakening and they were suffering increasing mortalities, an oysterman, impressed by the fast growth rate and the quality of the Pacific oyster (*Crassostrea gigas*) – it is very similar in appearance, taste and texture to the Portuguese oyster, and it is hardy and fast growing – tried importing some as spat. The results were good and more imports followed. Faced by a rising tide of imports of Pacifics and observing a concomitant increase in mortalities amongst Portuguese oysters, the *Institut Scientifique et Technique des Pêches Maritimes* 'proposed that the importation be stopped', fearing that an organism that killed the Portuguese oysters might be coming in with the Pacifics. But this measure 'was disapproved of by some of the oystermen' and not carried into effect. Two things then happened. Some Japanese experts came to France and concluded that the Pacific oysters imported into France were healthy – a proposition which does not tell one whether they were carrying with them organisms damaging to other kinds of oyster; and mortalities amongst the Portuguese became massive, causing increased economic pressure for the Pacifics to be admitted. In the words of Grizel and Héral, 'the mass mortalities' of the Portuguese at a time when the imported Pacifics 'appeared healthy', led to the official decision to introduce this exotic species to the French coast. Here most clearly one sees the lobbying power of the French oyster growers.

The Pacific oyster was then imported into France in amazingly large quantities under two programmes. Under one programme 562 tons of adult Pacific oysters were imported from British Columbia, most of them in the years 1971 to 1973, and laid in French waters to become breeding stock. Under the other programme no less than 10 thousand tons of spat were imported from Japan, also in the early 1970's. The number of spat in this tonnage is estimated by Grizel and Héral to have been 5 billion. The consignments of imports were inspected, samples were taken for analysis and all the spat was immersed in fresh water to kill predators before being laid in French waters. But with imports flowing in on this massive scale the chances of disease being brought in undetected must have been considerable. The only precedent, in Europe at least, for such a massive transportation of oysters over long distance from one environment to another was the importation at the end of the last century of American oysters to Britain. With those oysters came enemies of the native oyster that did a lot of damage in Britain, as we shall see in the next chapter.

At first the Pacific oysters grew at a remarkable pace in France; they were healthy; there was an abundance of nutrients in the water since the population of Portuguese oysters had died off; production soared. As the population of Pacifics grew, their rate of growth slowed down, but production was assisted by the spread at this time of the practice of using bags on trestles which, besides being more efficient than the traditional method of laying oysters on the seabed, increased the area that could be used for oyster layings. By 1980 a new peak in French oyster production had been reached.

In their conclusions Grizel and Héral (1991) recognise that the viral gill disease that killed the Portuguese oyster may have come in with the Pacific oysters, though they suggest two other possibilities: that it came from Portugal or that it had been present but dormant in Portuguese oysters growing in French waters and became active when the condition of those oysters deteriorated through overstocking. Their concluding remarks suggest that they are not very happy with what happened and would not like to see it repeated. The language is diplomatic, which is understandable since they are both employed by IFREMER, a Government research establishment, and work closely with the oyster growers of their area:

> Notwithstanding that the introduction of C. *gigas* (the Pacific oyster) in France continues to be a commercial success, it is important to underline that this kind of introduction can present considerable dangers, particularly from the zoosanitary point of view. It is essential when the situation is not dramatically urgent to take the maximum precautions during the importation and especially to follow ICES [the International Council for the Exploration of the Sea] recommendations concerning the introduction of non-indigenous species.

An American expert, Carl J. Sindermann, has suggested the possibility that the massive introduction of Pacific oysters to France may have been the cause not

only of the gill disease of the Portuguese oyster but also of *marteilia* and *bonamia*, the diseases of the native oyster that followed. He recognises that, despite extensive research, nobody knows the role that this massive introduction of the Pacific oyster, a non-indigenous species, may have played in disease outbreaks in the indigenous species. But he counsels caution, pointing out that the occurrence within a single decade of three major oyster diseases, each accompanyied by mass oyster mortalities, is unique in the long and well-documented history of oyster culture; and so is the scale on which new species were imported during this same period.[7]

The third innovation, the development on a commercial scale of the technique of breeding oysters in hatcheries, has been of less importance to France than to Britain. The Pacific oyster will breed in the warm waters of the southern part of the Atlantic coast of France, and spat is shipped from there to other parts of the country; hatchery-bred spat is used for only a proportion of French production of Pacific oysters. In Britain, where the waters are cold, production of Pacific oysters is wholly dependent on spat from hatcheries. The development of hatchery breeding in Britain and its implications are described in the next chapter.

Current problems

With French oyster production at a very high level for the third time in this century, oyster experts are anxious, understandably, whether for the third time there is not going to be a collapse. In particular, there is anxiety that disease may be striking again. The Portuguese oyster was wiped out in the late 1960's. Production of the native oyster, assailed by two diseases, is much reduced. The industry now depends predominantly on the Pacific oyster, and there is no reason to suppose that it is any more immune from disease than the other two types.

Messrs Grizel and Héral, having studied evidence for the Marennes-Oléron basin, have put forward the theory that the cycles in French oyster production can be explained by the tendency for the oyster growers to overstock the beds in relation to the supply of nutrients in the water, with cumulative bad effects: the rate of growth of the oysters slows down and they become thin; enfeebled, they suffer rising mortality rates when hit by hard weather conditions and other stresses and, most important, they become more vulnerable than usual to

OPPOSITE: *Aerial view of the vast oyster layings (Claires) at Marennes-Oléron.*

disease. The producers tend to react perversely as these conditions set in. Instead of reducing the quantity of oysters they put in the water, they go on putting out too many in an effort to maintain their income in the face of the low price of oysters caused by the over-production and the higher costs of production associated with slow growth and high mortalities. It is a pattern of behaviour that is well known to economists. It would pay the producers if they could all agree to limit the stock of oysters they put in the water to that quantity that is sustainable and profitable in the long run. But there is no mechanism for getting them all to agree to restrain themselves like that, let alone a mechanism for getting them to stick to an agreement if one is reached.

There is evidence that something along these lines may now be happening in France. The very high national production statistics suggest over-stocking. The rate of growth of oysters, at least on the Atlantic coast, has been slow; because growth is poor, there is a national shortage of large Pacific oysters; mortalities are said to have risen. The symptoms of the cycle are there and so, understandably, is fear of a new epidemic disease. Marennes-Oléron is the place where the problem is probably worst and certainly is best documented. In the late 1980's IFREMER presented their evidence of over-stocking and its consequences at a general consultation *(concertation générale)* between the representatives of the Government and the oyster growers of the area. It was agreed that the stock needed to be reduced so as to get a better yield and a higher rate of return. A decree *(arrêté)* by the Prefect of the Department was introduced in 1989 which is meant to limit both the proportion of a concession that can be devoted to breeding and the density of bags of oysters that could be put out to grow. The limit was set at 6,700 bags per hectare.[8]

The possibility is now being explored at Marennes-Oléron of finding suitable deep layings for oysters, at a depth of 10 to 12 metres, in waters that are now unused. The object is to transfer production to the new sites from the overstocked layings on the foreshore without increasing the total production of the area. If suitable sites are found, the technique used will be to dredge the oysters up once a year, as is the practice on the deep layings at Quiberon.[9] But this is a long-term project and meanwhile it is likely to be very difficult, if not impossible, to enforce on the oyster growers the limitations on the number of bags per hectare laid down in the prefect's decree. Over-production brings hard times, and in hard times it is hard to impose restraint.

Rebellious protests took place at the end of 1993 at Marennes-Oléron against the importation of Pacific oysters from abroad. The story of what happened was told in *L'Ostréiculteur Français*, the trade paper of the French oyster growers, under the headline, '*Marennes-Oléron: Haute Tension sur le Bassin*". Trouble started in early November 1993, when fuel oil was put into the oyster pits *(claires)* of the ex-president of the oyster finishers and merchants association of the area. He had imported Pacific oysters from Holland to the extent of 5 per cent of his total purchases, in order to be able to supply his customers with large oysters. The sight of the Dutch lorries bringing in the imported oysters maddened the local growers; it was surmised that, since Holland nowadays produces few oysters, the imports had really come from Korea or some other place outside the European Union; and there was fear that they might be carrying a virus from foreign parts. Fifteen days later, in spite of calls for calm and an end to vandalism, the houses of the nine oyster merchants of the island of *Oléron* were covered with graffiti saying such things as '*Halte aux importations*'. It was hoped that tension might ease if there were good sales of oysters over Christmas.[10] To calm things down, the authorities, in response to demands from the local oyster producers, rapidly mounted an intense burst of inspections, after which they were able to report to the producers on 11 January that they had inspected over 300 vehicles and about 200 oyster establishments; they had found some cases of wrong grading and of the incorrect description of produce but none of the fraudulent importation of oysters from countries outside the EU.[11] Producers in various parts of France continued to declare disquiet about the new EU import regime.[12]

Reports of what is happening in France are causing oyster growers and the authorities in other countries, for example, in Britain and Ireland, to fear that the emergence of a disease of Pacific oysters may be the cause of the poor growth and rising mortalities that are being experienced in France. These fears are understandable, for the emergence of disease is one of the outcomes that is predicted in the French model of over-stocking referred to earlier, and if there were a disease and it was allowed to spread the results could be disastrous for oyster growers throughout the single European market. On the other hand, fears of this kind can easily be exaggerated and can lead to wild rumours. The fact is that no disease has yet been identified.

Oyster beds in the British Isles.

CHAPTER TEN

Britain in the 20th century

IN THIS CENTURY production and consumption of oysters in Britain has been reduced to a trickle – though recently the seeds of a possible recovery have been visible. According to recent official figures, Great Britain is producing only about 10 million oysters a year while France is producing something like 2,000 million oysters a year. 200 oysters are produced in France for every oyster produced in Britain. The market for oysters in Britain has come near to extinction.

Causes of the decline

Since the end of the last century the British oyster fisheries have faced a succession of difficulties. Had the economic foundations of the industry been strong and Government policy positive, these difficulties might perhaps have been surmounted. But that was not the case. The industry consisted of a declining population of oystermen carrying on as they always had done, exerting the unfettered right to fish for any oysters that showed themselves on the public beds and tending the private beds and layings that had at one time or another been enclosed. As for Government policy, the fact that the industry had declined so far meant that by the beginning of this century there was no longer an 'Oyster Question' to be referred to a Select Committee; members of Parliament no longer paid attention to oysters; the policy of inaction bequeathed by the Royal Commission of 1866 was no longer challenged. Apart from the hesitant steps that were taken to deal with the cleanliness of oysters after the typhoid crisis of 1902, there is no trace of any move by the Government to do anything about the state of the oyster industry until after the second world war, and then the action taken did not amount to much.

The difficulties that hit the oyster growers make a daunting catalogue. Two pests described in chapter 4, the whelk tingle and the slipper limpet, were brought in with the American oysters that were imported and re-laid in British waters at the turn of the century. These had to be removed by extra dredging if oyster production was to be kept going.

The typhoid scare of 1902 caused a collapse in demand. Then there was great mortality of oysters in the early 1920's. This was popularly attributed to the dumping of surplus explosives off the mouth of the Thames and in other places after the end of the 1914-18 war, but a scientific investigation established no connection between the presence of explosives and mortality in oysters, nor was any organism found that could be held responsible. The fact that high mortality was experienced at practically all the oyster breeding grounds of Europe suggests strongly that the cause was an undetected malady.[1] With the oysters mostly dead, the slipper limpet increased greatly in density, smothering the oyster beds. 'On many oyster grounds this was the final blow and economic exploitation was rendered impossible.'[2]

Industrial pollution, damaging to oysters, must also have been on the increase as new industries emitting effluents were established on the Thames estuary and elsewhere. The oyster fisheries may also have been affected by the large amounts of London's rubbish that were dumped by barge in the Thames estuary. As early as 1888, Mr Fryer, the Inspector of Fisheries, estimated that at least 170,000 tonnes of house rubbish, known as 'dust', and 150,000 tonnes of street rubbish, known as 'slop', were being barged away down the Thames in a year.[3]

There were extremely cold winters in 1939-40, 1946-47 and 1962-63, which wiped out large numbers of oysters. Of these, the 1962-63 was the worst. It was the most severe winter for 200 years; it destroyed 95 per cent of the stock which was then about to become marketable.[4]

In the 1970s TBT (tributyl tin), a component of anti-fouling paints, did great damage to oysters and other shellfish if they were growing, as was often the case, in estuaries where boats were moored. While poisoning sea creatures and thereby preventing them growing on the bottoms of boats and ships, TBT also poisoned shellfish in the surrounding area. The Canadian Government issued a notice warning against the use of TBT in 1967; the French acted in 1982 after suffering great damage to their shellfish industry; the UK followed suit only in 1987, when the scientific evidence against TBT was found to be conclusive.[5]

Finally, there have been the oyster diseases that have hit Europe since the 1960's. The *maladie des branchies* that killed the Portuguese oyster was less serious for Britain than for France. Since Portuguese oysters would not breed in

British waters, Britain suffered only the loss of the small quantity that was still being imported for laying down and for immediate consumption.

The two diseases of the native oyster, *marteilia* which first afflicted French oysters in 1974, and *bonamia* which struck between 1979 and 1984, have been a serious threat. They have reduced production of natives to a fraction of its former level in France and the rest of the Continent, but their spread has been checked, or at least slowed down in Britain by orders controlling the deposit of shellfish. These regulations were first introduced in 1965 to control the spread of foreign pests already present in Britain, for example, the slipper limpet and whelk tingle, and to control the introduction of new pests and diseases from abroad. The regulations were strengthened and amended in 1974 and 1983. By and large they appear to have worked well, helped no doubt by the small size of the British oyster industry, which makes it relatively easy to police, and the law-abiding tradition of the country – or what remains of that tradition. Nevertheless some oysters infected with *bonamia* slipped through the British regulations to the River Fal in about 1980 and, before special control measures could be introduced, the disease had spread to the Helford River, to north- and mid-Essex and to some parts of the south coast.[6] Since that time the spread of the disease has largely been contained. But the entry into force of new all-European regulations for the control of the movement of shellfish within the single market may have increased the chances of oyster disease spreading, a point discussed in Chapter 12.

The extent of the decline

How far production and consumption have declined since the later years of the last century can be seen in Charts 1 and 2. The figures are derived from the official fishery statistics. They appear to be tolerably accurate; they are for England and Wales, but they closely represent trends in Great Britain as a whole: production in Scotland, which had been substantial in the 18th and early 19th centuries, came to less than 1 million a year at the beginning of this century; only in recent years has it become at all substantial again.

Chart 1 shows the production and imports of oysters. Chart 2 shows approximate consumption of oysters (as measured by production plus imports) and an index of the average real price of home-produced oysters.

Between the beginning and the end of the period, a matter of a century, consumption of oysters fell from 160 million to about 10 million a year. The greater part of this huge decline was the result of lower imports; they fell from

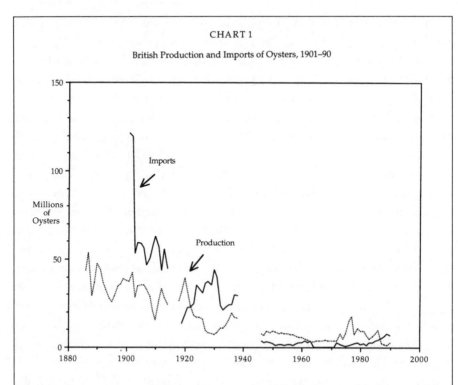

CHART 1

British Production and Imports of Oysters, 1901–90

Sources   1890–1912 from the twelfth and subsequent issues of the Annual Report of the Inspectors of Sea Fisheries; from 1913 onwards from annual Sea Fisheries Statistics.

Notes
1. The figures do not cover production in Britain of rock (Pacific) oysters and therefore understate total oyster production in recent years. See text.
2. The figures are for England and Wales; Scottish production was negligible from the beginning of the period until the last decade when Pacific oysters became important.
3. The import figures represent imports for consumption. Imports for relaying, which were substantial and were separately recorded for the period 1919–62, have been excluded since it appears that when sold for consumption they show up, in part at least, in the figures for production.

120 million at the turn of the century, nearly all obtained from the United States, to only a few millions a year after 1945. Production fell from about 40 million to under 5 million a year in the 1960's; recently it has been about 10 million a year.

The main phases of the massive decline in oyster production and consumption since the beginning of the century were these:

Before 1914: The damage done to demand for oysters by the typhoid scandal of 1902 shows up clearly on the two charts. From one year to the next consumption was halved – from 160 million to about 80 million; imports fell

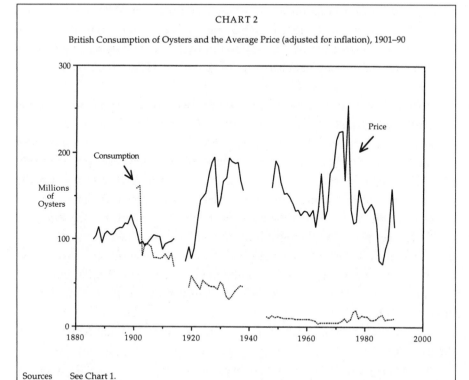

CHART 2

British Consumption of Oysters and the Average Price (adjusted for inflation), 1901–90

Sources   See Chart 1.

Notes

1. The figures labelled 'consumption' are the sum of the production and import figures in Chart 1. Exports
    were relatively small and for that reason were not recorded for most of the period.

2. The 'prices' are average values of oysters produced (i.e. the value of oysters produced divided by the
    quantity produced) which means they do not reflect changes in the price of imports; nor do they reflect
    changes in the proportion of different grades and types of oyster in the production figures.

more heavily than production; average real prices of home produced oysters fell
by 20 per cent or more and had not recovered by 1914.

The 1920's: Consumption almost halved once again – to about 45 million
compared with 80 million before 1918. This time lack of demand was not the
problem so much as a failure of supply, as is evident from the average real price
of home-produced oysters. It rose to about 80 per cent above the depressed
1914 level and well above the pre-1902 level. On the supply side, production,
after briefly recovering from the 1914-18 war, fell to under 10 million a year in
the late 1920's when unidentified disease was taking its toll here and abroad.
Imports, now mostly native oysters from the Continent, recovered but remained
well below the pre-war level.

The 1930's: Consumption fell by about one-third from 1930 to 1933 and then recovered gradually to the 1920's level. Production grew during the decade, assisted by an increase in imports of oysters for re-laying. Imports for consumption fell by one half between 1931 and 1933 and then recovered to some extent.

1946 to 1980: From the end of the second world war onwards the figures are pathetically small. Consumption after the war was down to about 10 million and stayed there. The decline was associated with a virtual cessation of imports. In the years just before the war, imports had again been coming mostly from the United States. For more than a decade during and after the war the general policy of restricting imports in order to save foreign exchange caused an interruption; and then in 1965 came the regulations to prevent the spread of existing oyster pests and the introduction from abroad of new pests. American imports effectively ceased with the start of the second world war. Production trickled along between 5 and 10 million until the early 1960's when the exceptionally hard winter of 1962-63 knocked it down to about 3 million. It did not rise much above that level until the late 1970's, when there were one or two exceptional spatfalls in the Solent where native oysters had reappeared in the early 1970's. In spite of the great reduction in the supply of oysters, the average real price of them declined between 1949 and the mid 1950's to below the pre-war level and remained at that lower level, apart from a surge in about 1970. That real average prices were lower when supplies were so greatly reduced implies that demand had died away during and after the war.

1981 onwards: Consumption continued at about 10 million a year or less. The traditional fishery statistics were based on landings of flat oysters and did not record production of Pacific oysters in bags on trestles. They therefore understated production significantly at the end of the 1980's when this form of production began to be important. Earlier in the decade, production fluctuated, causing, as you would expect, fluctuations in the opposite direction in the price of home produced oysters: when lower production made oysters scarce, the price rose and *vice versa*. But on average the real price for the 1980's was rather low compared with any period since 1914. Recently estimates by MAFF and its Scottish counterpart SOAFD (Scottish Office Agriculture and Fisheries Department) have become available of production of Pacific as well as native oysters. These put total production in Great Britain in 1992 at just under 10 million oysters, comprising about 6 million Pacific oysters and 3 million native oysters. Since figures for the value of production are not given, the average price cannot be estimated. Evidence from the trade suggests that the relative weakness of prices shown by the figures for the 1980's has persisted.

What is most remarkable about this history is that, despite the collapse in the supply of oysters, the price of home produced oysters, adjusted for inflation, was not much higher in 1990 than it had been at the beginning of the century. Evidently, demand for oysters had died away during the century.

The two markets

In order to see what happened to demand it is important to distinguish between the two traditional markets for oysters in Britain, the market for expensive natives and the market for cheap imported oysters, mostly of the cupped variety. The natives, of which Colchester and Whitstable were the classic supplying areas, were consumed by the rich in clubs, restaurants and oyster bars, and in their homes. The cheap oysters that were being imported from the United States at the end of the 19th century were consumed by the working people who in the mid-19th century oyster boom had consumed the coarse oysters from the Channel that were then sold on the streets. The American oysters, having been brought across the Atlantic in the winter and usually re-laid briefly, were sold in the summer, mostly at seaside resorts, race tracks and similar places. Oysters were not a basic food of the poor, any more than they had been in the mid-19th century; they were a treat, a minor luxury, a festive food eaten on a day out. The summer trade in imported oysters was concentrated in the north of England, with Blackpool a focal point. Since Liverpool was the port to which American oysters were shipped and many of them were re-laid in nearby English, Irish or Welsh waters, they were easily and cheaply supplied to northern markets.[7] In the south of England, the jellied eel seems to have taken the place of the oyster on shellfish stalls, alongside cockles and winkles which were sold in both north and south.

In the first half of this century the market for cheap oysters suffered a much more severe collapse than the market for natives. In the 1920's imports of oysters from America had fallen to an average of 11 million a year, compared with 41 million in the years 1910-1914 and 120 million at the turn of the century. In the 1930's they averaged 16 million. The supply of cheap oysters was supplemented by Portuguese oysters re-laid in British waters to grow and fatten, but the quantities were too small to change the picture. The fall in consumption of cheap oysters in the inter-war years cannot be attributed in any great degree to higher prices. Compared with the years 1910-14, the average price of imported oysters in the 1920's, adjusted for inflation, was up by only about 20 per cent, yet consumption was down by no less than 75 per cent.

What happened in the market for natives was strikingly different. Although the price of natives rose by 50 per cent, consumption in the 1920's stayed at the pre-war level. True, the market for cheap oysters recovered a bit in the 1930's and the market for native oysters went down, but this moderated rather than reversed the relative movement of the two markets. The evidence strongly indicates that demand for cheap oysters collapsed more completely than the demand for natives.

The extinction of demand

One can see many causes for the decline and fall in the demand for oysters in this century. To start with, in the absence of a decent regime for oyster hygiene, the fear of illness prompted by the 1902 scandal lived on, kept alive by recurrent reports of sickness or death caused by oysters.

Secondly, the price of oysters in the inter-war period and afterwards was always extremely high compared with the mid-19th century oyster boom. In this country, unlike France, oysters were never made cheap by surges in production.

Thirdly, changing economic and social conditions must have had an effect. The inter-war years were plagued by economic depression which caused particularly high unemployment in the north, the area where the market for cheap oysters was concentrated. These conditions are likely to have depressed demand for oysters by working men. On the other hand, the behaviour of those who bought the more expensive native oysters, mostly in the south, appears to have been more volatile. The 1920's were a period when those who had money were uninhibited about high living, a period when bright young things sought, initially at least, to recapture the gaiety of Edwardian life. It was the period portrayed by P.G. Wodehouse and Evelyn Waugh and, in America, by Scott Fitzgerald. It is not altogether surprising that demand for expensive oysters should have been strong in the 1920's, or that it should have weakened in the 1930's after the stock market crash. A third leader in *The Times*, one of those articles, now almost extinct, that comment facetiously on a passing event, conveys the flavour of the times – and pretty silly it is too. It was written in May 1933 after the opening at Brightlingsea of the first plant in Britain for the purification of oysters, one feature of which was that the water was heated:

The oyster may shut up but it is not silent.... It does not rest quietly in its bed; it is a regular raggle-taggle gypsy for wandering. It has a heart; and, belonging now to one gender and now to the other between the same pair of valves, it has a very complex and eventful sex-life. Moreover, so far from shrinking into its shell, the oyster has a matchless capacity for getting into the news. No film star – say, no other film star, for the oyster has got on to the films – no society beauty, lion tamer, or peerage-catcher can touch it.... And now the oysters have broken out in a new place. As the house-agent's daughter would have said, it makes one go h. and c. all over to learn that oysters want hot baths.[8]

The second world war and its aftermath shattered that mood. This time the war was longer, and after it there was no going back to pre-war frivolity; instead there was prolonged rationing and austerity, and there was continuing high taxation to finance the welfare state and the Cold War. Rationing lasted for about 10 years; and high taxation for much longer. It is not fanciful to believe that in these conditions the taste for oysters, always regarded in England as a rather frivolous article of consumption, was frowned upon. A strong whiff of that austere mood is to be found in the answer given in December 1949 to a question asked in Parliament by an oyster-loving cousin of mine who, God bless him, had introduced me to oysters a year or two earlier:

Mr F. Noel-Baker asked the Minister of Food when he will introduce a maximum controlled price for the retail sale of oysters, in view of the present high cost and variation in price.

Dr. Summerskill (Parliamentary Secretary to the Ministry of Food): I do not think there is any need to control this luxury foodstuff, particularly in view of the decision to decontrol the price of fish.

Once the long period of post-war austerity was over, the revival of good living did not take the form of a return to pre-war patterns of eating and drinking. The social structure had changed; the middle class had grown and become broader; domestic servants had vanished; middle-class housewives, and sometimes their husbands, did the cooking and began to give attention to gastronomy. There was growing interest in Continental cooking, aided by the importation of fresh foreign ingredients by rapid refrigerated transport; and there was a surge in wine consumption. But oysters did not figure in the new cornucopia. They were not offered at dinner parties or in the new restaurants.

The consumption of oysters by the rich lived on in traditional oyster bars, in some London hotel dining rooms and in a few new fish restaurants. Indeed there was quite a growth after the 1950's of bogus traditional oyster bars. These establishments, which still seem to flourish, are generally embellished with Dickensian facades, complete with leaded panes and interior furnishing to match. Most of the space is given over to tables and chairs, but there will typically be a small oyster bar on the ground floor where you can sit on a high stool and, having ordered a dozen oysters, see them opened before your eyes. It is all very satisfactory to the oyster-lover, if he can afford the price of the oysters, but he is bound to note that in these places few people are eating oysters. They are really fish restaurants – and they offer good fish – dressed up as oyster bars. Which is a curious comment on the reputation of oyster bars and oysters. It seems that oyster bars have come to be thought of as desirable places to go by people who are not oyster-eaters, as places with a ye olde flavour where you get good fish.

After 1945 the market for cheap oysters appears again to have collapsed more completely than the market for expensive oysters. Whereas the supply of native oysters to the expensive market, derived from home production and imports, always continued on a limited scale, the supply of cheap oysters was severely interrupted in the late 1960's when the supply of imported Portuguese oysters was banned because of disease; it took some time before there was a ready supply of hatchery-bred Pacific oysters in England. Meanwhile the shift in the class structure towards middle-class occupations and towards the new middle-class habits of consumption, together with the growth of cheap holidays in the sun abroad, diverted the younger generations from places like Blackpool.

The old market is not totally dead. In the summer of 1993 I found half a dozen or more seafood stalls or bars on or around the front at Blackpool selling oysters alongside cockles, whelks and other shellfish. But those who bought oysters were mostly old regulars having a few for old times sake; the young mostly bought other kinds of shellfish.

The extent of the decline in the oyster trade at Blackpool was described to me by Jim Bamber, an old hand whose family has been selling oysters there for several generations. He still helps his son on a seafood stall in the pleasure gardens. It stands amidst fairground machines and booths and is close to a larger-than-life model of a 'laughing sailor' which stands on a plinth, swaying mechanically and emitting recorded raucous laughter. The stall was impeccably clean, the oysters excellent. He described how, in the years between the wars,

Shellfish stall in the Pleasure Gardens at Blackpool seen both from a distance and from close to so as to show that oysters are on offer in a corner.

oysters would be sold on 'carts', wheeled stalls that were pushed onto the beach, some of them big enough for five or six fellows to stand round opening oysters; customers would start to come at five in the morning; and at high season his family might order 3 thousand oysters to sell in a week-end. There would be 15 or 16 carts on the beach in the summer season, many of them belonging to Irishmen who for the rest of the year returned to Ireland, often to a family farm. After the war the business recovered and went on fairly well until the mid-1960's. Then it collapsed and the Irish gave up coming. Bamber became philosophical. He expected the oyster trade to keep going one way or another. He quoted an old friend of his who had died a few years ago. 'Isn't it funny,' he had said, 'that people have been in all sorts of jobs, selling all sorts of things on stalls, they've done everything, but shellfish has lasted everyone out.'

With the decline in oyster consumption for more than a century the taste for oysters has progressively been lost. In each of many successive generations more people have grown up in Britain never having eaten an oyster, never having been offered one and perhaps never having seen one. The demand for an article depends upon people knowing it. If a food vanishes for long, the demand for it will surely die – until a new generation is persuaded to try it – if, one day, it is on offer again.

The seeds of revival

From this whole dismal story one might easily conclude that the British oyster, deserted by consumers, was finally on its deathbed, meekly pumping the last few gallons of polluted sea water through its diseased gills. But things are not so black. There have been several encouraging developments.

The first is the revival of native oysters on the natural beds in the Solent, an area that had been important as a source of young oysters for Essex dredger men until the first world war, when it was fished out. It is possible that the few oysters left on the long-abandoned beds gradually bred and produced the new population. An alternative explanation, favoured by most oyster experts, is that some imported oysters laid in adjacent waters produced larvae which were carried out to the old beds and settled there to produce the new population. What is known is this. In the mid-1950's about 100 tonnes of young Brittany oysters and a smaller quantity of Dutch half-grown oysters were deposited in the Beaulieu River and in the Newtown River on the Isle of Wight. Subsequent

The Helford river, one of the surviving sources of native oysters in England.

dredging in these areas for marketable oysters proved uneconomic; mortalities were observed and the enterprise was written off. But at the end of the 1960s an accumulation of unexploited oysters was noticed, and in 1971 the area was surveyed by Mr Denis Key of MAFF. In the Beaulieu River, the beds were found to be full of oysters of various ages; on Stanswood Bay in the Solent, dredgeful after dredgeful of beautiful young oysters was caught.[9]

So far *bonamia* has not done much damage in the area of the Solent, apart from the Beaulieu river, and oyster fishing in most of the area is regulated in a manner that helps preserve the stock. There are two several orders, each of which gives the oyster fishing rights to about 200 acres in the Solent to a group of fishermen; they are free to fish as much as they like in their area and to take oysters of any size, but out of self interest they limit their fishing to a few days a year. And there is a regulating order in favour of the Southern Sea Fisheries Committee for an area of over 17 thousand acres. The committee issues licences to fish for oysters to those who apply and limits the quantity of oysters taken by permitting fishing for oysters for only a limited number of days, typically thirty a year, and by permitting only oysters above a minimum size to be taken. In total a few hundred tons of native oysters are now produced each year from the Solent. Though modest, this revival of an old breeding area has been a significant event. The traditional breeding grounds of the East Coast are defunct, largely infected with *bonamia,* and native oysters continue to breed in only a few other places in the British Isles – principally in the South West of England, in Scotland and in Ireland.

Technical innovations

The second encouraging development has been the transformation of oyster production by the three innovations already mentioned: the use of plastic mesh bags on trestles to contain and protect oysters as they grow; the introduction of the Pacific oyster; and the successful breeding of Pacific oysters in hatcheries.[10] Of these developments, the last has been much more important to Britain than to France, where Pacific oysters will breed naturally.

Work on the breeding of oysters in hatcheries began before the second world war and was then pushed ahead in the 1950's. The technique that was developed consists of a series of steps: the oysters selected for breeding are first put into warmed water with cultured algae as food, in order to bring them into condition to spawn; the temperature of the water is then raised and lowered so as to induce them to spawn, or, alternatively, the oysters are opened and the

Young oysters at the Reculver hatchery in upwellers in which they are fed by a constant supply of aereated sea water full of algae.

eggs or sperm are extracted from them. The eggs or sperm, which are visibly distinct, are then inspected and collected together; the two are mixed to achieve fertilisation; and the mixture is put into special vessels for 24 hours, by the end of which larvae have been formed. The larvae are then put to grow in rearing tanks in which they feed and swim freely for about 12 days, after which they are ready to stick themselves to a suitable surface and turn into baby oysters or 'spat'. For this purpose, typically, a black plastic sheet is placed at the bottom of the rearing tank. The spat which collect on it are scraped off with a razor blade and are put in special tanks to grow. When they are 2 to 5 millimetres long, they are sold or they are put into outdoor tanks to grow further. At the different stages of the process, the temperature, salinity and purity of the water need to be carefully controlled, as well as the supply of nutrients; and conditions must be kept hygienic. A pamphlet issued by the MAFF fisheries laboratories describes the technique in detail. It warns that

> Despite many years of research, there are still considerable problems in the reliable hatchery production of bivalve species. Successful hatchery production of larvae and spat is related more to the skill and experience of the staff than to the excellence of the facilities and equipment.[11]

The spat is sold to oyster farmers at sizes ranging from 2-3 mm. to 10-20 mm. The larger the size the higher the price, a point that the oyster farmer will weigh against the consideration that the larger the size of spat he buys the lower will be the labour and equipment costs he incurs in tending his oysters until they are ready for market and the lower too will be the mortality rate of what he buys.

The introduction of the hatchery breeding of Pacific oysters was undertaken with great caution by the MAFF laboratory at Conwy in order to ensure that the new species would not bring with it disease or pests and would fit the habitat. The laboratory imported consignments of broodstock from Canada in 1965 and 1972. A long period of experiment and quarantine followed. Only in the late 1970's did the laboratory begin to supply broodstock to commercial hatcheries. Now the breeding of Pacific oysters is well established in Britain at a few commercial hatcheries.

Native oysters have also been bred in hatcheries, but not subsequently grown as successfully as Pacific oysters; and demand for native oyster seed has been inhibited by the presence in many places of *bonamia,* which kills off the young native oysters once they are put out in the sea.

The great importance of the development of hatchery breeding is that the supply of spat is no longer dependent on the caprice of nature: for Pacific oysters there is now a reliable and limitless supply of healthy spat available. Added to which, the Pacific oyster is hardy and grows rapidly; it does not mind the cold waters of the British coast although it will not breed regularly in them. Since it reaches marketable size in 3-4 years compared with 5-6 years for a native, it is relatively cheap to produce.

Oyster farming with these modern techniques, unlike the farming of fish, does not involve the use of artificial or packaged nutrients. In the hatchery, the parent oysters are supplied with the kinds of plankton on which they feed normally; it is simply provided in those proportions and in th0se conditions that will best induce breeding. Once placed in the sea in their mesh bags, the oysters feed on the plankton that exists naturally in the water.

The possibility of growing hatchery-bred Pacific oysters in cold waters means that the west coast of Scotland, where the waters are unpolluted and the Gulf Stream prevents extreme cold, now has potential for oyster farming. The west coast of Scotland is so indented with sea lochs and is so thickly surrounded with islands that the length of shore is far greater than that of the coast of France, which, by comparison, is almost straight. Moreover the sea lochs often provide the shelter and the mixture of salt and sweet water that oysters need. In England and Wales hatchery-bred Pacific oysters are farmed on various parts of the coast, often at places where native oysters were once produced.

The new oyster farmers

The prospect of growing Pacific oysters profitably on the shore has brought forth a new breed of oyster producer, different from the traditional oystermen. Oystermen following the traditional techniques are still to be found in those places where the native oyster survives. For example, the holders of concessions under the two several orders in the Solent are groups of inshore fishermen who go after many kinds of fish and are limited in the number of days they dredge for oysters for only a few days a year. They sell their catch of oysters to merchants who sell them on to buyers, mostly on the Continent but some in other parts of Britain, for example, at Mersea and Poole. The buyers, following the traditional practice, re-lay the oysters on their local foreshore to fatten and gain their final quality. Poaching is a problem around the Solent. Oysters are not re-laid in that area.

The new oyster farmers are very different. In the first place, they are not in any degree hunters. They do not go out to sea looking for the progeny of oysters that grow wild; nor do they place collectors on which the larvae of oysters may settle; they simply order young oysters from a hatchery.

Secondly, they work mostly with tractors on the foreshore, not with boats, though they will use boats or amphibious vehicles when trestles and bags are placed on banks that cannot be reached by tractor.

Thirdly, they need quite a lot of capital to invest in a stock of young oysters, in bags and trestles, in second-hand tractors and trailers, and in a shed on land in which periodically to handle and sort the oysters as they grow and in which to pack them before dispatch to customers. The packing shed must meet EU hygiene standards. The assets in which they have to invest – special sheds, tractors and trailers, bags and trestles – are inflexible; they are not like a fishing boat that can be turned to other kinds of fishing.

Finally, the new oyster farmer needs to be able to face quite a high risk on his initial investment. For although Pacific oysters are remarkably resistant to cold weather, they can suffer high mortalities if they are mishandled or if the water conditions prove unsuitable.

The new men who have responded to these demands are first and foremost entrepreneurs, men who are willing to take a risk in business; they are often middle class and well educated; and there is usually some special reason why they have taken to oyster farming. In Scotland the boom and subsequent slide in salmon farming made people aware of the possibilities of fish farming and has given those engaged in salmon farming a desire to diversify into oysters and other shellfish. John Noble of Loch Fyne and Mark Pattinson of Kishorn are examples of Scottish landowners who have become successful oyster farmers. Along the coast of England there is Christopher Kerrison, an old Etonian and former racing driver, who saw the chance of leasing the old Colchester oyster fishery; there is David Jarrad, a young man who, having been brought up in the London area, wanted to escape to the country; there is Philip Gibbon, a retired naval officer; or at Whitstable there is Dr John Bayes who runs a successful hatchery and grows Pacific oysters, having come into the industry from marine biology, bringing a scientific approach to the job.

Compared with France, with its well-established population of oyster growers backed by professional organisations and by professional training, the approach of the new oyster growers of England and Scotland is, perhaps inevitably, that of enterprising novices who learn the hard way. There is a useful leaflet produced in 1990 by one of the MAFF laboratories on the cultivation of Pacific oysters. This provides advice on where and how to grow them, a list of where to get hatchery oysters and equipment, and advice on the legal problems of establishing an oyster fishery. The novice may pay a brief visit to France to take a look at French practices; and one or two locals who have succeeded in establishing themselves now offer their services as advisers. But the general approach is, in British style, that of the amateur who plunges in and learns by doing; and it is undertaken without the support of a coherent Government policy towards the industry, a point to which we shall return. This does not mean that many people fail. Oyster growing, like cultivating a single species in a garden or on a farm, is not very complicated, but there are tricks and skills to be learnt if you are to get a good yield and consistently good quality.

A rather extreme example of the English amateur approach is provided by Richard Pinney who, with his wife, started the oystery and fish smokery at

Orford on the coast of Suffolk. In his memoirs he charmingly described how, having come to the east coast to live on a boat at the end of the war, his interest in reviving the local oyster beds was aroused when he was served fried oysters and bacon for breakfast at a local hotel and found them delectable.[12] Prevented by post-war import controls from importing oysters to restock the local beds, he turned his energies to discovering by experiment how to make mats from the local reeds, an activity by which he lived for a time. But when post-war restrictions were removed, he turned to learning by experiment how to farm oysters and how to smoke fish; and he even went on to discover how to breed oysters in his own oyster hatchery. He was plainly an extraordinary resourceful and tenacious man, a creative English eccentric and successful entrepreneur.

A second difference from the French is that the new British growers are much preoccupied with marketing their oysters, for example by trying to sell directly to consumers by mail order. The collapse in the past hundred years of popular demand for oysters in Britain means that there is not a large ready market. Selling by mail order is a way of enticing new consumers to buy oysters, and it brings the producer a much better price than selling through merchants. For their part, consumers may often buy by mail order because their local fishmonger does not have a regular supply of fresh oysters. In France the market is so large and every fishmonger so well supplied with oysters that the idea selling by mail order would be ridiculous. French oyster producers have marketing problems. For example, there are small producers who feel exploited by big producers who buy from them and then sell in bulk to Paris and other centres. But the French do not suffer from a lack of national demand for oysters.

A third difference is that the oyster growers of France are a continuing population consisting principally of families, many of which have maintained their concessions from one generation to another. This continuity has not prevented their metamorphosis from being fishers seeking oysters on natural banks to being farmers tending Pacific oysters in bags on trestles. On the contrary, the professional training and state support with which they are provided has helped them to adapt to new methods; the long-standing system of concessions has given them security and contact with the state: it has made them an effective lobby, comparable perhaps to the farmers of France or Britain. There has been nothing like the discontinuity that has occurred in Britain as a result of the almost total demise of traditional oyster farmers – and the traditional oyster-growing areas – now followed by a tentative influx of new men, many of them in Scotland, a largely new area.

Finally, British oyster growers are organised, for the purposes of exchanging views with one another and representing their interests to the Government and the public, in a very different way from their French counterparts. In France, as we have seen, all oyster producers are obliged by law to belong to their professional organisation, and it operates closely with the Government; for example, representatives of the producers take part in the allocation of oyster concessions. In Britain there is a trade association, the Shellfish Association of Great Britain (SAGB), founded in 1969, of which membership is voluntary. It is the direct descendent, through reorganisation, of the Oyster Merchants and Planters Association which was formed by the Fishmongers Company in the wake of the oyster scandal of 1902. The old association was dominated by merchants who, when oysters were still commonly traded through Billingsgate Market, had greater financial interest in the oyster, and greater ability to put forward their views, than the traditional growers dispersed around the coast. The SAGB is very different. It represents shellfish merchants and processors as well as growers, but in the case of the oyster, which is only one of the shellfish within its remit, the voice of the new oyster growers is now dominant; the merchants are no longer important. The SAGB runs annual conferences at which professional papers on technical and marketing problems are presented and discussed; it organises specialist committees to consider policy issues that affect its members, such as the control of the re-laying of oysters and methods of purification of oysters under the new EU regulations; and it provides advice to members. Its director, Dr Edwards, is a marine biologist who had a long career with MAFF. Altogether its approach is modern and professional. But, despite enjoying the benefit of being sponsored by the Fishmongers Company and having offices in the Fishmongers Hall, it remains a small, stretched, voluntary organisation, operating in a country where the consumption per head of shellfish is very low compared with France and many other Continental countries.

The prospects for demand

There are signs that we could be seeing the beginnings of a revival of demand for oysters. Some of the new oyster growers have found that if they set up a stall at a food fair, a race meeting or an agricultural show, and encourage people to come and try oysters, they get a good response; young people are ready to try oysters for the first time and many take to them. In London, that great trend-setter, Sir Terence Conran, has opened a number of restaurants

The modest scale of British oyster farming today: oyster trestles at Essex (right), Loch Fyne (below) and Kishorn (bottom).

that make a point of displaying and offering oysters. More than one chain of supermarkets has started selling oysters at some of its branches, though the quantity they stock at each branch is so trivial that they are often sold out. And yet another sign that demand may be stirring is that oyster knives may now be found on sale in some of those shops that sell smart kitchenware imported from abroad.

All these signs can be read to support the notion that there is a potential market, possibly a large one, amongst the broad new middle class whose members are interested in experimenting with new foods in competition with their friends and neighbours. They have tried most of what the Continent has to offer. Smoked salmon, which was a luxury, has become progressively cheaper and more accessible to the point where it has become almost commonplace as a result of a glut of farmed salmon. The oyster, one feels, must have a chance of coming into fashion again. One of the important pre-conditions of such a revival in the demand for oysters, namely that they should be clean and known to be clean so that people may eat them without fear for the after-effects they may suffer, has at last been fulfilled thanks to the new EU hygiene regime (Chapter 12).

Government policy

After the second world war an effort was made to restore oyster production. The initiative for this unprecedented adoption of a positive policy towards the oyster in Britain appears to have come not from the ministers, whose attitude to oysters at that time could, as we have seen, be disdainful, but from within the Government's fisheries research community. The moving spirit was Dr H.A. Cole who, having returned after the war to work on oyster rearing, was made head of shellfish research in 1953.[13] He persuaded his superiors that oyster fisheries needed reviving as a national resource. With the aim of restoring the breeding stock, research was done into the breeding cycles and growing conditions of native oysters, and also the control of predators. But the attempt to help the industry was not confined to biological research. Rather, the approach appears to have been thoroughly pragmatic and to have addressed the practical problems of restoring the industry to prosperity. For example, it was decided that improved mechanisation of the industry was required, and methods of dealing with dredged material on a production line basis were developed.[14]

There were some good breeding seasons in the late 1950's and things looked promising, but then the stock of native oysters in English waters was largely wiped out by the hard winter of 1962-63. In the face of that disaster, it was decided that it was no good relying on natural events for a steady supply of young oysters. Attention was turned to hatchery breeding. Natives were bred successfully in hatcheries, but the spat so produced were too delicate to be an attractive commercial proposition. There followed the development of the hatchery production of Pacific oysters which, as we have seen, was highly successful.

In the past decade, the policy of reducing the role of government and leaving applied research to industry appears to have caused the MAFF laboratories to concentrate on 'scientific work' and draw back from research closely related to the profitable operation of the industry. This does not mean that what is now being done is unimportant. On the contrary, there is a great deal of research still to be done on oysters and other shellfish, and on the relationship of their survival and growth to the condition of the waters in which they live. These problems have become more important as pollution has become worse. And the laboratories now have a lot of new work to do monitoring the condition of oysters so as to ensure that the waters from which they come conform to the standards of cleanliness set in the new EU regulations.

It is not clear that greater help to the industry would require more funds rather than a clear reversal of the policy of the past decade which has tended to reinforce the traditional feeling amongst British civil servants that to work too directly for the benefit of private industry is improper. It may be that with closer relations with people in the industry, greater willingness to give advice and to produce up-to-date booklets that dealt with immediate problems, the Government scientists could contribute significantly to the development of the industry at little or no cost. But they would need encouragement to go in that direction. That there should be such a change with reference to fisheries of all kinds was strongly recommended in July 1993 in a report by the Agriculture Committee of the House of Commons:

> It is absolutely vital that scientists in England and Wales bestir themselves to expand contacts with fishermen, for instance by taking the opportunity to travel on commercial fishing expeditions. It would also be desirable for scientists to invite fishermen to accompany them on research voyages or to their laboratories for discussions. The Government should also give urgent consideration to other means of

encouraging better communication between scientists and fishermen throughout the UK.[15]

The second way in which the Government has been active since the second world war has been in the introduction of the regulations, mentioned earlier in this chapter, to prevent the importation and spread of diseases, pests and parasites of the oyster. In this they have been commendably successful so far. The working of these regulations, and the new EU regime which took their place in January 1993, is described in chapter 12.

But the main point that stands out in a comparison of Britain with France is the absence in Britain of a coherent Government policy towards the production of oysters – and other shellfish. The research laboratories make their contribution; the regulators keep out disease, pests and parasites of the oyster; and the civil servants represent Britain in the negotiation of new regulations in Brussels. For the rest, the oyster growers are left to respond to market forces within an incoherent framework of higgledy-piggledy institutions. Nowhere is this more true than in the matter of obtaining oyster concessions.

CHAPTER ELEVEN

Oyster concessions and the Crown Estate

IN FRANCE THE ownership of the foreshore and the seabed within territorial waters is coherent and straightforward and so, as we have seen, is the procedure for getting an oyster concession.

In Britain there is no such coherence. The ownership of the foreshore and territorial seabed was already complex when the Royal Commission reported in 1866. It will be recalled that there were old manorial rights granted before Magna Carta (and also disputed claims to such rights); and that fishing rights had been conferred on some boroughs, for example Colchester, by act of Parliament or royal charter. For the rest, the foreshore and the territorial seabed belonged to the Crown or to the duchies of Cornwall and Lancaster, two appendages of the Crown; and there was a public right of fishery. The position as regards ownership is the same today. The Crown owns no less than 1,700 miles of foreshore out of the total of 3,200 miles in England, Wales and Northern Ireland; and in Scotland it owns about the same proportion – 55 per cent. The two duchies own about 300 miles of foreshore. But since 1866 there have been the most bizarre changes in the management of the area belonging to the Crown. These changes were introduced with no regard for the interests of the shellfish industry. Yet they have had major implications for it.

The first change, which usually goes unnoticed, took place in 1866. Early in that year the management of the foreshore and the territorial seabed, and the right to any income derived from it, were transferred from the Commissioners of Woods, who managed the Crown Estate at that time, to the Board of Trade. The ultimate title to the foreshore and territorial seabed remained with the Crown, but for reasons of administrative and political convenience the beneficial ownership was sold to the Government, to be administered by the

Board of Trade. Also in 1866 came the introduction of several and regulating orders, described in chapter 5, which were intended to provide a new means of enclosing the foreshore and seabed for shellfish farming but largely failed in their purpose because the costs and difficulties of obtaining orders were so great. By these two measures – the purchase of the foreshore and territorial seabed and the introduction of a defective procedure for granting concessions – the Government unwittingly paralysed enclosure of the foreshore and seabed for the purpose of conserving and farming shellfish for nearly a century. The Board of Trade effectively owned the unenclosed coast (apart from the area belonging to the two duchies); it alone could grant new concessions; but the method at its disposal was ineffectual.

The position has been transformed again since 1949 when the Government, almost casually, handed back the management of the foreshore and the territorial seabed, and the income from it, to the Commissioners of the Crown Lands, the successors of the Commissioners of Woods. Remarkably, this was done by means of a clause in a Coast Protection Act, the purpose of which was to stop the erosion of the coast by the sea; the interests of the shellfish industry were never even referred to. But the transfer has been beneficial, fortuitously, to shellfish farming compared with what went before. For it has meant that shellfish farmers now have the possibility of obtaining leases from the Crown Estate on the many parts of the coast that belong to the Crown.

The outcome of this tangled history is that anyone who today, seeking to become an oyster grower, looks for a site in Britain, will find that around the coast the right to dredge or cultivate oysters is held in the following ways:

1. Under manorial titles – claims to which are sometimes disputed by the Crown or by rival private claimants.
2. By royal charters or pre-1866 private acts of Parliament conferring rights on boroughs.
3. Under several orders granted by the Government to individuals or to co-operatives and similar bodies.
4. Under regulating orders granted by the Government to local authorities, harbour boards or sea fisheries committees (formed by a local authority or several neighbouring local authorities), which give the recipients of the order the power to licence fishing, limit it and make charges for it.
5. Under regulating orders the recipient of which is given the power to grant leases to individuals, co-operatives or similar bodies.

6. By sea fisheries committees which have obtained several orders that give them the power to grant sub-leases.

7. By harbour authorities or local authorities to which the Crown Estate Commissioners or the duchies of Cornwall or Lancaster have leased their rights to the foreshore, giving the latter the power to sub-lease moorings and fisheries.

8. Where none of these seven kinds of title is to be found, by the Crown Estate Commissioners or the two duchies.

The minimum requirements of the new entrant are a claim of some kind to a part of the foreshore; a bit of land behind the shore on which to have a shed and space for gear; access and reasonable transport to the site; and permission from the government departments responsible for preventing oyster disease and human disease. He will find three main alternatives ways of getting a concession: to find a place where an existing title exists and seek to get a lease from the owner of that title or to buy it; to go for a lease from the Crown; or to go for a several order.

A private lease or title

Private titles and delegated public ownership (e.g. in the hands of harbour authorities) are as common in Scotland as in England and Wales. In England and Wales they are concentrated in those parts of the east and south coast where there was once intense oyster farming.

Obtaining a private title, once a seller is found, is often straightforward. For example, Christopher Kerrison obtained from the Colchester Borough Council the lease of the fishery rights and shore facilities of the old Colchester oyster fishery after it had lost value as a result of the hard winter of 1962-63 and other tribulations. In Suffolk, Mr Pinney obtained a lease without difficulty from a landowner whose family had established their title to Butley Creek. But in some cases the complexity of the ownership of the coast can cause remarkable difficulties to the oyster farmer seeking a lease. An extreme example is the case of David Jarrad. He in 1989 took over from an oyster grower a licence from Lord Courtenay, the Lord of the Manor of Kenton, to grow oysters on a stretch of foreshore on the estuary of the river Exe in Devon. In seeking to renew the lease he discovered that the title to the area was disputed by the Crown Estate Commissioners. Indeed his lawyer found that the dispute had been unresolved for over 150 years and that when the South Devon Railway was built along that stretch of the coast by Brunel, the railway company, in order to get the land it needed without unacceptable delay, bought it from both parties to the dispute paying twice. Mr Jarrad eventually got his licence after the dispute had been settled on the steps of a law court. A further problem for David Jarrad is that there is no space on the coast for a shed, purification plant and holding tanks. He has therefore established these facilities at a farm three miles from the coast to which he transports sea water for his purifying and holding tanks in a tanker behind a tractor.

Crown lease or several order

The root of the difference between a several order and a lease from the Crown Estate Commissioners, which is not quite the same in Scotland as in England and Wales, is this. What the Crown owns (except where it has yielded rights to others) is the soil of the foreshore and the soil below the territorial waters, not the water above that soil, nor the fish in that water, nor the shellfish lying on the bottom (except for mussels and oysters in Scotland). If you want to attach anything to the bottom – a structure, a pipeline, a mooring or a trestle to carry oysters – you need the permission of the Crown Estate Commissioners and you must be ready to pay rent to them. A lease does no more than permit you to attach things to the bottom on the terms specified in it. A lease for shellfish farming does not stop the public right of fishery: the public may come and fish in the water above a leased bed. But the public are guilty of theft if they take oysters from any private bed 'if it is sufficiently marked out or sufficiently known as such'.[1]

Several and regulating orders forbid the public from fishing for oysters – or for whatever type of shellfish is specified in the order – in the area to which they apply. In other words, they are a means of locally suspending the public right of fishery with respect to oysters. The public is permitted to fish over the specified area only with line and hook, or with nets solely adapted to catching floating fish.[2] In England and Wales, several orders are needed by those who seek the exclusive right to conserve and gather native oysters on natural beds, except where there is an ancient title to a natural bed. For it follows from the fact that oysters of that type grow naturally on the seabed, that the public has the right to take them if there is not a several order – or a regulating order or an ancient title – to stop them.

In Scottish law the position is somewhat different. In Scotland the Crown owns for its own benefit not just the soil beneath the foreshore and the territorial waters but also oysters and mussels that lie in natural banks on that soil. In England the notion that natural oyster or mussel beds were part of the disposable property of the Crown was brought to an end by Magna Carta, which asserted the common right of fishery and stopped the monarch from enclosing the foreshore and territorial seabed for his or her personal use, or granting exclusive rights over it to anyone else. But this constraint on the rights of the Crown was never assimilated into the law of Scotland.

That native oysters and mussels on natural beds belong to the Crown in Scotland was ruled in a series of judgements in the Scottish courts, mostly in the 19th century. The disputes before the courts were over mussels, but it was held that oysters and mussels should be should be treated alike – and differently from other shellfish. The principal argument for treating them differently from other shellfish was that their conservation required that it should be possible for the Crown to put them into private ownership so as to safeguard them from unrestrained fishing by the public. But there was never agreement on the nature of the Crown's right to oysters and mussels. On one view it was part of the Crown's right to the soil below the foreshore and territorial seabed, since concentrated banks of immobile mussels and oysters amounted to part of that soil. On another view the Crown held the right of fishing for mussels and oysters.

The implications of this difference between English and Scottish law are not great. In Scotland today the Crown Estate Commissioners aim to control the collecting of oysters and mussels from natural beds in its ownership by means of collecting licences, and the farming of oysters on trestles or other structures by means of farming leases, as in England and Wales.

Since a several or regulating order from the Government is indispensable only for the purpose of getting exclusive rights in England and Wales to natural oyster beds (where no old private rights exist), and the procedure for getting either kind of order is costly and difficult, it is understandable that there are few of them. In 1993 there were 18 several orders and 3 regulating orders for oyster fisheries in England and Wales, none for oyster fisheries in Scotland where there is the alternative of the collecting licence from the Crown Estate.

The procedure for getting a fish farming lease from the Crown Estate Commissioners is not as expensive, formal and slow as the procedure for getting a several or regulating order, but it has become more formal for reasons that have largely to do with salmon farming. After the Crown Estate Commissioners had given many leases for salmon farming in the 1970's there were objections to the ugliness of the large numbers of rafts supporting netted enclosures for salmon, and there were objections to pollution attributed to salmon farming. In response, the Government declined to introduce new planning legislation. It went instead for an arrangement whereby the Crown Estate Commissioners introduced for Scotland a consultation and appraisal system and an advisory committee, consisting of representatives of the interested public bodies, to which contentious cases can be referred. The same approach to appraisal and consultation has been adopted in England and Wales, but there are so few applications that it has not yet been considered necessary to introduce an advisory committee. In England and Wales there are only 11 Crown Estate leases for shellfish farming, all for oysters, and one for fin fish farming. In Scotland there are 255 Crown Estate leases for shellfish farming, of which 80 are for oyster farming; and 284 leases for fin fish farming, mostly for salmon.

To sum up, in Britain the location of oyster farms is the result of individuals looking at possible sites and struggling, in the face of possible legal difficulties and public objections, to get a lease for the site that looks most promising; in France it is the result of decisions taken jointly by Government agencies in close consultation with the producers, which determine, in the face of any public objections, broadly where oyster farming will take place and on what scale; the would-be oyster farmer then applies, in the manner described in chapter 9, for a concession within that framework. To a Briton, the French oyster industry appears to be strategically planned, concentrated in places where it has intense, sometimes irritating, relations with the government. To a Frenchman the British industry looks market-driven yet constrained by an incomprehensible legacy of royal and private property rights; it appears to be lacking in Government guidance and support; altogether disorderly. At the heart of the tangle of property rights are the Crown Estate Commissioners, a body about which few Britons, let alone any foreigners, know anything. Nor is it easy to explain what it is.

In brief, the Crown Estate Commissioners run something akin to a property company which is entrusted with the curious task of managing for the benefit of the Treasury property that formally belongs to the Crown. A Frenchman might call it an anachronism, a misshapen product of centuries of wheeler-dealing between monarch and parliament, an institution typically British and totally devoid of logic. An Englishman is more likely to feel pride in the long ancestry and grand name of this inherited institution, to be amused by the strange deals that have shaped it over many centuries, and to be content that it works in its own way. It has a long history which, for the benefit of readers who may wish to know more, is described in Appendix B (page 185).

CHAPTER TWELVE

The impact of the single European market

THE INTRODUCTION OF the single European market has brought with it two important changes for the oyster industry, one that looks beneficial, one that looks as if it could be damaging, conceivably disastrous. The beneficial change is the introduction of new measures to prevent consumers being supplied with bad oysters. The potentially damaging change is the introduction of rules for the free movement of oysters around the single market for re-laying which have weakened our ability to stop our oyster beds being infected by imported oysters carrying diseases of the oyster. Since diseases of the oyster can have devastating effects, this risk is a matter of concern to all who are interested in the survival of oysters in this country.

The new hygiene regulations

The new hygiene regulations follow, with substantial modification, those developed in France. They are the outcome of several years of negotiation among the member nations of the European Community. The main argument was between those nations which saw little prospect of cleaning up their coastal waters in shellfish-producing areas and held that all shellfish should be put through a process of purification; and those, with France in the lead, which held that water should be graded and only where it was found that the water in a producing area was impure should purification or the transfer of oysters to cleaner water be required. The latter system was adopted. It provides a reward for clean water that is lacking in the first system.

The new regime was introduced by means of a directive of the Council of the European Commission to be enforced by national legislation.[1] The classification of waters is done by taking samples of molluscs from each production area and testing them for contamination with sewage bacteria. In Britain the job is done by local environmental health officers – the modern equivalent of public health officers – working for local authorities in co-operation with scientists from MAFF. The waters are put into four classes:

A – molluscs can be sent for direct human consumption;

B – they can be sent only after going through a purification plant or being re-laid in an approved clean water area or being heat treated (which oysters cannot be since they are usually eaten raw);

C – they must be re-laid for at least two months in clean water or be heat treated.

All other areas – harvesting prohibited. This applies to all areas where the water has not been tested, as well as to those where it has been found to be excessively dirty.

Further parts of the directive provide that all places where oysters are packed and handled as they are moved from the oyster bed to the consumer must conform to high standards of sanitation and cleanliness, and that each package of oysters must bear a durable waterproof health mark which shows the identity of the dispatch centre and the date on which the contents were wrapped. This health mark is a European version of the *étiquette sanitaire*, introduced in France more than 50 years ago (chapter 8).

In Britain it was always true that action from the centre – which until Brussels came along meant action in London – was needed if a single comprehensive system of monitoring and preventive action was to be introduced throughout the country. That required two things: the political will to take action, and a belief that it was the centre that should act. But in Britain direct action by the centre in matters such as public health, instead of being regarded as natural, as it is in France, has been regarded in Britain as a last resort, a form of 'intervention' that should be avoided if at all possible. The pre-1993 British shellfish regulations operated on precisely that basis. Local health officials had to chase after one another from one area to another reporting bad oysters and calling for investigation; the minister acted as an officer of last resort if there was an appeal to him. Only when oyster hygiene became a matter to be negotiated as part of the arrangements for the single market did London use its powers over local authorities to instruct them to apply a coherent preventive system to safeguard consumers from polluted oysters.

Under the new system local authority officers guided by the scientists from

MAFF do the sampling and analysis, and MAFF issues the resulting classification of producing areas. To smooth the introduction of the classification system, MAFF and the Department of Health encouraged local authorities to establish Shellfish Liaison Committees to coordinate the activities of adjacent authorities and keep in touch with local shellfishermen. These bodies, which in British style depend on voluntary cooperation and were created in response to a particular problem, not as part of a general design, have apparently worked well in some areas.

The results of the October 1993 classification for England and Wales, shown below, are rather bleak. The first column refers to all beds where any type of bivalve mollusc (cockle, mussel or oyster) is produced; the second to beds where oysters, and sometimes other bivalve molluscs as well, are produced:

	ALL MOLLUSCS	OYSTERS
A –	17	12
B –	94	40
C –	45	9
Unclassified	8	2
TOTAL	164	63

These results confirm the impression, which one gets from evidence about British beaches, that our coastal waters are often seriously polluted with sewage. That the 'all mollusc' beds are shown to be dirtier than the oyster beds is not surprising, or necessarily disturbing. Molluscs other than oysters are mostly cooked, and thereby purified, before being consumed.

The figures for oysters, with 9 out of 63 placed in category C (which requires that the oysters be re-laid in clean water for two months or heat treated) and two unclassified (which requires that harvesting be prohibited), are not pretty. One can reflect that it is not surprising that fear of illness has put British consumers off oysters; and, more cheerfully, that the new regulations should improve matters and permit one to eat oysters with the same confidence in Britain as in France, though it must be remembered that the French probably enjoy better immunity from poisoning than the British precisely because they eat so many more oysters and other shellfish. Moreoever a system has yet to be developed for testing oysters and other shellfish for the presence of viruses.

The fundamental solution to the problem of oyster hygiene is to stop pollution. Since in Britain we now have a National Rivers Authority and regional water companies, the organisations that are required for a systematic attack on the problem are in place: at last we have something like the organisational structure that was called for at the beginning of the century. Added to which we have the EU, which has been setting European standards for the cleanliness of beaches and concerning itself with other aspects of pollution. But the government, for economic reasons, is not rushing to enforce those standards. Moreover we still lack in Britain any mechanism for selecting areas for shellfish farming and ensuring that in those areas the water is clean and that the other conditions for oyster farming are satisfied, in particular that leases are available.

The regulation of oyster movements

Under the pre-January 1993 regime for regulating the movement of oysters so as to keep out oyster disease, the government had the power to prohibit, by ministerial order, the deposit of shellfish and the importation of shellfish from abroad. The entire coast was divided into areas according to the prevalence and intensity of major pests and diseases, and the deposit in any area of molluscan shellfish taken from outside that area was forbidden unless a licence had been obtained. There were two types of licence, general licences which permitted the deposit of molluscs anywhere within the area from which they were taken and between areas with similar types and levels of infestation; and special licences which were required if molluscs from an infested area were to be deposited in an area that was less infested or free of infestation. As we have seen in chapter 10, action was taken under these regulations sufficiently quickly and effectively to delay greatly the spread in Britain of *bonamia* and *marteilia*, the two diseases that have done so much damage to the native oyster.

There are three elements to the new European system. First, oysters going directly for consumption (without re-laying or temporary immersion) may be moved without restraint within the single market, provided they show no signs of disease and do not come from an oyster farm that has been closed for animal health reasons. Second, imports of oysters from outside the single market are all regulated regardless of whether they are going directly for consumption or are to be re-laid. Thirdly, there are rules governing the movement of oysters within the single market for re-laying. These are the most sensitive part of the regime, for when oysters are re-laid in the water they are very likely to pass on any diseases or parasites they carry.

The core of the new rules governing re-laying is a list of diseases of oysters arrived at by negotiation. Oysters that are certified to have come from areas that are free of the listed diseases may be moved freely for re-laying within the single market; the internal movement for re-laying of all other oysters is restricted. This is not very different from the old British system. But for the new system to be effective in stopping the spread of oyster disease, two conditions need to be satisfied: all the national authorities enforcing the system must be competent and reliable; and secondly, the list of diseases must be comprehensive and flexible; it must be possible to amend the list quickly or to impose temporary restrictions when there are reasonable grounds for thinking a new disease may be present. There are grounds for concern over both these requirements.

As regards the first, there is good reason to believe that when the new regime came into force at the beginning of 1993 the newer and poorer members of the single market did not all possess the technical and administrative facilities, or the experience, required to operate the new regime effectively. How long it will take them to come up to scratch it is hard to say.

As regards the second requirement – a comprehensive and flexible list – only *bonamia* and *marteilia*, the two major diseases of the native oyster, have been put on the list. Nothing has been done to deal with the risk that a new disease may be the cause of the slow growth and high mortalities of Pacific oysters in the south-west of France. On the contrary, just after the new regime came into force in January 1993 the French pushed through an amendment to allow Pacific oysters for re-laying to be moved freely to all areas, including those, mostly in the British Isles, that are still free of the two listed diseases. The interest of the French growers, suffering from an excess population of feeble, possibly diseased, Pacific oysters was to be able to export them for re-laying in rich clean waters where they might recover and fatten. The British Isles, in particular Ireland and Scotland, have lots of water that is very attractive for that purpose.

The argument used for allowing the free movement of Pacific oysters for re-laying was that the Pacific oyster does not itself suffer or carry the two listed diseases, *bonamia* and *marteilia*. To deal with the risk that a consignment of Pacific oysters may accidentally include infected native oysters, or may include Pacific oysters that bear the infected spat of native oysters attached to their shells, it was agreed that each consignment must be accompanied by a document from the inspecting service of the country from which the oysters are sent. The document must certify that the consignment does not contain species other than Pacific oysters.

Almost immediately there was trouble. Within a week of the amendment being passed, a lorry load of half-grown Pacific oysters was sent for re-laying from France to Ireland where it was found upon close examination that about 1 per cent of the oysters had the spat of native oysters on them.[2] Since then steps have been taken to improve the inspection of consignments of Pacific oysters for re-laying to see if they include native oysters or other molluscs that could carry infection. French oysters have continued to be re-laid in Irish waters; and it has been reported that at one place Pacific oysters belonging to a local enterprise that were growing well have ceased to grow properly and have been suffering high mortalities since oysters from France were put in the water nearby.

The possibility that a disease of the Pacific oyster has been brought into Ireland is disquieting. But it is important not to be alarmist. In September 1994, well after the news of the problems in Ireland, it was reported that no disease had yet been identified by the French scientists who have been watching the retarded growth and rising mortalities amongst the Pacific oysters on the southern Atlantic coast and have been testing oysters from that area for disease.[3] Meanwhile the Shellfish Association of Great Britain has advised its members against taking in imported oysters for re-laying. This seems an eminently reasonable action, but one is bound to ask whether it is sufficient. You cannot rely on everyone to respond to a call for voluntary action. Moreover the French have the right within the European Union to get over this kind of embargo by leasing oyster farms in Britain, if they can get over the difficulties described in the last chapter that face anyone trying to get an oyster lease here.

It is not the case that there is a simple conflict of interests between the French producers unanimously backing the free movement of oysters for re-laying and the producers of other countries afraid of admitting French oysters. The French oyster producers have themselves been opposing the importation of oysters into France for re-laying on the grounds that they may bring disease;[4] and within France there is concern about the possible spread of disease from one area to another. Rather, it is a general problem: the long run interests of producers and consumers in all countries within the EU, including France, may be put at risk by the short-sighted pursuit of their short-run interests by producers in one area; that area now happens to be in France, but it is the kind of behaviour that could occur in any country and with respect to many kinds of produce.

The fundamental problem with the new system is that agreement to put a new disease on the list is likely to be reached only when there is conclusive evidence of its presence, including its identification, which may take a long time, or may never be achieved. Meanwhile the disease may have spread far and wide. What is needed is that precautionary restrictions should be imposed when there is reasonable suspicion of disease. That is unlikely to be achieved by international agreement. For, even if there is international agreement in favour of precautionary restrictions, it is likely that, when it comes to any particular case, the negotiators of one or a few countries, instructed to represent the short-sighted interests of their producers, will obstruct action until it is too late. Only national precautionary action, for a period sufficient to allow scientific investigations to be carried to a conclusion, can be relied upon to be effective.

The normal objection to allowing the national imposition of trade restrictions for precautionary reasons is that the restrictions will be used by governments to give economic protection to their domestic producers. But in the present case there is no question of interfering with the free movement of oysters for consumption: there are no good grounds for challenging that part of the new single market regime. It is only the movement of oysters for re-laying that is at issue. The economic benefits of the free movement of Pacific oysters for re-laying within the single market need to be weighed against its probable long-run costs. Now that we have fast refrigerated lorries, there cannot be much need, if any, for oysters that are carried from one point to another in the single market for consumption to be re-laid so that they may recover from their journey before being offered to consumers. Moreover the need to transport stocks of Pacific oysters for breeding has been reduced or removed by the advent of hatcheries. What remains and is at issue is the benefit of being able to take growing Pacific oysters from areas where their numbers are excessive in relation to the mass of water to areas where there are surplus waters in relation to the stock of oysters, remembering that there is the alternative of increasing production in the clean waters by introducing hatchery spat or spat from clean waters. The French fear that if national precautionary action is allowed, limitations on the movement of shellfish for relaying will be unstoppable and damaging.

A great deal is at stake. The Portuguese oyster survives only in Portugal. The European native oyster survives healthily only in a few disease-free places in Europe. If a third species of oyster, the Pacific, is wiped out by disease, it is not clear what future, if any, the oyster industry will have. There are other species in the world – the American *Crassostrea virginica* and perhaps the Sydney rock oyster – but it is far from clear whether and how quickly production of these could safely be developed in Europe; and if hasty and uncontrolled importation took place again, for which there would surely be pressure in France from their powerful population of oyster growers who would once again be in financial distress, a new species farmed at high densities might soon be lost to disease.

When confronted by this problem it is natural to think about the measures that are used to prevent the spread of disease amongst farm animals, for example, foot and mouth disease. But it soon becomes apparent that the spread of disease in farm animals is easy to check compared with disease in shellfish. Farm animals are kept fenced in; germs do not travel far if modest precautions are taken; a herd can easily be counted and destroyed, and the owner compensated. In the case of oysters, infection travels though the water; and in waters where a species breeds naturally, for example, the native oyster in England or the Pacific oyster in the warmer parts of the French coast, oysters will be dispersed all over the place; you can scarcely hope to gather in an infected population and destroy it. The only feasible method of stopping the spread of disease is to regulate movement between large areas of different disease status. That was how the old British system worked and it is the element in the new European system that needs to be reinforced.

CHAPTER THIRTEEN

Conclusion

WHAT HAPPENED TO the oyster in Britain and France is an example of the problem of conserving exhaustible species in the face of the advance of population, industry and technology. It is a problem that is now attracting attention around the world. Pressure groups campaign for the protection of particular species; public concern for conservation of the environment, including natural resources, has become a significant force in national and international politics; and theoretical economists have been considering what is the optimum rate at which exhaustible resources should be exploited.[1] But these developments, which are still of uncertain political efficacy, are recent. The great decline of the oyster in Britain took place in an earlier and more ignorant world.

The oyster has suffered all the possible afflictions that man can impose on an exhaustible species: over-fishing; poisoning by industrial pollution and anti-fouling paint; contamination by sewage; the spread of oyster disease as improvements in transport have permitted the rapid movement over longer and longer distances of oysters to be re-laid in local waters; and also the spread, in the same manner, of predators and competitors of the oyster.

The things that can be done, and in some measure are now being done, to counter these afflictions have always been rather obvious. Overfishing can be restrained by government regulations or by the transfer of public beds to private owners (who can be expected to have a financial interest in conserving a breeding stock). Industrial pollution can be restrained by regulation or by taxation. The transmission of diseases and pests from area to area can, with luck, be checked by quarantine measures. What matters is whether politicians decide to take action along these lines and whether there is a system of public administration attuned to the planning and execution of such action. And that is where Britain, as we have seen, differs most strikingly from France. The difference in the physical climates of the two countries might have meant that measures to conserve the oyster would have been slower to produce results in Britain than in France, but physical climate alone cannot explain the difference between what has happened to the oyster in Britain and France. In the pristine era before the industrial revolution and the coming of the railway, oysters were as abundant in Britain as in France, and they were subject to the same kind of cycles. One must look to other explanations.

In France the oyster is seen as a part of French life, an asset which in the national interest must be safeguarded. The first explanation for this that comes to mind is that the French, unlike us, take food seriously. But that is only a part of the story. At least as important is the tradition of economic government derived from Colbert according to which it is the task of the government, for the sake of the strength of the nation, to create and foster industry, agriculture and other economic activities, and to help them when they are in difficulty. That approach was applied to the economic development of France, where the government took the lead in providing scientific and technical education, building railways and roads, creating banks and fostering industrialistion. And it lives on. To this day it is taken for granted in France that the government should act effectively when a part of the French national economy is threatened by foreign competition or is in trouble of other kinds. Invoking this belief, French farmers and fishermen – and, as we have seen, oyster farmers – become rebellious in a manner quite alien to their English counterparts when their livelihood is threatened by competition or by changes in regulations.

As regards internal public administration, the outstanding feature of France is that the structure of internal government and the legal system, including the ownership of the foreshore, are coherent and that power is centralised. This has been important to the history of the oyster. Detailed decrees can be laid down in Paris and sent down, through the imperial system of internal government that was codified by Napoleon, to be enforced with some discretion by the prefect of each locality. It was in this political setting that Coste persuaded Napoleon III that action was needed to save and restore the breeding stock of oysters in France, that Napoleon III ordered that what Coste recommended should be done, that the community of oyster growers was preserved, supported, modernised and given formal links with the Government, and that the oyster growers became a well organised and vocal force in their respective regions.

Britain is very different. When in the middle of the 19th century there was evidence here of an oyster shortage and political concern about it, the old, and admittedly not very effective, tradition of sending orders through the Admiralty that fishing should be restricted was gone. Parliament ruled; the industrial revolution had made Britain the leading industrial nation in the world – though other nations were catching up rapidly; the thinking of the government, and of the Royal Commission and the Select Committees that considered the oyster question, was dominated by the idea that the government should not act to preserve the oyster – to do so would be to interfere with the principles of *laissez-faire* and upset the processes of competition. That the British do not take food as seriously as the French is no doubt one reason for this refusal to act to preserve the oyster. But as we have seen, the dominant reason was that, in the aftermath of the political battle over the reform of the Corn Laws, *laissez-faire* was embraced by its supporters as an absolute dogma; the common sense idea of taking steps to save the breeding stock of oysters was treated as heresy.

It is also true that the system of internal government in Britain is very different from that in France. In Britain, modern local government was established by evolution and compromise; the structure of authority is not logically defined; and local autonomy, at least until the recent intrusions by London and Brussels, has been much greater than in France. For this reason, British governments might have found it difficult to take effective action to support the oyster had they wanted to do so. But for the most part our governments have not wanted to act.

The muddled way in which the ownership and management of the foreshore and seabed were shunted between the Crown Estate and the Government is another example of how the evolution of British institutions has not been helpful to the oyster growers, or to the preservation of the oyster, compared with what happened in France – though that is a high standard of comparison, and the position in Britain is now better than it was.

The post-war period

During and after the second world war adherence to *laissez-faire* was displaced by belief in economic planning, but by that time the decline in the production and consumption of oysters had gone so far in Britain that the oyster, regarded as a luxury in an age of austerity, was not on the economic and political agenda. Nevertheless important things were done for the oyster, principally through the expansion of the work of the MAFF research laboratories. Their most visible achievement has been the introduction into Britain of the hatchery breeding of Pacific oysters, but they have also done a great deal both by way of research and advice to growers, and by providing advice to the government on policy and helping in the enforcement of regulations. If the prospect for oyster production in Britain has been markedly improved by action of any kind by British governments, it has been through the work of the MAFF fisheries laboratories and the accident that in 1949 the Crown Estate gained, and subsequently has exercised, the power to grant leases for oyster-growing on the foreshore. Of the two bits of European legislation that have recently come into force, the laws relating to the hygiene of oysters look beneficial: they should increase the confidence of consumers. But the laws relating to the movement of oysters for re-laying look dangerous since, as they stand, they increase the risk that pests and diseases of the oyster, which have already caused so much damage, will be spread rather than contained.

As for the future, the nature of the oyster problem has been substantially changed by scientific and political developments. On the scientific side, any kind of oyster, for example the Pacific, that can be successfully grown from hatchery spat is no longer an exhaustible species in the same sense as before. For, with hatcheries, the supply of young oysters ceases to depend directly on the preservation of a large natural breeding stock of oysters on the foreshore and seabed, and comes to depend in the first place on the preservation of a small brood stock at hatcheries, backed by a variety of breeding lines if it is to retain vitality and the oyster population is not to be excessively vulnerable to a single disease. Advances in genetics and genetic engineering are opening up new possibilities for the oyster, as they are for other species. For example, French scientists are at work trying to develop a type of native oyster that is immune to bonamia; the MAFF laboratories are working on the development of a modified and improved strain of Pacific oyster.

On the political side, policy making is becoming more international. This is partly because we are members of the EU, and partly because international action is increasingly needed to deal with the problems of controlling the spread of diseases, predators and competitors of the oyster, including the risks associated with the introduction of new species of oysters. Such action often needs to be taken on a global rather than just an European scale. The necessary international institutions exist in the form of the EU and the The International Council for the Exploration of the Sea. What should concern British producers and consumers of oysters is that the Government should represent their interests effectively. The oyster producers have a good apparatus, in the form of the Shellfish Association of Great Britain, for communicating their views to MAFF; and the ministry gets advice on policy from the scientists at its laboratories. Compared with France, there is no evidence that technical appraisal of what needs to be done is lacking. Rather, the weakness of Britain is that our governments may generally be less forceful than the French at getting their way in international negotiations, added to which the oyster stands less high in the political consciouness of our officials and ministers than in the political consciousness of their French counterparts. The potential for a revival of the oyster in Britain is not yet appreciated.

There are many things that could be done in Britain without international cooperation. To bring consumers back to the oyster a marketing effort is required that provides the public with information about oysters, about their merits today and about how to approach them. And it requires that the industry should concern itself, and be seen by the public to concern itself, with the quality of oysters, seeking higher standards and inviting the public to take part in judging standards. In such a fragmented industry these things are not likely to be achieved unless there is some collective action. The kind of steps that might both improve standards within the industry and serve to rouse the interest and confidence of consumers are the production of good information leaflets for fishmongers, restaurants and households telling them how to judge and handle oysters and serve them; the introduction of a standard classification system for oysters; and the introduction of oyster tastings organised by the industry. On the production side, it would be a blessing if the tangle of institutions which decide these matters could introduce a more coherent policy for coastal usage so that part or parts of the coast were allocated exclusively to the production of oysters and other shellfish. If that were done, there might develop one or more concentrated areas of production where skills, training, research, marketing and other ancillary facilities were developed profitably, where, in other words, the potential external and internal economies of scale were exploited.

There is scope for Anglo-French cooperation in producing a revival of oyster production in Britain. We have under-utilised clean waters; they have expertise and experience. Is the idea of a colony of French oyster growers in Scotland, using local hatchery-bred spat too fanciful? Or the idea of establishing in Britain one or more courses in oyster culture based on the French model and with French experts on the staff? Today there is very little contact between the oyster growers of the two countries. The civil servants and scientists meet at international gatherings, but the growers of the two countries live in different worlds, knowing little about each other, each afraid of diseases or competition emanating from the other country. It is high time there were meetings between them at which common interests and cooperation were discussed.

The classification and labelling of Pacific oysters (Huîtres creuses) *in France*

Three variables are employed: the unopened weight of the oysters; the relationship of the weight of the flesh of the oysters to their unopened weight; and whether they have been fattened in *claires*.
The categorisation by weight is as follows:

Description	Number	Weight in grams	
		Normally	*Huîtres speciales de claires*
Très Grosses	1	110 and above	120 and above
Grosses	2	80 to 109	90 to 119
Moyennes	3	65 to 79	75 to 89
Moyennes	4	50 to 64	60 to 74
Petites	5	40 to 49	50 to 59
Petites	6	30 to 39	

Often only the number is given. When the descriptions (*Petites* etc.) are used, the sub-division into the smaller numerical categories may be omitted: *Petites* then means 30 to 49 and *Moyennes* means 50 to 79. In the case of *Huîtres spéciales de claires*, the type which, as explained below, has been fattened to the maximum, the categories, as shown above, are 10 grams heavier than for all other Pacific oysters.

As regards quality (*qualité*), meaning the relationship between the weight of flesh in an oyster and the unopened weight of that oyster, oysters for which the relationship is in the range 6.5 to 9.0 per cent are classified as *fines*; those for which the figure is more than 9.0 are classified *spéciales*. Other oysters, i.e. those below 6.5, are unclassified as regards quality.

Oysters that have been fattened in *claires* come in two categories according to the duration of their immersion in *claires* and the density with which the *claires* have been filled with oysters. (The lower the density the greater the supply of nutrients for each oyster.) Their quality (flesh weight to crude weight) is also taken into account. The precise rules are as follows:

Huîtres fines de claires must have been immersed in *claires* for a minimum of one month at a maximum density of 20 oysters per square metre, and the quality index (flesh weight to unopened weight) must be in the range 6.5 and 9.0.

Huîtres spéciales de claires must have been immersed in *claires* for a minimum of two months at a maximum density of 10 oysters per square metre, and the quality index must be greater than 9.0.

The French regulations lay down the size of samples to be taken for the purpose of classifying oysters by weight and what margins of tolerance are allowed. They also specify precisely how oysters are to be measured for quality. Twenty oysters are to be taken from a batch as a sample; they are to be weighed to the nearest gram; they are to be opened; the flesh is to be removed, leaving none behind, and placed on an absorbant paper; when the flesh of all 20 oysters has been placed on the paper, another absorbant paper is to be placed on top and the oysters are to be left for five minutes while water is absorbed. Then the flesh is to be weighed and that weight, multiplied by 100 is to be divided by the unopened weight.[1]

APPENDIX B

The history of the Crown Estate and the management of the foreshore

The general history

The King is deemed to have had the ultimate title to all the land in the realm after the Norman conquest, but part of it was immediately yielded to men whose support he needed; in the following centuries Crown land was sold, often to pay for wars, or given away by the monarch to persons he or she wished to reward; and then, during the period of commonwealth, further Crown land was irreversibly lost, with the result that at the restoration of the monarchy in 1660 little Crown land remained to provide the monarch with an income. In particular, knight tenure was abolished, a step of considerable social and financial importance:

> The military tenure had originally been created as a means of national defence. But in the course of ages whatever was useful in the institution had disappeared; and nothing was left but ceremonies and grievances. A landed proprietor who held an estate under the Crown by knight service – and it was thus that most of the soil of England was held – had to pay a large fine on coming to his property. He could not alienate an acre without purchasing a licence. When he died, if his domains descended to an infant, the sovereign was guardian, and was not only entitled to great part of the rents during the minority, but could require the ward, under heavy penalties, to marry a person of suitable rank. The chief bait which attracted a needy sycophant to the court was the hope of obtaining, as the reward for servility and flattery, a royal letter to an heiress. These abuses had perished with the monarchy. That they should not revive with

it was the wish of every landed gentleman of the kingdom. They were, therefore, solemnly abolished by statute; and no relic of the ancient tenures in chivalry was suffered to remain, except those honorary services which are still, at a coronation, rendered to the person of the sovereign by some lords of manors.[1]

To support Charles II after this loss of royal land, parliament in 1660 for the first time provided an income to the monarch, but it was not adequate, particularly in the face of the Dutch War of 1667. He therefore disposed of more Crown land, and so later did William III when he needed to reward those who had helped him to the throne. Parliament objected to these practices, for they meant that the monarch augmented his spending by depleting the assets of his successors and so enlarged the claims that the successors would make on Parliament. This difference between parliament and the monarch was resolved slowly in several steps. In 1698 parliament granted William III a fixed income for the support of his household to be financed from customs and excise duties and from the 'hereditary revenues', which included the profit from the Crown lands. Then in 1702, by which time there had been so many sales and grants that income from the Crown estates was down to £6,000 a year, an Act was passed on the accession of Queen Anne which stopped the sovereign freely disposing of land; henceforth it was to be let only for limited periods and at commercial rents.

The next important change came in 1760 when George III came to the throne. This time a tight grip was taken on the Crown lands: the king surrendered to the Exchequer for his lifetime the income from the royal lands and received in exchange a fixed civil list. Since then all our monarchs have committed themselves to this contract to the point where it 'may now be reckoned among those constitutional conventions that it would be very hard to discontinue'.[2]

But there were two exceptions to this surrender of royal wealth which are relevant to oyster concessions today. George III did not surrender the Duchies of Cornwall or Lancaster, nor has any succeeding sovereign done so. In consequence, it is to these duchies that application must be made for concessions on the coasts of the west country and Lancashire, except where there are manorial titles or where the duchies have yielded or leased their rights to others who can sub-let.

While the basic contract between sovereign and parliament has remained unchallenged until today, the way in which the royal lands are managed has been changed many times.

Management of the Crown Estate

As part of the reforms of the machinery of government at the end of the eighteenth century, the royal lands were completely surveyed and a board was established to manage the estate, entitled 'The Commission of Woods, Forests and Land Revenues'. This board employed John Nash as architect and commissioned him to plan the creation of Regent's Park and the surrounding terraces on an area belonging to the Crown on which the leases were falling in, and also to plan Regent Street, a new thoroughfare to connect Regent's Park to Westminster and Whitehall. This early development, financed by loans, is rightly acclaimed as the greatest achievement of the managers of the royal lands. It produced one the most handsome areas of London, now of great value.

At first the board consisted of three commissioners, a minister and two permanent officials. In 1832 responsibility for works and public buildings was merged with responsibility for royal lands, but in 1851 the two were separated again; responsibility for royal palaces and public buildings was placed in a separate works department with a parliamentary spokesman; responsibility for the royal lands was entrusted to the Commissioners of Her Majesty's Wood, Forest and Land Revenues. The commissioners, of whom there were two, were both officials.

The essential task of this second body – to manage the revenue-earning Crown lands – has not changed since 1851. What has changed is who manages the Crown lands, how far ministers tell them what to do, and what they are called. Their name has been changed twice, first to Commissioners of Crown Lands and then to Crown Estate Commissioners.

In 1906 the Liberal government, 'anxious to further its declared policy of multiplying small-holdings',[3] put the minister responsible for agriculture on the board, which subsequently consisted of him and one official. In 1943 the Secretary of State for Scotland was added by the war-time coalition government. It is not clear what influence, if any, these ministers had upon the investment and management policy of the board. But in the 1950's there was a scandal, the Crichel Down case. Some land in Dorset, having been appropriated as a bombing range by the Air Ministry before the second world war, was no longer needed by the military; it was let by the Commissioners of Crown Lands to a farmer without the original owner being given a chance to get it back; there was an outcry, followed by an enquiry in which some civil servants were severely criticised; the Minister of Agriculture, Sir William Dugdale, to whom the civil servants were responsible, followed the honourable but now breached tradition that ministers should assume responsibility for the actions of their civil servants and resigned.

After this episode there was a public enquiry into the best way to manage the Crown lands in the mid-20th century. Its report was forthright:

> The Commissioners of Crown Lands do not meet and take decisions as a Commission. Since 1906, Ministers of Agriculture have taken a particular interest as Commissioners in the administration of the agricultural estates in England and Wales. Since 1943, Secretaries of State for Scotland have performed a similar service for the Scottish estates. These benefits are however outweighed by the artificiality of a Commission which includes two Ministers and an official, and by the risk of using, or even appearing to use, trust moneys to further government policy. The duties of a Minister of Agriculture may conflict with the duties of a trustee for the Crown agricultural estates. This we think has caused difficulty, and few Ministers of Agriculture have been, as such, particularly interested in the urban properties. In practice, the Permanent Commissioner (appointed from within the civil service) heads a small government department for which the two Ministers are responsible to Parliament. He seeks the approval of one or other of the Ministers at his discretion but is 'out on a limb' with a wide and lonely responsibility. For many purposes, he is his own chairman, management board, general manager and finance officer.[4]

The committee of enquiry proposed an arrangement designed to reconcile the lingering title of the sovereign, the need for public control, and the objective of political independence, a solution singularly British:

> We therefore recommend a new statutory board of trustees, to be known perhaps as the 'Crown Estate Trustees'. The relations of the board with the Sovereign as owner of the estate, and with the immediate advisers of the Sovereign, would naturally remain, as now, close and not on a formal basis. We should expect one of the principal duties of its chairman to be to seek the Sovereign's consent on such matters as the more important capital transactions and the administration of the Windsor estate.
>
> The board should be a public authority, but not a government department in the sense of an organ of executive government. ....We appreciate and endorse the need for trustees to be independent.

Parliament are however entitled to the whole surplus income during one reign. ...There must therefore be powers to ensure the possibility of control at least over policy and major matters of management. A specified Minister of the Crown should have power to give directions (whether general or specific) to the board, the Treasury should have a power of control over staffing and expenditure, the administrative head of the office should be accounting officer for the board's accounts and should appear before the Public Accounts Committee, the Comptroller and Auditor General should audit the accounts, and the board should be required to submit an annual report and accounts to Parliament.

The extent to which the powers of control are used must be for the decision of the Government and Parliament. We do however respectfully advise that the board should be more, not less, independent than the present Commissioners and that they should be given defined powers and duties as trustees and allowed to work them out with the minimum of direction or control.[5]

In an admirably succinct summary of its findings at the end of the report, the following propositions were put forward with reference to the anomalous constitutional position that was being proposed for the new body :

The rights of the Sovereign and of Parliament should be secured.
The board should enjoy a substantial measure of independence as trustees.
They should be protected from any suspicion of subsidising government expenditure.
The statutory requirements about the size and composition of the board should not be too precise and detailed.
The responsible Minister should not have a special interest as Minister in the use or control of land.
The general duties of the board should be written into statute.[6]

The committee's recommendations were adopted with minor changes, such as the adoption of the title 'Crown Estate Commissioners' rather than 'Crown Estate Trustees', and were initially implemented in the Crown Estate Act 1956.

Parliament gave powers of direction over the new board to two ministers. At first, these were the Lord Privy Seal and the Secretary of State for Scotland, but a few years later the Chancellor of the Exchequer replaced the Lord Privy

Seal. It appears that at first they were able to stand back. The official history published in 1960 tells us that, while the ministers are 'naturally kept acquainted with what the Commissioners are doing, it has not yet been found necessary to exercise the "powers of direction" conferred upon them'.[7]

After the new Commissioners had gained some experience of their job and its problems, a second Crown Estate Act was passed in 1961 which released them from some old constraints on their freedom of action and laid down their general statutory duty as follows:

> It shall be the general duty of the Commissioners, while maintaining the Crown Estate as an estate in land (with such proportion of cash or investments as seems to them to be required for the discharge of their functions) to maintain and enhance its value and the return obtained from it, but with due regard to the requirements of good management.[8]

The injunction in the last clause is as economical as the injunction applied to new Fellows of Trinity College, Cambridge, upon their admission. They are required to promise loyally to observe the 'good customs of the College' which are nowhere defined. It is not a bad formula for making people behave themselves.

Under the new regime, the management of the estates seems generally to have gone well. The estate was valued at £1.7 billion in 1993, having been worth about £2.5 billion at the height of the property boom. The restoration of the terraces round Regent's Park has resurrected an island of beauty which in some measure offsets the uglification of so much of the rest of London; and, whether one likes it or not, the fact that the estate has the anomalous status of belonging to the Crown while its income goes to the Exchequer must have protected it from privatisation. It is hard to believe that this accumulation of marketable real estate would not have been put up for sale in recent years if it had belonged outright to the government.

The management of the foreshore

How the management of the foreshore came to be transferred to the government in 1866 and then back to the Commissioners of Crown Lands in 1949 is a story of decisions made upon administrative grounds of which Parliament was scarcely made aware; little of the story is to be found in the published records of government; the foreshore seems to have been so valueless and unimportant, an open domain where everyone enjoyed the public right of fishing and disposed of their effluents and rubbish, that no one seems to have cared what happened to it.

The case for the first transfer was made in a letter to the Treasury on 28 December 1865 from Mr Farrer, the permanent secretary of the Board of Trade whose mastery of the problems of the foreshore and oyster fisheries was displayed in his evidence to the Select Committee of 1876. He said that the Office of Woods, responsible for the Crown lands, had granted some land in Harwich harbour to a railway company for the building of a pier; the pier might interfere with navigation for the protection of which the Board of Trade was responsible; but the Board of Trade had not been consulted. It appeared to the Board of Trade that the Treasury should consider whether the anomaly of having two departments of state with different objectives concerned with the foreshore should not be put an end to. If the whole management of the Crown's rights and duties with respect to the foreshore could be placed in the hands of the Board of Trade there would be the following advantages:

1st. Persons seeking to construct works upon the foreshore would have to seek the assent of one, instead of two departments. Considering the expense of plans and the trouble of dealing with two offices, each having a different object in view, this advantage would be considerable.

2nd. The department charged with the duty of protecting navigation would, through the medium of a legal title to the soil in cases where that title is vested in the Crown, be furnished with powers enabling it to perform that duty much more efficiently than it can at present perform it, with its very inadequate powers.

3rd. The Board of Trade possesses in the officers of Customs and of the Coast Guard a more efficient machinery for watching the foreshore than is at the disposal of the Office of Woods, and in dealing with the Crown's rights to wreck it already has in its possession much information which would be of value in dealing with questions affecting the foreshore.

4th. Double management of the Crown's rights and conflict of jurisdiction of two departments would be avoided.

On the other hand it is not improbable that if the Board of Trade are empowered to deal with the foreshore with a view to the public interest generally, the revenue derived from it by them may be less than that derived from it by a department whose sole duty is to treat it as property.[9]

The Commissioners of Woods, consulted by the Treasury, wrote on 1 February

1866 saying that since they had difficulty in managing the foreshore, they would be glad to hand it over to the Board of Trade, if compensation was paid. In this connection, they reminded the Treasury that it had recently told the Commissioners that it was their duty to assert their rights of property for the benefit of the public 'and for the protection of the interests of the Sovereign in reversion', which seems to imply that the Treasury still entertained the notion that the monarch might claim back the Crown lands. But perhaps the reference to the reversion of the property to the Crown was only a ritual formula.

On 14 February 1866, only six weeks after the Board of Trade had written to the Treasury proposing the transfer, the Secretary to the Treasury wrote saying that the Lords Commissioners of Her Majesty's Treasury agreed with the proposal and that a Bill should be prepared in communication with the Commissioners of Woods. From the remarkable speed with which the decision was reached and the harmony between the views of the Board of Trade and the Commissioners of Woods it is reasonable to suppose that the two sides had agreed in advance, probably over lunch, what should be done. The wheels of government work smoothly when oiled by creative collusion.

The transfer was put to Parliament as one of a miscellany of tidying-up measures to do with the Crown lands. It is remarkable that in introducing the transfer the Chancellor of the Exchequer did not rely on the internal arguments on which the decision had been based, namely the arguments of the Board of Trade and the Commissioners of Woods concerning the problems caused by having two departments dealing with the foreshore. He said instead that it was a way of ensuring that the Crown was no longer involved in quarrels with local people over the ownership of the foreshore. His words were these:

> The third Resolution... was prepared with reference to the foreshores, which formed a subject of discussion and of conflicting claims between the Crown and local parties. In the opinion of the Government the purchase of these rights would be a great advantage, and as the Crown estates owed a very large sum to the public, they thought a convenient method of making the purchase would be by a deduction from the amount of the debt so owing. It was also their opinion that the management of the foreshores might be more properly placed in the hands of the Board of Trade, and it would therefore be transferred from the Commissioners of Crown Lands to that Board.[10]

The sum of £496,000, arrived at by two arbitrators after lengthy investigations, was paid by the Government for the transfer of the foreshore. It was met by the cancellation of debt owed by the Commissioners of Woods, who then ran the Crown Estate, to the Exchequer.[11] This seems to have been debt incurred in financing the development of Regent's Park.

In December 1866, after the foreshore had been transferred to the Board of Trade, Mr Farrer listed the tasks he saw for the Board of Trade to perform as managers of the foreshore. These were four: first, to find out where the Crown had parted with its rights to the foreshore, where it had not done so, and where the matter was in doubt; secondly, to prevent encroachments on the foreshore; thirdly, to watch Bills that may affect the foreshore; and fourthly to sell or lease the soil of the foreshore when it is expedient to do so.

Later in the memorandum Mr Farrer refers to the possibility of granting licences to oyster and mussel fisheries, in which case a small royalty might be taken on the produce; and he notes that like the Office of Woods, whose rules they had inherited, the Board of Trade must not part with land at less than its true value.[12] By this time the Royal Commission on Sea Fisheries had reported and its recommendations had been accepted by the Government.

The return of the foreshore

The foreshore was handed back to the Commissioners of Crown Lands in 1949 by the post-war Labour administration. The government department making the transfer was the Ministry of Transport which had inherited responsibility for the foreshore from the Ministry of Shipping, to which it had been transferred from the Board of Trade in 1939. The minutes of a meeting held at the Treasury in April 1946 record that the Ministry of Transport had asked to be relieved of responsibility for protection of the coast from erosion by the sea, which had apparently become a potentially tiresome and costly problem; at the same time they wanted to be relieved of foreshore administration which no longer fitted in with the ministry's work.[13] It was recommended that the management of the Crown foreshore should be restored to the Commissioners of Crown Lands and that until the necessary legislation could be passed the Commissioners should be asked to manage it on an agency basis for the Ministry of Transport.

The transfer to the Commissioners of Crown Lands was enacted as part of the Coast Protection Act 1949. In introducing the Bill to Parliament, the spokesman for the Government gave no explanation why the foreshore was now to be transferred to the Commissioners of Crown Lands; a member said he did not think the transfer was contentious. Beyond that, nothing was said about the transfer as the Bill went through Parliament. The attention of the legislators was focused on such matters as the problems of coastal erosion in particular areas, the powers of the local authorities, and the extent to which the central government should provide funds for protective works. Nothing was paid by the Commissioners of Crown Lands for the return of the foreshore. It seems to have been regarded as valueless.

Nor was much attention paid to the foreshore in 1956 and 1961 when, after the Crichel Down affair, the two bills were introduced which laid down the constitution and tasks of the new Crown Estate Commissioners. In 1956, Mr Mitchison for the Labour party said that the management of the foreshore should be put into the hands of the local authorities. He argued that its management by the Crown was an absurd anachronism which produced objectionable results, of which he cited two, both rather idiosyncratic: the public, he said, had a common law right to go fishing on the foreshore but not swimming; and secondly, a point with respect to which he admitted a personal interest, he had been charged half-a-crown by the Commissioners of Crown Lands for taking seaweed from the shore of the west coast of Scotland for use, as was the local custom, as manure on his farm on that coast.

In 1961, one member objected to the transfer of ministerial oversight of the Commissioners from ministers who had a departmental interest in the usage of land to those who did not; and two members, Mr Donnelly from the Labour benches, and Mr Nicholas Ridley from the Conservative benches, raised a case in which the Commissioners, exercising their monopoly power, had recently tried to charge a very high rent to oil companies seeking to develop Milford Haven as an oil port. The Solicitor General replied that the Commissioners had first asked for £60,000 a year, and that agreement was later reached on a provisional rent of £6,000 with the final amount to be between £1,000 and £10,000, which, he said, 'I think was worked out as a result of the strenuous protests of the Honourable Member for Pembroke (Mr Donnelly)'.[14] The Solicitor General further said that the Government had now laid it down that in future the practice would be for the Commissioners to bring in the district valuer where there was a dispute over the price to be charged. From this it appears that the Commissioners' over-enthusiastic initial use of their new profit-maximising mandate had caused ministers to act to restrain them.

The expanding task

The machinery for the management of the Crown lands set up after Crichel

Down was not designed with an eye to the task of managing the foreshore and seabed, but that task has grown and changed out of all recognition in recent years for three reasons:

1. There has been a huge increase in demands for the use of the foreshore by the oil industry, which must get leases for pipelines, jetties and such things; by the yachting community, who pay rent to the Crown Estate for marinas and moorings; and by the fish-farming industry who must pay for moored enclosures containing salmon or other fish.
2. The domain of the Crown, which owns the seabed to the limit of territorial waters, has increased as the limit to those waters has been extended to twelve miles.
3. There has been a surge of concern for the environment and an increase in legislation, made in Brussels and London, for its protection, to which the managers of the Crown Estate must somehow respond, since the remit of local authorities as regards planning and environmental issues does not extend to the foreshore and territorial sea.

These developments have made the foreshore valuable: in 1992/93 the gross surplus of the marine estates, including fish farming, of the Crown Estate was £12 millions, and their capital value was put at £114 millions.[15] Until the late 1960s, the income was negligible.

What has happened is reflected in the annual reports of the Crown Estate Commissioners. The space devoted to the foreshore and to the problems of managing it have gradually increased. In the 1960's, references were short and mostly about leases for the extraction of gravel. By the 1970's there were references to the new oil industry in Scotland and the need to take account of amenity and environmental factors, and also references to marinas for yachts and to fish farming. In 1984 the Commissioners were actively seeking ways of positive management. By the end of the 1980's the Crown Estate Commissioners had assumed responsibility, subject to the guidance of the Secretary of State for Scotland, for planning where fish farming should take place in Scotland and new consultative machinery was in place. The use of the foreshore and territorial waters for purposes other than fish farming is subject to statutory controls administered by a variety of government departments. But gone as regards fish farming was the post-Crichel Down doctrine that the Crown Estate Commissioners should not be an agency of government answerable to a minister with an interest in what the Commissioners were doing with the real estate they manage. The abandonment of that doctrine came about, slowly, for political reasons that are not hard to trace.

Coastal planning

In the early 1980's the Government appointed a committee to consider the functions and powers of the local councils of the Scottish islands. The Council of the Western Isles told the committee that they were increasingly faced with problems over the use of the sea, in particular the sea lochs; since their planning authority did not extend beyond dry land and the discretion of the Crown Estate Commissioners was limited to whether or not to grant a lease, they suggested that their planning power should be extended. The Government, in the shape of the Scottish Development Department, took the view that planning legislation was not the right way to control sea-based developments; the appropriate form of control was legislation specifically framed for the purpose.

The report came down rather on the side of the Council of the Western Isles:

> It is our opinion that a more structured form of control is needed to deal with increasing development activity in the sea, and we recommend that the Government's present study be carried through as a matter of urgency with the object of introducing a form of control which should at the very least involve consultation with the local authorities concerned. In view of the responsibilities of the local authority for land-based developments it seems to us appropriate to give control to the planning authority, but we have not conducted a detailed investigation of the issues, and we therefore stop short of a positive recommendation on this point, although we think it must be given serious consideration.[16]

The reaction of the Government, after it had considered the report, was neither to extend the planning powers of the local authorities nor to introduce new legislation giving statutory powers to any other body to regulate the use of the foreshore and seabed in Scotland. Instead the problem was passed to the Crown Estate Commissioners who agreed that they would establish a consultation procedure for the consideration of fish farming applications. In the next few years, the Commissioners set about improving their ability to do that job and for that purpose established consultation procedures which would enable them 'to *plan* the needs of this rapidly growing industry in a way which necessarily takes into account all the wider aspects and views'.[17] [my italics] The Secretary of State for Scotland, having reviewed these consultation procedures, said they were working well and that the Government had again concluded that a convincing case had not been made out for an extension of planning control, but they accepted that steps should be taken to enable contentious cases to be discussed more fully and to introduce an independent element into the decision-making process on such cases. He then descrbed the proposed steps as follows:

> I have therefore agreed with the commissioners that they will establish an advisory committee, to consider lease applications referred to it. The chairman and deputy chairman of the advisory committee will be appointed by me and the following statutory bodies will be invited to participate as members of the committee: the relevant district or general planning authority, the Countryside Commission for Scotland, the Nature Conservancy Council, the Highlands and Islands development board, the relevant river purification authority and the Department of Agriculture and Fisheries for Scotland.
>
> Should the committee decide that any case raises particularly difficult or wide-ranging issues it will be open to the chairman to advise the commissioners to refer the case to me for my advice before a decision is taken. The commissioners have undertaken that where such a recommendation is made they will refer the case to me and take particular account of my advice in reaching their decision.[18]

The committee was set up to deal with leases for salmon farming, but contentious applications for oyster leases could always be referred to it. In England and Wales the Crown Estate follows the same consultation procedures as in Scotland. If the flow of applications for fish or shellfish leases south of the border became more intense, it can be expected that an advisory committee similar to that for Scotland would be established for England and Wales

What all this means is that a body which at its creation by Parliament in 1961 was given the task of acting as a profit-maximising but virtuous property company at arm's length from any minister with a close interest in its decisions, and whose commissioners 'were neither established nor empowered to act as a regulatory body with overall responsibility for coastal development',[19] was told less than thirty years later to perform that very task with respect to fish farming and to do so under the supervision of the minister with the closest interest in the way it was done.

It is not surprising nor necessarily deplorable that this happened. To a government that believed strongly in reducing the powers of government, including local authorities, the possibility of leaving the job to the Crown Estate Commissioners must have appeared attractive and economical, compared with the alternative of introducing legislation to give planning powers over fish and shellfish farming to some branch of central or local government. Moreover this is but a minor and little noticed part of a bigger debate about the management of the coast. Many people have become concerned about the conservation of the coast, the prevention of flooding and the conservation of the many forms of wildlife whose habitat is in the coastal waters or on the shore and adjacent land. Some politicians are exercised about the problem; and so is Brussels, though the policy of the Government is to insist on subsidiarity, meaning that it aims to prevent, or at least limit, the power of Brussels to intervene.

In 1992 the House of Commons Environment Committee produced a report on coastal zone protection and planning which called on the Government to take a strategic view and to create a hierarchy of coastal zone management plans from the national to the regional and local levels. The Government in two discussion documents described the incredible tangle of bits and pieces of regulation that now influence developments below the low water mark and declared that it rejected the approach proposed by the House of Commons committee.[20] It took the view that,

> local authorities and other agencies will be expected to work together on a voluntary basis, informed by an understanding of national and regional issues provided by national policy statements and by bodies *such as* the National Rivers Authority, English Nature, the Countryside Commission, The Countryside Commission for Wales, the Sports Councils and Regional Councils for Sport and Recreation, regional coastal defence groups and Sea Fisheries Committees. [my italics]

One wonders how on earth voluntary co-operation amongst all these agencies, and anyone else who cares to join in, is expected to achieve results when power is so fragmented and there is no clear mechanism for pulling things together. In the two Government papers, shellfish are barely mentioned, nor is the role of the Crown Estate Commissioners in shaping what happens to the coast. It looks as if the whole business of coastal planning is a muddle which the Government is trying to patch up sufficiently to quieten the environmental lobby without spending money. It would take quite an optimist to believe that this policy will produce a coherent policy for allocating parts of the coast to shellfish farming and keeping them clean.

Footnotes

Chapter One

[1] Mary Saul, *Shells, an Illustrated Guide*, Hamlyn, London 1974, pp.62-3.

[2] John Butterfield, 'The circulation in diabetes, from HL523 to the NO era', *The Lancet*, Aug 28, 1993.

[3] *The Letters of Charles Dickens*, ed. House, Storey and Tillotson, Oxford, 1974, vol 3, p.244

[4] *Ibid.* p.291-2

[5] G.O. Trevelyan, ed., *The Life and Letters of Lord Macaulay*, 1878, vol II, p.281.

[6] Lewis Carroll, 'Through the Looking-Glass', Complete Works, Nonesuch, London, 1939, p.172.

[7] Saki (H.H.Monro), 'The Match-maker', *The Chronicles of Clovis*, London, 1911.

[8] Ogden Nash, *Collected Verses from 1929 On*, Dent, London, 1961, p.288.

[9] John Gay, *Trivia*, Part III, London, 1721.

[10] Lord Byron, *Don Juan*, Canto XIV, LXXXI.

[11] H. Gerson and E.H. ter Kuile, *Art and Architecture in Belgium*, 1600-1800, Harmondsworth, 1960, p.161.

Chapter Two

[1] H.A. Cole, *Oyster Cultivation in Britain*, MAFF Laboratory, Burnham-on-Crouch, 1956, pp.41-2.

[2] D. Rice, 'Seafood and Good Health', *Proceedings of the 24th Annual Shellfish Conference*, Shellfish Association of Great Britain, London, 1993.

[3] There is a school of thought that when you open your oysters you should pour away the liquor and then let them stand in the lower shell for half an hour, during which time the shell will partially fill with a liquor of superior

taste that has emerged from the body of the open oyster.

⁴ *The Times*, 3 December 1994, p.18.

Chapter Three

¹ Charles Dickens, *The Posthumous Papers of the Pickwick Club*, Vol I, p.229, London Edition, Caxton Publishing Co.

² Charles Dickens, *Sketches by Boz*, Vol II, London Edition, Caxton Publishing Co., pp.379-383.

³ Charles Dickens, *Great Expectations*, vol II, Chap XXX, p.179, London edition, Caxton Publishing Co.

⁴ Henry Mayhew, *London Labour and the London Poor; a Cyclopaedia of the Condition and Earnings of Those That Work, Those That Cannot Work, and Those That Will Not Work*, London, 1851.

⁵ *Ibid*. p.62.

⁶ H. Sutherland Edwards, *Personal Recollections*, Cassell, London, 1900, p.60.

⁷ Mayhew, *op.cit.* p.65.

⁸ *Ibid*. p.75.

⁹ *Ibid*, p.78.

¹⁰ The figure is cited in John R. Philpots, *Oysters and all about them*, London, 1890, p.348; and it is presumably the basis for the statement in *The Cambridge Natural History*, Macmillan, 1927, that 'It has been computed that the quantity [of oysters] annually produced in Great Britain amounts to no less than sixteen hundred million,' a statement which, since it includes no date, might unfortunately be taken by the reader to mean that in 1927 production was of that size, rather than about 10 million, the official statistic for that year.

¹¹ J.P. Hore and Edward Jex, *The Deterioration of Oyster and Trawl Fisheries of England*, London, 1880, p.9.

¹² *Ibid*, p.11.

¹³ *Ibid*. p.16.

¹⁴ *Letters and Papers, Foreign and Domestic, of the Reign of Henry VIII*, ed. J.S. Brewer, London, 1867, Vol III, para 907.

¹⁵ Robert Tyler, *The Emperor Charles the Fifth*, George Allen and Unwin, 1956, p.271.

¹⁶ Henry Laver, FSA, *The Colchester Oyster Fishery*, Colne Fishery Board, Colchester, 1916, pp.42-3.

¹⁷ W.D. Christie, *A Life of Anthony Ashley Cooper, First Earl of Shaftesbury*,

Macmillan, 1871, vol 1, Appendix I, 'A Fragment of Autobiography, from birth (1621) to 1639', pp.xiv-xvii.

[18] Hore and Jex, *op. cit.* p.22.

[19] *The Diary of Samuel Pepys*, ed. R. Latham and W. Mathews, Bell and Hyman, London, 1983, Vol xi (Index), pp.108-9.

[20] Philip Morant, *The History and Antiquities of Colchester*, 1748, p.87 cites the following lines from Cokayne:

> The old luxurious Romans vaunts did make
> Of gustful oysters took in Lake Lucrine:
> Your Essex better hath, and such perchance
> As tempted Caesar first to pass from France.

[21] Thomas Fuller, D.D., *The History of the Worthies of England*, London, 1662, p.281.

[22] J.H. Plumb, "Sir Robert Walpole's Food", *The Gourmet's Companion*, ed. Cyril Ray, Eyre and Spottiswoode, London, 1963, p.372.

[23] *Boswell's Life of Johnson*, ed. George Birkbeck Hill, revised edition, Oxford, 1934, vol. iv, p.197.

[24] Mr John Aloysius Blake, giving evidence before the Select Committee on Oyster Fisheries on 4 May, 1876.

[25] The *Report of the Royal Commission on Sea Fisheries*, 1866, p.lxxxvii, says the deep Channel beds were discovered very shortly after 1852; in Mayhew, in the passage we have quoted, the date is put at 1848.

[26] *Ibid*, p.lxxxvii.

[27] *Ibid.* p.xc.

[28] *Ibid.* p. xcii, and C.E. Dove, "The Colne Oyster Fishery", a draft chapter for *The Victoria History of the County of Essex* volume on Colchester, forthcoming.

[29] Hervey Benham, *Once upon a Tide*, London, 1971, p.132.

[30] *Ibid.* p.132.

[31] *Ibid.* p.134.

[32] Hervey Benham, *Last Stronghold of Sail*, London,1948, p.87.

[33] John R. Wennersten, *The Oyster Wars of Chesapeake Bay*, Tidewater Publishers, Centreville, Maryland, 1981, pp.123-6.

[34] *Lucullus: Or Palatable Essays, in which are merged "The Oyster," "The Lobster," and "Sport And Its Pleasures."* by the author of *"The Queen's Messenger," "The Bric-a-Brac Hunter,"* &c. Remington and Co, London,

1878, pp.1-2.

35 *Ibid.* pp.108-9.

36 *Ibid.* pp.84-5.

37 *Ibid.* pp.158-62.

38 *Ibid.* p.168.

39 John R. Philpots, *op. cit.*

40 'Parliamentary Papers relative to the Complaints made against Mr Grenville-Murray as Her Majesty's Consul-General at Odessa and to his dismissal from Her Majesty's Service', *Parliamentary Papers*, 1868-69, LX1V, pp.353-658.

Chapter Four

1 This section is based on a number of sources. Most useful were H.A. Cole, *Oyster Cultivation in Britain – a Manuel of Current Practice*, HMSO, London 1956; and H.A. Cole, "Benthos and the Shellfish of Commerce" in *Sea Fisheries – Their Investigation in the United Kingdom*, ed. Michael Graham, London, 1956. pp.148-162.

2 Ogden Nash, *Collected Verse from 1929 On*, London, 1961.

3 Y. Fauvel, *Conchyliculture en Méditerranée: Histoire sans Marée*, IFREMER, Direction des Ressources Vivantes, 1987.

4 For a formal exposition and economic analysis see Richard J. Agnello and Lawrence P. Donnelley, 'Property Rights and Efficiency in the Oyster Industry', *The Journal of Law and Economics*, 1975, pp.521-533.

5 Dr James Murie, *Report on the Sea Fisheries and Fishing Industries of the Thames Estuary*, Kent and Essex Sea fisheries Committee, 1903, pp.14-15.

6 *The Victoria History of the County of Essex*, ed W. Page and J.R Round, vol. 2 p.426.

Chapter Five

1 Adam Smith, *Wealth of Nations*, book IV, chap 5.

2 J.T. Jenkins, *The Sea Fisheries*, Constable, London, 1920, pp.160-1.

3 Copy of translation of a report made to the Minister of Marine in France, by M.G. Bouchon Brandely, secretary of the College of France, relative to Oyster Culture on the Shores of the Channel and of the Ocean, published in the *Journal Officiel de la Republique Française*, of the 22nd day of January 1877 and presented to the House of Commons on 17 May 1877.

4 Sir William Blackstone, *Commentaries on the Laws of England*, London,

1825, Book 2, p.50.

[5] *Halsbury's Laws of England*, London, 1977, vol 18, para. 609.

[6] *Report of the Royal Commission on Sea Fisheries*, 1866, p.c.

[7] Stuart A. Moore, *A History of the Foreshore and the Law Relating Thereto*, 3rd ed., Stevens and Haynes, London 1888, p.xxxiv. See also The Duke of Richmond, House of Lords, June 19 1868, cols.1823-1831 and the Lord Chancellor, *ibid.* cols.1831-1834.

[8] *Parliamentary Report, House of Commons*, 3 June 1863, Cols. 261-276.

[9] *Ibid.* 8 June 1863, Col. 515.

[10] *Report of the Royal Commission, op.cit.* p.xv.

[11] *Ibid.* p.lxxxii.

[12] *Ibid.* p.lxxxvi.

[13] *Ibid.* p.xciv.

[14] *Ibid.* p.xcv.

[15] *Ibid.* p.xcvii.

[16] *Ibid.* p.cv.

[17] *First Report of the Commissioners of the Irish Fishery Inquiry*, 1836, pp.xvi-xvii.

[18] *Report of Royal Commission, op.cit.*, p.lxxix.

[19] *Dictionary of National Biography.*

[20] *Ibid.*

[21] 'Oysters and the Oyster Question,' *The English Illustrated Magazine*, 1883-84, p.115-6.

[22] Professor Sir Michael Foster and Professor Ray Lankester (ed) *The Scientific Memoirs of Thomas Henry Huxley*, supplementary volume,London, Macmillan, 1893, p.89.

[23] *The English Illustrated Magazine, op. cit.*, p.117.

[24] *Ibid.*, p.121

[25] William Irvine, *Apes, Angels and Victorians*. A joint biography of Darwin and Huxley, Weidenfeld & Nicolson, London, 1955, p.233.

[26] *Parliamentary Report, House of Commons*, April 9, 1866, col. 894.

[27] See Mr Stephen Cave, House of Commons, February 24 1868, cols. 1075-6; and The Duke of Richmond, House of Lords, May 14 1868, co. 239.

[28] Mr T.H. Farrer, giving evidence to the Select Committee on Oyster Fisheries, on 20 March 1876.

[29] *Ibid.*

[30] *Report of the Select Committee on Oyster Fisheries, 1876.*

31 *Report of the Select Committee on Sea Fisheries, 1893.*
32 *Minutes of Evidence taken before the Select Committee on Oyster Fisheries,* 6 April 1876, p.114, Mr F. Pennell.

Chapter 6

1 Joseph Pichot-Louvet, *Les Huîtres de Cancale,* Cancale, 1982, mimeo.
2 C.W. Cole, *Colbert and a Century of French Mercantilism*, vol. 1, pp.460-4, Frank Cass, London, 1964; and E.H. Jenkins, *A History of the French Navy,* Macdonald and Jane's, London 1973.
3 *L' Huître et St. Vaast: une Longue Histoire,* Collège Guillaume Fouace de Saint-Vaast-la-Hougue, 1990.
4 Pliny, *Natural History, with an English Translation by H. Rackham,* Loeb, Book IX, para 168.
5 M. Coste, *Voyage d'Exploration sur le Littoral de la France et de l'Italie,* 2nd ed., Paris,1861, reprint by the Museé Maritime de la Tremblade, 1993, p.95.
6 M.G. Bouchon-Brandely, Report on Oyster Culture on the Shores of the Channel, made to the French Minister of Marine, in January, 1877, and submitted in translation to the House of Commons by the Board of Trade on 17 May 1877; and J. Pichot-Louvet, *op. cit.*.
7 Bouchon-Brandely, *op. cit.*, p.2.
8 Coste, *op. cit.*, p.162.
9 *Ibid.* pp.167-176.
10 *Ibid.* pp.177-183.
11 Mr F. Buckland, *Minutes of Evidence of the Royal Commission on Sea Fisheries, 1866,* 16 March 1865, p.1320; Noel P. Wilkins, *Ponds, Passes and Parcs: Aquaculture in Victorian Ireland,* Dublin, 1989, p.45-6.
12 Noel P. Wilkins, *op. cit.* Dublin, 1989, p.44.
13 Jean Roche et Henri Bouxin, *Le Laboratoire de Concarneau et son Centenaire,* Le Tendre, Concarneau, 1959, p.11.
14 *Ann. Mag. Nat. Hist.* NS, 1838, 2, pp.183-198
15 Adrian Desmond, Huxley: *the Devil's Disciple,* Michael Joseph, London, 1994.
16 Personal communication from M. Thibault .
17 M. Thibault, 'La redécouverte de la fécondation artificielle de la truite en France au milieu du XIX siècle; les raisons de l'engouement et ses conséquences,' in *Colloque Homme, Animal et Société*, 13-16 mai 1987, Inst. Et. Polit., Toulouse

18 H. Cholmondeley Pennell Esq, *Report on the Oyster and Mussel Fisheries of France and the Applicabilty of the French System to British Waters,* made to the Board of Trade and presented to Parliament in 1868.

19 H. Cholmondely Pennell, *op. cit.* p.5.

20 M. Brocchi, *Oyster Culture in France,* copy of a Translation of a Report made to the Minister of Marine in France by M. Brocchi, relative to Oyster Culture on the Shores of the Channel and of the Ocean, published in the *Journal Officiel de la République Française* of 8th November 1881, submitted to the House of Commons dated 1 August 1882.

21 Brocchi, *Traité d'Ostréiculture,* Paris 1883.

22 Bashford Dean, 'Present Methods of Oyster-culture in France', *Bulletin of the United States Fish Commission for 1890.*

23 Major J. Hayes, Inspector of Irish Fisheries, *Report on the Principal Oyster Fisheries of France,* presented to both houses of Parliament, 1878; W.E. Hall, paper on the oyster fisheries of France, *Report of the Select Committee on Oyster Fisheries, 1876,* Appendix 16; and Brocchi, *op. cit.*

24 Brocchi, *op. cit.,*

25 Y. Fauvel, 'Du Golfe du Lion a l'étang de Thau', *La Pêche Maritime,* Jan 1987, p.34.

Chapter 7

1 Oliver Macdonagh, 'Ideas and institutions, 1830-45'; and R.B. McDowell, 'Administration and the public services', in W.E. Vaughan (ed.), *A New History of Ireland,* Vol.V, pp.206-9 and 547-8.

2 See 'Historical Sketch of the British and Irish Fisheries,' compiled by Sir T. Charles Morgan, Appendix I, to *The First Report of the Commissioners of the Irish Fishery Inquiry,* 1836.

3 *First Report of the Commissioners of the Irish Fisheries,* Minutes of Evidence, Balbriggan, 7 December 1835, resolution read at the start of the hearing by Mr G.A. Hamilton.

4 Noel P. Wilkins, *op. cit.* p.122

5 *Report of the Royal Commission, 1866, op.cit.,* p.lxv.

6 *Report of the Commissioners Appointed to Inquire into Salmon Fisheries (England and Wales),* 1861, pp.xxii-xxxvi.

7 Noel P. Wilkins, *op. cit.,* p.200.

8 *Ibid.,* p.205-6.

Chapter 8

1 *Ninth Annual Report of the Inspectors on Sea Fisheries (England and Wales)*, pp.25-6
2 *Eleventh Annual Report of the Inspectors on Sea Fisheries (England and Wales)*, p.26.
3 Lord Harris, *Parliamentary Report, House of Lords*, 18 May 1899, cols. 897-901.
4 Lord Harris, *Parliamentary Report, House of Lords*, 31 July 1899, cols. 827-9.
5 *Annual Report under the Acts relating to Sea Fisheries (England and Wales) 1903*, pp.xl-xlvi.
6 W.M. Frazer, *A History of Public Health, 1834-1939*, Bailliere Tindall and Cox, London 1950.
7 *Fourth Report of the Royal Commission on Sewage Pollution appointed in 1898 to Inquire and Report What Methods of Treating and Disposing of Sewage may properly be Adopted: Pollution of Tidal Waters with Special Reference to Contamination of Shellfish*, Cd. 1883, 1904.
8 *Oysters and Other Shell Fish*, Report of the Fishmongers Company, London, December 1902 to June 1905. p.5.
9 *The Times*, 6 January, 1903.
10 *The Times*, 10 January, 1903
11 *Memorandum on the Public Health (Shell-fish) Regulations, 1915, of the Local Government Board*, Oyster Merchants and Planters Associstion, Fishmongers Hall, London, 23 July 1915.
12 Letter from Mr H.C. Monro, Secretary of the Local Government Board, to the clerks of local authorities informing them of the Public Health (Shell-fish) Regulations, 17th February 1915.
13 Arthur J. Lee, *The Ministry of Agriculture, Fisheries and Foodstuff's Directorate of Fisheries Research: its Origins and Development* MAFF, Lowestoft,p.256; and 1992, Mr Peter French, 'Oyster fishing in Essex' in the Proceedings of the 20th Annual Conference of the Shellfish Association of Great Britain, 1989.
14 Dr Eric Edwards, 'Shellfish Developments in Britain and Ireland', Shellfish Association of Great Britain, 1988.
15 See Louis Lambert, 'Le Controle Sanitaire des Coquillages Comestibles' in *Les Coquillages Comestibles*, Presses Universitaires de la France, 1950, pp.110-127; and Report by Mr Charles Fryer on Shell-fish and Sewage

Contamination, *Annual Report of Proceedings under Acts Relating to Sea Fisheries for 1904,* pp.xxvi-xxvii.

[16] Louis Lambert, *op.cit.* p.126.

Chapter 9

[1] *L'Ostréiculteur Français,* November 1994, p.5, reported that production in 1994 was expected to reach 150,000 tonnes.

[2] Decret du 22 Mars 1983 fixant le régime de l'authorisation des exploitations de cultures marines, modifié par le décret no. 87-756 du 14 septembre 1987.

[3] IFREMER, Annual Report, 1990, English version, p.58.

[4] For a description of these innovations see B.E. Spencer, *Cultivation of Pacific Oysters,* MAFF Directorate of Fisheries Research, Laboratory Leaflet No. 63, Lowestoft, 1990, p.34.

[5] *L'Ostréiculteur Français ,* Janvrier 1994, p.7.

[6] Henri Grizel and Maurice Héral, 'Introduction into France of the Japanese oyster *(Crassostrea gigas)'* J. Cons. Int. Explor. Mer 47: 399-403.

[7] Carl J. Sindermann, 'Disease Risks associated with Importation of nonindigenous Marine Animals', *Marine Fisheries Review,* 54(3), 1993.

[8] 'Modèle de production du bassin de Marennes-Oléron', *Activités d'IFREMER en Poitou-Charentes, Bilan de la Convention IFREMER, contrat du IX Plan, 1984-88.*

[9] *L'Ostréiculteur Français,* Janvrier 1994, p.11.

[10] *Ibid.* p.10.

[11] *Ibid.* Fevrier 1994, p.24.

[12] *Ibid.,* Mars 1994, pp.10 and 24.

Chapter 10

[1] H.A. Cole, 'Benthos and the shellfish of commerce', in *Sea Fisheries – Their Investigation in the United Kingdom,* ed. Michael Graham, London 1956, pp.149-150; and Gilbert Barnabé, ed. *Aquaculture,* Paris 1989, p.347.

[2] H.A. Cole, *op. cit.,* p.152.

[3] Report of Mr C. E. Fryer, Inspector of Fisheries, on the Injury alleged to have been caused to the Fisheries by the Deposit of Rubbish in the Estuary of the River Thames, Board of Trade, April 17, 1888.

[4] Denis Key of the MAFF Fisheries Laboratories Lowestoft, 'The Native Oyster Fisheries of England and Wales', the Dr Walne Memorial Lecture, at

the 22nd Annual Shellfish Conference of the Shellfish Association of Great Britain, May 1991, p.7.

[5] B.E. Spencer, *op. cit.,* p.11; Phillip Gibbon, Water Quality in the Shellfish Industry, Marine Forum Presentation, 9 June 1993, p.7; Dennis Key, op. cit. TP 16-17 and Parliamentary Report, House of Commons, 22 April 1985, Cols. 368-369 and 22 February 1987, cols. 200.

[6] S.D. Utting and B.E. Spencer, 'Introductions of marine bivalve molluscs into the United Kingdom for commercial culture – case histories', ICES mar. Sci. Symp., 194, 1992, p.86.

[7] For the description of the import trade from America at the turn of the century see the evidence given by Mr Charles Petrie to the Select Committee on Sea Fisheries on 8 May 1893.

[8] *The Times,* 11 May 1933.

[9] Denis Key, *op. cit.*

[10] For a description of these innovations see B.E. Spencer, *op. cit.,* p.34.

[11] S.D. Utting and B.E. Spencer, *The hatchery culture of bivalve molusc larvae and juveniles,* MAFF Directorate of Fisheries Research, Laboratory Leaflet No. 68, Lowestoft, 1991.

[12] Richard Pinney, *Smoked Salmon and Oysters – A Feast of Suffolk Memories,* The Butley-Orford Oysterage, 1984.

[13] Arthur J. Lee, *op. cit.,* p.175.

[14] Denis Key, *op. cit.,* pp.6-7.

[15] *The Effects of Conservation Measures on the UK Sea Fishing Industy,* Sixth Report, Agriculture Committee, House of Commons, Session 1992-93, 20 July 1993, p.xi.

Chapter 11
[1] Sea Fisheries (Shellfish) Act 1967.
[2] *Ibid.*

Chapter 12
[1] Council Directive 91/492/EEC of 15 July 1991 'laying down the conditions for the production and the placing on the market of live bivalve molluscs'
[2] David Hugh-Jones, 'The importation of half-grown C. gigas from France for re-laying in English and Irish waters', Shellfish Conference, London, May 1993.

³ *L'Ostréiculteur Française*, Septembre 1994, p.5.
⁴ See Chapter 9.

Chapter 13
¹ P.S. Dasgupta and G.M. Heal, *Economic Theory and Exhaustible Resources*, Cambridge University Press, 1979.

Appendix A
¹ *Norme Française, Huîtres creuses, dénominations et classification*, Association Française de Normalisation, NF V 45-056, September, 1985

Appendix B
¹ Lord Macaulay, *The History of England from the Accession of James II*, London, 1860, vol. 1, p.154.
² *The Crown Estate: an Historical Essay*, HMSO, 1960, p.16.
³ *Ibid.*, p.17.
⁴ *Report of the Committee on Crown Lands*, Cmd 9483, HMSO, 1955, pp.4-5.
⁵ *Ibid.* pp.5-6.
⁶ *Ibid.*, p.12.
⁷ *The Crown Estate: an Historical Essay*, op. cit. p.25.
⁸ Crown Estate Act 1961 (9 and 10 Elizabeth II, 55), 1.(3).
⁹ Correspondence between the Treasury and the Board of Trade as to the Transfer to the latter of the Management of certain Rights of the Crown in Tidal Lands, Parliamentary Papers 1866, LX, 467-8
¹⁰ Parliamentary Report, House of Commons, April 9 1866, Col. 960.
¹¹ Foreshores: Copy of Treasury Warrant dated 30th June 1868, providing for the Compensation to be made to the Land Revenue for the Crown's Foreshore Rights transferred to the Lords of the Committee of Privy Council for Trade, under Act 29 & 30 Vict. c. 62, Parliamentary Papers 1867-68, XL, 413-5.
¹² See memorandum by Mr T.H. Farrer of the Board of Trade, House of Lords Papers, 1867, 127 cited by Stuart A. Moore, *op. cit.*, p.597.
¹³ PRO T 227-1096
¹⁴ Parliamentary Report, House of Commons, 28 June 1961, Col. 617.
¹⁵ *The Crown Estate, The Commissioners Report for the year ended 31 March 1993*, pp.53 and 55.

16 Report of the Committee of Inquiry into the Functions and Powers of the Islands Councils of Scotland, chairman Sir David Montgomery, Bt., Cmnd. 9216, April 1984, p.49, para. 7.14.

17 Report of the Crown Estate Commissioners for the year ended 31 March 1986, p.14, para 93.

18 Parliamentary Report, House of Commons, Written Answers, 19 December 1988, Cols 88-90.

19 William Howarth *The Law of Aquaculture*, Fishery News Books, 1990, p.20.

20 *Managing the Coast – a Review of Coastal Management Plans in England and Wales and the powers supporting them,* and, *Development Below the Low Water Mark – A Review of Regulation in England and Wales,* Department of the Environment and the Welsh Office, October 1993. See also *'Managing the Coast'* and *'Development Below Low Water',* *Comments on the DOE/Welsh Office Discussion Papers,* Marine Conservation Society, January 1994.

Index of Names and Places